The Cinema of the Precariat

The Cinema of the Precariat

The Exploited, Underemployed, and Temp Workers of the World

Tom Zaniello

BLOOMSBURY ACADEMIC
NEW YORK • LONDON • OXFORD • NEW DELHI • SYDNEY

BLOOMSBURY ACADEMIC
Bloomsbury Publishing Inc
1385 Broadway, New York, NY 10018, USA
50 Bedford Square, London, WC1B 3DP, UK
29 Earlsfort Terrace, Dublin 2, Ireland

BLOOMSBURY, BLOOMSBURY ACADEMIC and the Diana logo are trademarks of
Bloomsbury Publishing Plc

First published in the United States of America 2020
This paperback edition published in 2021

Copyright © Tom Zaniello, 2020

For legal purposes the Acknowledgments on p. ix constitute an
extension of this copyright page.

Cover design by Eleanor Rose | Cover photograph: Scene from season 1 of the
TV series Chernobyl, 2019 © Collection Christophel / ArenaPAL

All rights reserved. No part of this publication may be reproduced or transmitted
in any form or by any means, electronic or mechanical, including photocopying,
recording, or any information storage or retrieval system, without prior
permission in writing from the publishers.

Bloomsbury Publishing Inc does not have any control over, or responsibility for, any
third-party websites referred to or in this book. All internet addresses given in this
book were correct at the time of going to press. The author and publisher regret any
inconvenience caused if addresses have changed or sites have ceased to exist,
but can accept no responsibility for any such changes.

Library of Congress Cataloging-in-Publication Data

Names: Zaniello, Tom, 1943-author.
Title: The cinema of the precariat: the exploited, underemployed, and temp
workers of the world / Tom Zaniello.
Description: New York: Bloomsbury Academic, 2019. |
Includes bibliographical references and index.
Identifiers: LCCN 2019035759 (print) | LCCN 2019035760 (ebook) |
ISBN 9781501349201 (hardback) | ISBN 9781501349218 (epub) |
ISBN 9781501349225 (pdf)
Subjects: LCSH: Precarious employment in motion pictures. |
Working class in motion pictures. | Poor in motion pictures.
Classification: LCC PN1995.9.P6579 Z36 2019 (print) |
LCC PN1995.9.P6579 (ebook) | DDC 791.43/655–dc23
LC record available at https://lccn.loc.gov/2019035759
LC ebook record available at https://lccn.loc.gov/2019035760

ISBN: HB: 978-1-5013-4920-1
PB: 978-1-5013-8584-1
ePDF: 978-1-5013-4922-5
eBook: 978-1-5013-4921-8

Typeset by Deanta Global Publishing Services, Chennai, India

To find out more about our authors and books visit
www.bloomsbury.com and sign up for our newsletters.

This book is dedicated to Maci, Basti, Fitz, Phoebe, and Bel, my grandchildren, with high hopes that they will grow up in a safe and fair world.

*It is the dark urge for personal freedom, which
drives the workers to work in a foreign land.*
—Max Weber, *Developments on the Placement of the Farm Workers from
East of the Elbe River* (1894)

*Oh, Saint Precario,
Protector of us all, precarious of the earth,
Give us paid maternal leave,
Protect chain store workers, call-center angels
And all the flexible workers, hanging by a thread.*
—Poster, The Chain Store Workers of Milan (2004)

Contents

List of Figures	viii
Acknowledgments	ix
Preface: Making Invisible Workers Visible	x
Introduction: Who Are the Precariat?	1
1 *Harvest of Shame*: The First Series of Films about the Precariat	17
2 Internal Migration in China	31
3 *Daughters of a Lesser God*: Women of the Precariat	41
4 Scavengers of the World, Unite!	49
5 Epidemic Cinema and Catastrophic Mise-en-Scène	65
6 Precious Cargo: The Creation of Wealth by the Global Precariat	85
7 The Cyberprecariat in the Alt-Future	95
8 Video Games as Cinema—All Work, All Play	105
9 The 1 Percent: A Top-Down Conclusion—Fifty Films about Capitalism in the Twenty-First Century	121
10 The 99 Percent: A Bottom-Up Conclusion—Alt-Labor and Organizing the Unorganized	137
Bibliography	161
Index	186

Figures

I.1	Israeli police raid from *Manpower*	11
I.2	Demonstration against Walmart. *Talking to the Wall*	14
1.1	Edward R. Murrow in *Harvest of Shame*	20
2.1	Dismantling a German coke factory from *Losers and Winners*	38
4.1	Recycling in the First World (Manhattan)	51
4.2	Main Street, Willet's Point	62
5.1	Inside a Chernobyl reactor from *Pripyat*	70
5.2	Director Judith Helfand with National Guard general flying over potentially deadly zip-code areas from *Cooked: Survival by Zip Code*	74
5.3	Impressed African American precariat workers on the levees from *The Great Flood*	75
6.1	Sanabhai at his salt flats from *My Name Is Salt*	92
6.2	Food factory workers on break from *Our Daily Bread*	93
8.1	Refinery for processing oil from tar sands from *Petropolis*	114
9.1	On front lines of anti-capitalism from *Capitalism*	126
9.2	Demonstration from *97% Owned*	133
10.1	Karen Nussbaum from *Raises Not Roses: The Story of 9to5*	142
10.2	Banner of San Precario from Milan	147
10.3	Installation by Oliver Ressler in *We Have a Situation Here*	157

Acknowledgments

I am indebted to the following filmmakers, writers, and film festival organizers who have helped to shape my view of the cinema of the precariat:

- David Bacon
- Ramin Bahrani
- Wang Bing
- Steven Bognar
- Anna Burton
- Grady Clay
- Dick Couto
- Mike Davis
- Kai Erikson
- Mark Finch
- Chris Garlock
- Jon Garlock
- Alex Gibney
- Dennis Grunes
- Judith Helfand
- Hsiao-Hung Pai
- Anne Lewis
- Mike Leigh
- Sherry Linkon
- Ken Loach
- Kyri Lydersen
- Kevin Lynch
- Peggy Parsons
- Mimi Pickering
- Julia Reichert
- Alex Rivera
- John Russo
- Guy Standing
- Raymond Williams
- Judith Williamson

Preface

Making Invisible Workers Visible

We see the "invisible" workers of the precariat every day. They are "illegal immigrants," fast-food workers, waiters and waitresses, manicurists and hairstylists, restaurant cooks, Uber and Lyft drivers, retail clerks, day laborers, landscape workers, migrant workers, child laborers, farmers, seasonal workers, house cleaners, nannies, domestic workers, hotel and motel workers, *carwasheros*, tech workers, adjunct professors, convict labor, so-called "guest workers," and even androids.

But there is a real danger that they will remain invisible. They are, by and large, exploited and underemployed temp workers, often undocumented if they are immigrants, not to mention barely tolerated in some countries as guest workers. There is almost a one-to-one correlation between the shrinking unionized share of any country's workforce and the corresponding expansion of the precariat.

This book is intended to keep the precariat visible. What better means of achieving that goal than by accessing their cinematic lives? This book will be the first detailed study of their extensive cinematic record, an exploration of their work and lives in the last twenty-five years, and a rediscovery of their even earlier exploitation by employers worldwide. It discusses 300 films and related visual media, a representative but not exhaustive selection that takes the measure of the precariat worldwide.

Each chapter focuses on a subclass of the precariat or a contested zone of labor or the evolving political manifestation of the struggles of the unorganized and the dispossessed. The book also challenges the limitations of traditional film studies by including video games, film installations, and agitprop films that circulate on YouTube and other websites as important variations on a too traditionally narrow definition of the cinema. The precariat, in newness and scale, can be a challenging concept, so one of the best ways to understand its scope and importance is by simply viewing the films discussed in this book.

The Cinema of the Precariat is the natural sequel to my previous books, *Working Stiffs, Union Maids, Reds, and Riffraff: An Expanded Guide to Films about Labor* (2003) and *The Cinema of Globalization: A Guide to Films about the New Economic Order* (2007), both of which included feature films, documentaries, television films, made-for-cable films, and online films—categories that are no longer as strictly defined as they once were. Netflix, for example, routinely streams feature films that are sometimes released in theatres simultaneously. A documentary may appear online but it is not a "made for television" film.

This is the first book of film and/or cultural studies that focuses almost entirely on the precariat. Although the cinematic portrayal of migrant workers, retail workers, and miners has received some of the attention it deserves (certainly in my two earlier books), this book also for the first time analyzes scavengers, recyclers, shantytown and garbage city residents, home factory and small workplace workers, and what can only be called the cyberprecariat (androids and technologically modified human workers).

From the more than 550 films analyzed in those two earlier volumes, I have selected only thirteen to discuss in a new framework in the current volume, six of which are essential to an understanding of the series of films, including—and generated by—Edward R. Murrow's landmark documentary of migrant labor, *Harvest of Shame* (1960, United States), that I have designated as "the first series of films about the precariat." This series, like all of the other films in the earlier two volumes, never used the term "precariat," although the precariat as we understand it today appears often in those films, especially migrant laborers throughout the twentieth century and retail workers in the later third of the century in their calculated exploitation by Big Box stores like Walmart.

Among the hundreds of bewildering film choices available nowadays, this book offers the reader reliable guidance to the films bringing to life the economic, political, and social dilemmas faced by millions in the global workforce and their families. Unlike my earlier film guides, however, this book has self-contained essay chapters, not alphabetical entries for the films.

The chapters that follow are comprised of four related groups.

Chapters 1 to 4 discuss the first extensive cinematic series of films about American migrant workers, the massive internal migration of Chinese workers, and the exploitation of some of the most vulnerable members of the precariat—women, child laborers, scavengers, and recyclers.

Chapters 5 and 6 follow two special classes of precariat cinema—films of epidemics and catastrophes and films chronicling the exploitation of workers mining precious metals and harvesting common foodstuffs. Both classes of films involve the workers of the precariat as either victims of cataclysmic events or the underpaid creators of international wealth—when it comes to the scale of danger inherent in oil and coal extraction often the two classes overlap.

Chapters 7 and 8 turn toward the latest manifestations of the precariat in futuristic and alternative-media films as well as the no longer purely speculative employment of a cyberprecariat and an android class of workers.

Chapters 9 and 10 develop parallel sets of conclusions about, colloquially, the 1 percent and the 99 percent, respectively. Chapter 9 details films about capitalism that rarely even discuss workers of any kind, much less the precariat. Chapter 10 chronicles new forms of worker organization and forms of mass protest, including the new "spectacles" of cinematically inspired protests, especially installation art and agitprop films.

In my earlier volumes on labor films, I was an early adaptor of the term *transnational cinema* for films coproduced by two or more countries, often, but not always, the United States and another country. While such a coproduction did not necessarily negate or reduce the influence of Hollywood, it vastly improved the global reach of many countries whose films had not always been readily available for viewing in the First World. In any case, independent feature films and documentaries had always provided non-American directors and producers more latitude and control. I have discontinued the use of the term *international films*, however, which in the United States and the United Kingdom has historically meant "everywhere else but here."

This book is designed to be useful to both students and teachers in a number of different disciplines, as well as activists, film professionals, and programmers working in community and other venues—especially labor, environmental, and social justice arenas. Those readers who have or have had jobs in the precariat should also be especially interested in the films in this volume. Does their new class of global labor really include both scavengers at city dumps and migrant farm workers, baristas and adjunct college instructors, miners and nannies, not to mention themselves?

Of course, surveying all possible films about the precariat would be quixotic, so my goal has been to include as many of the important contemporary films, both documentary and feature, both long and short, as well as historically relevant ones. Part of my mission is to call attention to films that I believe have been neglected or ignored.

Our "contemporary moment," argue Michael Curtin and Kevin Sanson, the editors of *Precarious Creativity: Global Media, Local Labor* (2016), is "a particularly critical historical juncture, a point in time when corporate consolidation, digital technologies, and the globalization of production" have significantly altered the "forms and everyday practices of screen media production." Hollywood and TV have yielded their cinematic hegemony to the internet as well as to such diverse forms as video games and installations at both art galleries and political happenings. This "moment" has also allowed filmmakers to include the precariat as an essential arena of their concern.

Although there has been to date no book solely devoted to the cinema of the precariat, there have been some other helpful studies of the precariat as it relates to the media and culture in general. The British Film Institute's *Global Hollywood* series (2001 and 2005) focused on the impact of precarious labor (low pay, irregular hours, and no traditional benefits of any kind) on both traditional craft workers and intellectual/artistic staff in the film industry, while an earlier study, David Morley and Kevin Robins's *Spaces of Identity* (1995), delineated the changes in cultural identity on a local scale wrought by international communications technology. The end of Western ethnocentrism may in effect free former colonized cultures to embrace new technologies and artistic forms.

Every film or video game discussed is identified by release date, country or countries of origin, and director (dir.) or producer (pro.) if the work is part of a wider series or commissioning agent. The origin of quotations of dialogue from the films discussed should be obvious from context. For quotations from—or references to—printed or internet sources, I use parenthetical or in-line citations. I should also add that Walmart officially dropped the dash and capital M in its name in 2017, so "Walmart" is used throughout the book.

Introduction

Who Are the Precariat?

The precariat is now a vast global workforce whose transitory and tenuous relationship with their employers makes most of them liable for termination or furlough at any time. But they still continue to work, for these are likely the only jobs they can get. Ironically, quite a few count themselves as lucky when they join the growing mass of migratory laborers in every continent in the world who are forced to cross borders to find work.

Guy Standing, the leading chronicler of the precariat, and the former director of the Socio-Economic Security Programme of the United Nation's International Labour Organization, argues that the precariat lacks opportunities for advancement as well as "health and safety regulations, training, and stable income." They have no collective representation before their employer and no access to any job protection.

Not surprisingly, the precariat is especially difficult to organize, but some new forms of collective leadership and action have emerged, using strategy and tactics reminiscent of Latino organizations like the Coalition of Immokalee Workers that began in Florida 1993 or the Occupy Wall Street movement that began in New York City in 2011. Labor organizers both traditional and maverick as well as community leaders and activists across the progressive political spectrum have been attempting to recruit these unrepresented workers operating in the streets, in the fields, in workplaces, in the media, and in cyberspace (see Chapter 10).

As the precariat finds itself more and more concentrated in urban configurations—whether it be in a cleaning service in an American city or building skyscrapers in a global megalopolis such as Dubai or making Mardi Gras beads in a Chinese factory city or scavenging in a Guatemalan city dump—filmmakers turn toward both traditional documentary and online innovative forms to present their vision of cultures in crisis. Even politically progressive video game makers have contributed to the variety of new forms dramatizing the precariat.

Historically, we know that no metropolis could exist without a working class. Now we would argue that no megalopolis could exist without such precariat-intensive zones as airport complexes, tech corridors, immigrant districts, *favelas*, shopping (mega) malls, resorts, corporate estates, export processing zones (EPZs), container ports, street markets, shantytowns, and even garbage cities.

If the field of working-class studies lays claim to the study of the workers of the world, especially how they are represented in literature, art, theater, and film, then it must come to terms with the latest category that is also global: the precariat. The precariat is in effect the workforce with the most unstable conditions since they may be furloughed or terminated at any time. These workers of the world are now beset—ironically, when they are lucky—with employment situations such as *zero-hour contracts* (United Kingdom), *casual employment* (Australia), *low-hour contracts* (Iceland), *mini jobs* (Germany), *subcontracted labor* (India), *non-hukou migration* (China), and *McJobs* or *the gig economy* (United States), rather than working with a fair contract or a union. In fact, the vast majority of workers, underpaid and underemployed, have no contract of any kind.

The precariat is not a new phenomenon, but it has come into prominence in part because of what David Weil in *The Fissured Workplace* (2014) analyzes as the widespread severing or "fissuring" of a company's traditional working force into part-time and contracted labor. The precariat has also expanded because of the kind of jobs that have arisen and have been popularly characterized—mistakenly, I believe—as the "gig" economy, in which workers take on a job for Uber or a restaurant as if they were deliberately choosing the equivalent of a band's or performer's "gig" or job of entertainment work. The metaphor is reductive and too casual.

Both Andrew Ross's *Nice Work If You Can Get It: Life and Labor in Precarious Times* (2009) and Guy Standing's *The Precariat: The New Dangerous Class* (2011) argue that the precariat's incredible growth has now virtually replaced the traditional proletariat. Standing also stresses its post-globalization and transitional status: "A new mass class is emerging—the precariat—characterized by chronic uncertainty and insecurity." They "consist of millions of people relegated to bits-and-pieces living, in and out of casual flexible jobs, unable to build an occupational identity or career." Although there is a tendency to regard them as simply a new working class, they are "unlike anything in the past. Part comes from old working-class communities, part from migrants and minorities, and part from the educated, who do not see themselves in the old class categories." Nevertheless, they are "wanted by the global market system" and are not a lumpenproletariat or "underclass."

As the leading analyst of the precariat, Standing has tracked in *A Precariat Charter: From Denizens to Citizens* (2014) one of the origins of the concept of the precariat in the "growth of labor market flexibility," arguing that the "neo-liberal [economic] model" resulted in more "economic insecurity and fragmented societies." His empathy with the working classes followed Alfred Marshall's insistence that economists must "get into the factories" to understand their true constituency.

But what if many of the factories are gone as a result of international competition, deindustrialization, and the one-sided repercussions of the Global Financial Crisis of 2008? Alex Foti in *General Theory of the Precariat: Great Recession, Revolution, Reaction* (2017) demonstrates that "a new precarious class has superseded the old working class: the service precariat of the 21st century [is] the analogue of the industrial proletariat of the 20th century."

Although the precariat is clearly a worldwide phenomenon, Standing's principal interest has been this "class in the making" in the industrialized West. As such it shares some of the "primitive rebel" attitudes that marked the demonstrations and organizations of the Occupy Wall Street movement after the Global Financial Crisis of 2008. One of these proto-rebels—and our first cinematic exemplar of the precariat in this book—was captured by Ken Loach, the cinematic master of working-class films in the UK, in his Cannes Film Festival–winning film *I, Daniel Blake* (United Kingdom, 2014).

The titular hero of the movie, Daniel Blake, is a carpenter (joiner) whose heart attack at work has convinced his doctor that he should stop working. Social services, however, after administering some byzantine tests, deem him fit to work. If he doesn't find work soon, he will be denied unemployment and other support benefits. He has difficulty mastering a welfare state maze worthy of Kafka but finds a new friend in related unfortunate circumstances, a single mom with two children. The four of them join forces to avoid living in the council (city government) hostel to which they have been assigned.

With *I, Daniel Blake* Loach is returning in spirit to his first successful film, *Cathy Come Home* (1966, United Kingdom), one of the first British films to condemn the policy of breaking up families in catastrophic economic situations, but also more sardonically to another of his films, *Riff-Raff* (1991, United Kingdom), in which homeless workers build homes for other people. Although the former was a "teleplay" produced for British television in the 1960s and the latter a theatrical release of the 1990s, Loach's social realist style and emphasis on the precariat has remained remarkably consistent; *Cathy Come Home* eventually challenged the concept of a "made for TV" film because it has become a cinematic classic whose later audiences would have no idea that it was originally intended "only" for television distribution. It has been argued that *Cathy Come Home* helped displace "art television," works based on the writer rather than the director as auteur (see Caughie and Brandt). Loach has become the auteur of the precariat, as he himself has recognized. When his most recent film, *Sorry We Missed You* (2019, United Kingdom), about a worker caught in a self-subsidized Uber-like delivery service scam, premiered at the Cannes Film Festival, Loach stated, "If we believe in the free market, then that leads to the big corporations taking power, that leads to this competition to lower wages, and that leads to precarious work" (Mumford).

Daniel Blake is also a literal victim of that process: Just before he has a fatal heart attack, he writes his creed on the job center wall; when the film was released, his statement was also projected on the wall of the British Parliament: "I am not a client, a customer, nor a service user. I am not a shirker, a scrounger, a beggar nor a thief. I am not a national insurance number, nor a blip on a screen. I paid my dues, never a penny short, and was proud to do so. . . . My name is Daniel Blake, I am a man, not a dog. As such I demand my rights."

The following year, Daniel Blake had a French cinematic double in *The Measure of a Man* (2015, France, dir. Stephane Brize), whose original French title was *La Loi du Marche*—"the law of the market"—about a worker laid off from a decent job who struggles for a year with inadequate unemployment checks. His entry into the precariat after his family life collapses from unpaid bills leads him to become a security guard spying on desperate shoppers. Many of his old workmates are still fighting—foolishly, he believes—in the union campaign against his former company. Joining the precariat seems a safe, if inevitable, choice.

Another European counterpart to Ken Loach's approach to working-class films is the Belgian filmmaking team of Jean-Pierre and Luc Dardenne, who dramatized a similar dilemma with a young woman working in a small factory in *Two Days, One Night* (Belgium, 2014). In this instance, however, it is her coworkers who at first force her out of her job because management offers them a substantial bonus to work extra time to make up for her redundancy. She too goes on an odyssey, visiting all her coworkers in an attempt to have them change their decision in her favor.

These are working-class Europeans being pushed down into the precariat, "still a class-in-the-making, divided within itself," in Standing's analysis. They may be ready to reject "old mainstream political traditions" after their "primitive rebel stage" during the massive demonstrations and occupations that followed the Global Financial Crisis in 2008, but they are not yet in reach of "socioeconomic security, control of time, quality space, knowledge (or education), financial knowledge and financial capital." They will become a "transformative class" only when they can "struggle for redistribution of the key assets needed for a good life in a good society in the twenty-first century."

We know there is a substantial cinema of this "class in the making," whatever it might be called. The term *precariat* will need—as *globalization* before it—a conceptual framework as well as a social cartography. One trendsetting instance in which the precariat in fact erodes the traditional proletariat is the rise of two-tier union membership in the United States by the Teamsters for the United Parcel Service and the United Auto Workers for auto manufacturers by which established union workers and new part-time, sometimes temporary, workers have different contracts.

With these partial exceptions in mind, unlike the traditional proletariat who fought for union recognition, members of the precariat are almost uniformly ineligible for any traditional union, but some of them have turned to other forms of self-organization, based on locale (the Coalition of Immokalee Workers in Florida), through protest movements (the worldwide Occupy movements), or by cross-ethnic organizing of service workers (OUR Walmart).

While for a time it seemed that youth would be a marker for the precariat—for example, 20 percent of sixteen- to twenty-four-year-olds in Britain are out of work—other class and occupational markers seem to define the precariat more fully. The preponderance of employment brokers or self-appointed contractors or employment agencies have been a feature of the precariat in both Western and non-Western countries. New industries—call centers, Big Box stores for food and goods—are exclusively staffed by temporary workers. In the not-so-distant past, most factories, offices, and work sites (cranes at docks, for example) were obviously stationery and the workers had to come to their sites, making union organizing possible. Now there are even fleets of fishing ships at sea, whose workers catch, process, and package fish, sometimes even with a specific supermarket label, that never dock for great periods of time.

Standing's analysis is that the precariat is "not yet a class in the Marxian sense" but "a class in the making," only "approaching a consciousness of common vulnerability." The precariat "consists not just of everybody in insecure jobs" such as temps, part-timers, call center workers, and other outsourced arrangements, but it also consists of those no longer in control of their lives, economic or otherwise. Thus, Standing's assessment is that there exists—using Raymond Williams's formulation from a previous generation—a "structure of feeling" in society that is greater than the actual job description of the workers but a consciousness of precarity that not only runs through their work life but also is dominant in their family and social context.

The precariat does not have what the proletariat once did when it belonged "to a community of pride, status, ethics, and solidarity." It is difficult to avoid the assumption that the precariat has been the primary victim of globalization, "which put faith in labor market flexibility, the commodification of everything, and the restructuring of social protection." Ironically, Standing concludes that in the UK, for example, it is the very Labour Party under the guise of the New Labour slogans that has expanded the precariat. When the European Union tried to extend equal rights to temporary workers, the New Labour movement was in the forefront of blocking it. Without the "trinity of equality, liberty, and fraternity" that epitomizes the progressive proletariat, the precariat can become "dangerous," this is recruited to neofascism or in the US Trumpism (Standing, August 2011). One argument from the left (Choonara and Breman) was that emphasizing the precariat as a class was neither politically progressive nor of value conceptually: there was the danger that the precariat and the proletariat would not find common ground.

Economically and politically, Standing's solution is the Basic Income, a guaranteed payment for all, a proposal that is resisted by the forces Noam Chomsky has described in 2012 as the plutonomy—the dominance of the elite, the rich, the one percenters. Even Alan Greenspan, Chomsky argued, believed that a successful economy depended on "growing worker insecurity" (*Occupy*). Citigroup investment group, for example, had sent out to its investors a remarkable call in 2005 to seize the slogan, "Plutonomy: Buying Luxury," since "the world is divided into two blocs—the plutonomy and the rest." A large part of the "rest" is, of course, the precariat. Within three years, Citigroup was one of the investment banks that would have gone into bankruptcy in the Global Financial Crisis in 2008 if it had not been rescued by the US government.

Standing defines Basic Income as "a right, paid in cash (or equivalent) to all individuals regardless of age, gender, marital status, work status and work history." His global research concludes that "the twentieth-century income distribution system has broken down," but Basic Income would recognize "that current economic and social policies are producing unsustainable inequalities and injustices."

The class most affected by these changes is, of course, the precariat, "consisting of millions of people facing unstable, insecure labor, a lack of occupational identity, declining and increasingly volatile real wages, loss of benefits and chronic indebtedness." Basic Income is not a quixotic crusade for Standing for the alternatives are far worse: "Without a new income distribution system . . . the drift to the far right, which underpinned Brexit in the United Kingdom and the triumph of Donald Trump in 2016 in the USA . . . will only grow stronger" (Standing 2017).

Standing's model for his drive to publicize the role of precarity in contemporary economics and the opportunity to achieve the Basic Income is the sociologist and political visionary Barbara Wootton, little known outside the UK for her numerous successes in politically progressive campaigns such as workman's compensation, work hours, prison reform, and many others. Standing begins his book *On Basic Income* (2017) with her belief that "it is from the champions of the impossible rather than the slaves of the possible that evolution draws its creative force."

Because the precariat is an international presence, I have included films from around the world. There is no question that the majority of the world's workers now—and, perhaps, have for many generations, even centuries—fit most definitions of the precariat. People with steady jobs and good income, however, make the precariat in their midst invisible, especially in urban areas. In Washington, DC, for example, where I live, the firefighters, police, teachers, nurses, and other professionals have traditional proletarian and salariat jobs: they often have unions, earn a decent living wage, and have health and retirement benefits. Yet adjunct faculty in the area at colleges and universities who the American Federated Teachers call the highest-educated low-pay workers in America have no benefits of any kind, often receive inadequate announcements about re-employment semester to semester, and often work second or third jobs such as babysitting or bartending to survive.

In *The Precariat: The New Dangerous Class*, Standing uses a seven-tier class analysis that is one of the best measures of the new complexity of work in the world, although its origins is in the class system of the UK, Europe, and other relatively advanced economies in the Far East. But the precariat is an incredibly elastic classification that would include both Uber drivers in New York City and pedal cab drivers in Bombay, both recyclers of e-waste in China and the Dalits of India who service latrines, and both tomato pickers in Immokalee and diamond miners in Sierra Leone, in short any class of workers whose society has created a class of workers without recourse to job security or benefits.

What would be the center of traditional Marxist analysis of workers in society according to Standing is the "old working class" or the *proletariat*, often unionized and employed full time. The *precariat* is a class level lower, and its essence is "existential insecurity," dismissible at the will of a supervisor, with no benefits, much less a contract. Beyond the ability to do physical labor, the precariat's qualifications and job profile do not often match. The British Broadcasting Service (BBC) did its own classification in its Great British Class Survey in 2013. Although similar to Standing's pyramid of seven classes, the BBC's survey did differ in its placement of two distinct classes at the bottom—the "emergent service workers" and the "precarious proletariat"—both of whom would be subsumed by Standing's more capacious category of the precariat.

Just above Standing's proletariat are the *salariat* who have secure employment, "with pensions, paid holidays, and medical leave," and above them the *proficiens* who are typically college grads with the specialized training of experts. Below the precariat are the *unemployed* and *lumpen precariat* (also known as the lumpenproletariat)—those who are neither working nor actively seeking work. Standing's analysis of the lumpen "as socially ill misfits living off the dregs of society" seems to encompass both the homeless and criminals, two classes of individuals whose status is certainly precarious by any social measure we can devise, although they cannot or do not want to have even casual employment. At the top of Standing's pyramid are the *plutocrats* and the *elite*, the very wealthy and the governing or ruling classes of the world.

Two recent films provide helpful and dramatic guides to the intricacies of the three lowest levels of Standing's schema. *Sollers Point* (2017, United States/France, dir. Matthew Porterfield), a film set in a postindustrial and ravaged section of Baltimore, closely follows a young man, a former drug dealer from the neighborhood who has been released from jail and seeks a comeback to his life in Sollers Point, near Dundalk, the site of the now-closed Bethlehem Steel plant, and the legendary war horse of Baltimorean labor history. He navigates his father's friends—the last generation of the local unionized proletariat—and does various odd jobs to survive in the precariat, such as selling scrap metal, picking up rides for pay at the bus stops, trying without success to enroll in a vocational HVAC (heating, ventilation, and air conditioning) program, and even considers a community college art program. He fails at most of these endeavors and is sucked back into the lumpenproletariat, which includes black and white drug dealers as well as a white supremacy gang he "needed" for protection when he was inside prison.

Similarly, the Japanese film *Shoplifters* (2018, Japan, dir. Hirokazu Koreeda) dramatizes a lovable quasi-family of rogues who survive by negotiating all the lower rungs of Standing's pyramid. Director Koreeda said he was influenced by Ken Loach and the Dardenne brothers, the British and Belgian masters of precariat filmmaking, respectively. The father has a janitor-like job at a high-rise construction site when he is not actively shoplifting with his adopted son. His wife works in a laundry and steals any valuables she finds in the customers' dry cleaning. Another, a teenage girl, works as a sex worker in a peep-show parlor where she exposes herself according to the customers' written request lists. The older woman whom they call grandmother, the apparent owner of the tiny house they all live in, has a pension but is open to any scam going to keep the family afloat. In many ways they are a lumpenproletarian lot who accept their precariat jobs as long as a steady stream of shoplifted food and goods arrives home. They do care for each other, however, and dare you to approve of them.

These two films emphasize why the cinema of the precariat must be surveyed globally. The subjects of the films are inevitably the pawns of globalization, the economic phenomenon of multinational corporations that create and move goods and services at the lowest cost for the maximum profit. Its political clout comes from powerful organizations: the World Bank (WB), the World Trade Organization (WTO), and the International Monetary Fund (IMF). Its modus vivendi is the reflection of neoliberal economics that has literally capitalized on new technologies, transportation options, and digitalized logistic and financial systems. Containerized shipping has been the physical means of transnational business, but deregulation of banking and environmental laws as well as privatizing public resources has meant that raw materials, sources of energy, mineral wealth, and even drinking water have become commodities for sale. Outsourcing labor costs and securing offshore and usually tax-free sites have strengthened the corporate leadership.

The precariat internationally is often linked with migratory labor and immigrants. It may be, as Max Weber wrote of the Polish farm workers who emigrated "from East of the Elbe River" into Germany, that it was "the dark urge for personal freedom" that propelled them "to work in a foreign land," but then as well as now the complications of their migration are twofold. Will they be allowed to stay in their adopted land, and how will they get work that will let them survive? Because virtually every country has an influx of foreign workers and because inevitably they take the jobs that define the precariat, the cinema of the precariat is particularly rich in films that offer multiple workers' viewpoints. Most immigrants travel to the United States or other economically thriving countries like Germany, Israel, or the United Kingdom for jobs, freedom from oppression back home or from personal and family trauma. Those who come for jobs may not realize that globalization is responsible for the change in their economic situations in their countries of origin. Whatever the reason, inevitably they become part of the precariat of their host country. Some countries, like China, have a massive internal migration, where millions travel great distances within their own country in search of precariat work.

Unlike the Chinese internal migration that has been in place for the last thirty years, most patterns of immigration from country to county have endured for decades, if not longer. Typically, the older arrivals retain their native language but their children are soon bilingual. As soon as possible, immigrants and their children take jobs and join the precariat, willingly or not. In many cases chance has determined their exit from their native country, but work determines their lives after they arrive.

The situation in other robust economies, like Israel's, is similar. *Manpower* (2014, Israel, dir. Noam Kaplan) weaves four interrelated stories of Tel Aviv's surprisingly diverse representatives of its "manpower," half holding precarious jobs, the other half more secure employment or military status but with their own dangers of balancing on the edge of social mobility. The two seemingly most secure jobs are those of a policeman and a would-be soldier. The former leads a unit charged with vigorously pursuing a policy with civilian outliers called "Leave at Will"—that is, if they willingly take the government's deal and leave, Israel will become more white and Jewish. They focus on a Nigerian housecleaner who fears deportation but tries to support the president of his African Workers Union, a man also the target of the police squad.

Another teenager, who was born in Israel of a Thai mother and therefore not officially Jewish, nonetheless, wants to join the Israeli Defense Force as a means of fitting in. In the meantime, he is working in a fast-food restaurant where his good looks help him survive. A Jewish cabdriver whose Filipino wife, son, and grandson are leaving Israel completes the cast that reflects the replacement of Arab labor by guest workers from Thailand, Nigeria, and many other African nations, none of whom come under the Israeli "law of return."

The director includes numerous revealing incidents. In pursuit of the union president, the police pick out an African and ask him, "Who are you?" "Nobody," he says. "Are you in the union?" they ask him. When he replies affirmatively, they "arrest" him. When the teenager goes in for his military interview, they ask him to sing an Israeli song in Hebrew from a pop radio station. He succeeds, albeit feebly (Figure I.1).

Workers at the Walmart chain of stores represent one of the largest concentration of the precariat outside of China and India. The irony is that this Walmartization of the precariat is happening in one of the most prosperous of the First World nations. It is to these Walmart workers that the cinema of the precariat has turned repeatedly to expose many jobs that seem invisible to all except those who actually do the work. These workers were once called wage slaves or temp slaves, the latter the title of a magazine, *Temp Slave!*, published in the 1990s, just before the explosion of digitalization but after President Ronald Reagan had fired 15,000 air traffic controllers as the first step in a long, mostly Republican, drive to destroy unions' and workers' rights. *Temp Slave!* chronicled the precariat before the term existed. Jeff Kelly, its editor, argued that temp workers were not only used for cheap labor, but were also used to "make full timers think twice about raising questions about work conditions since the threat of replacement by a temp is all the more possible."

Figure I.1 Israeli police raid from *Manpower*. Courtesy Gum Films.

Barbara Ehrenreich's best seller, *Nickel and Dimed: On (Not) Getting by in America* (2001), is based on an experiment in which she is her own guinea pig. Could she survive by cleaning houses, waitressing, and clerking at Walmart? She discovers that unless you avoid paying for a place to sleep by living with a relative or take an equally bad-paying second job, you will be stuck in the precariat indefinitely.

It is no accident that one of Ehrenreich's choices for work was Walmart, the Big Box chain that controls the largest ever-changing cadres of the precariat. Before the precariat even had its current name, the widespread exploitation of Walmart workers throughout the United States and the virtually forced migration of millions of Chinese workers to new industrial cities to make the goods Walmart sold epitomized how globalization had reordered the working world.

On the surface, Walmart was *the* all-American store. Rarely outdone by competitors, Walmart's blockbuster and holiday sales, the giant American flags flying over the store, and the over-friendly staff resonated with patriotism. The fact of the matter is that eventually all of Walmart's goods were made in massive Chinese factories, whose workers were often migrants from the cities, driven to those factories by the end of the traditional Chinese "iron rice bowl" of state-supported jobs that came with free health and other public services.

The best wage for American Walmart workers is currently just under $14/hour, although the number of hours they work can vary radically, from ten to thirty-four a week—the epitome of the situation for the underemployed precariat. Walmart is the leading corporate target of lawsuits, especially for its refusal to pay overtime, locking in workers overnight, not paying them for working off the clock, and a myriad of racial and sexual acts of discrimination. Not surprisingly, their employee turnover is in the 50 percent range. Virtually no Walmart store in North America is unionized; only China and Germany have unionized Walmart workers. Until stopped by a lawsuit, Walmart routinely took out "dead peasant" insurance for as many as 350,000 workers with itself as beneficiary in case of death.

Sam Walton's rise to the elite class was facilitated by the work of a sizeable percentage of the American precariat. Five of his heirs—wife and four children—rank in the top twenty-five of the wealthiest Americans with approximately $18 billion each. These five heirs have as much money as the bottom 41.5 percent of all Americans combined. The current CEO earns $35 million, while the turnover for the underemployed first-year workers is 70 percent. According to Congressman Alan Grayson (Rep., Florida), Walmart employees make up a number of his state's largest group of food stamp and Medicaid recipients. The range of the precariat employed directly or indirectly by Walmart is staggering. Erika Smiley, the co-executive director of Jobs with Justice, has carefully deconstructed the Walmart empire beyond the 2.2 million members of the precariat it employs directly. Indirectly, Walmart controls the Louisiana seafood workers through exclusive contracts as well as the workers at the Hyatt hotel chain in which Walmart has invested a billion dollars.

No other corporate employer of the precariat has attracted more filmmakers, both feature and documentary, than Walmart. Its omnipresence in the American suburban world generates both customers and critics. In fact, the Walmartization of the precariat led most industries in their reduction of quality jobs for workers, unionized or not.

Working Stiffs, Union Maids, Reds, and Riffraff and *The Cinema of Globalization* have already discussed in detail many of the Walmart films through 2006, including three feature films, a TV series, and more than fifteen documentaries, a remarkable selection about a single Big Box store chain. Even when Walmart fails to penetrate a targeted community, a documentary charts the contest: *Talking to the Wall* (2012, United States, dir. Steve Alves), for example, surveys communities who have successfully resisted Walmart, arguing that low prices never offset the generous welcome package—paid for by people's taxes—that officials use to bribe Walmart to settle in. Ironically, the film argues, it is not "the story of an American bargain" (Figure I.2).

Walmart has been the target of one of the developing alt-labor groups, Organization United for Respect (OUR) at Walmart, that focuses on the low pay, lack of affordable healthcare, and a safe workplace of 2 million workers, many of whom are barely a step away from poverty even as they work "part time," since all Walmart workers are part-time. Their agitprop documentary, *Dear Walmart* (2019, United States, dir. Kiley Kraskouskas and Michael Blaine), follows both activists and rank-and-file leaders who take credit in forcing Walmart to raise the hourly minimum wage to $9. In a peculiarly Walmart gesture of spite, Walmart shut down a number of stores where activists were centered. Therefore, they were not "fired" for their activity, their jobs just disappeared.

A different and even more elaborate anti-Walmart defense originated from a radical community theatrical troupe in New York City called Reverend Billy and the Church of Stop Shopping. In their film, *What Would Jesus Buy?* (2007, United States, dir. Ron Van Alkemade), their "pastor" delivers sermons across America about the commercialization of Christmas and the necessity of not

Figure I.2 Demonstration against Walmart. *Talking to the Wall.* Photo by *Greenfield Recorder.* Courtesy Steve Alves.

buying as much at Walmart. Reverend Billy, aka Bill Talen, began on a NYC subway platform preaching against Shopocalypse and the Big Box culture. Over fifty arrests for disturbing the peace have not waylaid his crusade. He has more arrests than The Yes Men.

Walmart continues to draw very critical cinematic coverage. Although the NBC series *Superstore* (2016–17) was at first set at a K-Mart, the policies of the store named Super Cloud 9 mimic Walmart closely as well, with no maternity leave, no health insurance, no overtime, and extremely limited bathroom and lunch breaks. The series focuses on managerial staff, although at least one "associate," as workers in these stores tend to be called, is an undocumented immigrant and another—like the Walmart worker Natalie Portman played in *Where the Heart Is* (2000, United States, dir. Matt Williams)—gives birth in the store.

At the end of the twentieth century, Walmart was one of the two companies in the news for their successful maneuvering in the age of globalization: the Big Box chain had mastered the supply chain of Chinese-produced goods through digitalization and containerized shipping. The other company, Enron, an energy company that soon turned into a financial conglomerate, was a success story for the end of the century. But only Walmart, sticking to the letter of the law, survived. Enron, who followed neither the letter nor the spirit of the law, collapsed and its executives went off to jail. Twenty thousand Enron workers lost their jobs, millions lost their investments, and Enron joined a growing list of failed corporations. Of the triumvirate who led the cheating at the top at Enron, only Kenneth Lay, the CEO, escaped jail by dying. His COO, Jeffrey Skilling, spent twelve years in jail, while the CFO, Andrew Fastow, spent six. It was a rare moment when the 1 percent paid for their criminal leadership. (Don Blankenship, CEO of Massey Energy responsible for the Upper Big Bridge mine disaster in 2010, spent a year in jail, one of the few coal executives ever to do so despite a century of corporate negligence.) The precariat, however, remained at Walmart stores everywhere.

The cinematic record of Enron and Walmart was exhaustively surveyed in my earlier labor films books. Enron is old, bad news, and has left the screening room. Since Walmart has survived, of course, a number of later films—see Chapter 10—have tried to take the measure of the company's continued exploitation of their workers through low pay and controlled work hours, the latter always part time to avoid federal regulations on full-time labor.

1

Harvest of Shame: The First Series of Films about the Precariat

Edward R. Murrow's *Harvest of Shame* (United States, 1960) is *the* classic of early investigative journalism in the media. It inspired two major series of now little known but quite compelling film sequels in the late 1960s, the 1970s, and the 1990s, almost exclusively for American broadcast TV, capturing a major cohort of the precariat: white, black, and Latino migrant workers and farm laborers.

Murrow's television broadcast was an extremely influential breakthrough for public opinion about migrant workers, but an earlier film, a remarkable protest song, and a Pulitzer Prize–winning story had prepared the way for the reappearance in popular culture of the workers Murrow will call the "forgotten people" and who we would now see as some of the first unappreciated but finally recognized members of the precariat.

In 1952, Billie Davis, a young white woman, described her "hobo" life as a migrant worker with her family in "I Was a Hobo Kid," an essay for the *Saturday Evening Post* and the *Reader's Digest*. Later, she said that her "people were the true homeless migrant workers." She became a pop culture heroine for her remarkable journey from hobo camps to university graduate school. The National Education Association (NEA) saw her grit and her self-made life as an ideal symbol for the power of transformative education and sponsored a docudrama of her life, *A Desk for Billie* (1952, United States, dir. Irving Rusinow).

Billie's fervor for reading and writing was kindled by the accommodation and kindness she received at a school in Fort Laramie, Wyoming, where she was given her first school desk—hence the title of her filmed story—although she estimated that she had already attended about forty different schools as her family crisscrossed the country, picking hops in Oregon, vegetables in Idaho, and fruits in Texas and Florida, as well as harvesting wheat in Kansas.

The family also had a little household industry: making baskets and crepe paper flowers for sale in weekend markets, an especially important financial sideline for the young girl because it helped her go to school during the week. Her father regarded cutting the willows for basket weaving at a nearby river as an antidote for his life of toil: "I'm sick of doing the rich man's dirty work," he would say. At church, Billie heard that she was "a child of God," which made her believe that she "wouldn't be a bum." Her dream was to be a "real person and live in a house," frustrated that even at the best of locations, such as Bakersfield, California, they lived in migrant labor shacks with no electricity or running water.

They all put up with a lot of abuse. "Look at the gypsies and dirty bums," townies would say, "Those gypsies have lice and probably steal chickens." Sunday school as well as her discovery that she could go to a library and read books for "free" saved her. What she didn't have, however, was an address she could use for a library card. She also credits the Salvation Army for rescuing her and sending her off to a leadership training school. Eventually, with money saved from working in an aircraft factory in Bakerfield, she left the world of the migrants behind.

Billie's laboring family were homegrown Americans from a long tradition of the poor, white working class. But farm labor was already changing by the time Billie graduated. Idaho, for example, one of the states Billie's family worked in, had an extremely regulated flow of migrant laborers from Texas: they were of Mexican ancestry but they were all American citizens with social security numbers. The labor shortages during the Second World War were history, and a new pool of workers was needed. They were recruited in part by the Amalgamated Sugar Company as the bracero program was gradually being abandoned, in part because of a growing number of sizeable bracero strikes in Idaho. Mexico objected to the treatment of the braceros during the strikes in 1946 and suspended bracero travel to Idaho (Foy).

It is clear, then, why the state, according to a promotional film, *Idaho's Summer Citizens*, made by the state's Employment Security Agency in the mid- to late 1950s—since the migrant teenagers liked "rock-n-roll"—was very keen to schedule the workers with as much precision as the different crops required, using an Annual Worker Plan. The agency sponsored the fiesta we see in the film, one of their "migrant appreciation" days (Hodges). They seem to have lived in some of the old Farm Security Administration Labor Camps in Eagle Pass and Carville.

Farmers from other states, with government support and encouragement, had begun to employ workers on a temporary basis directly from Mexico as early as the 1940s. Labor's most famous folksinger, Woody Guthrie, had already written about a tragedy of twenty-eight of these braceros, as they were known, literally "those who work with their arms," who were being sent back to Mexico when their plane crashed in Fresno's Los Gatos Canyon in 1948.

Woody's song, "Deportees" (also known as "Plane Wreck at Los Gatos"), went on to have a distinguished performance record, having been recorded and/or sung by the Kingston Trio, Judy Collins, Joan Baez, Pete Seeger, Bob Dylan, and Woody's son, Arlo Guthrie. With rare exception, the national news stories had never listed the names of the deceased, just referring to them as "deportees," although they had entered the country legally under this program that gave them limited visas to work on selected farms. Guthrie's song asked if using "deportees" who were treated like "outlaws" and "thieves" was the "best way" to grow fruit.

Murrow's *Harvest of Shame* was filmed at the end of the 1950s, only twenty years after John Steinbeck portrayed the iconic farming family, the fictional Joads, whose story was adapted in *The Grapes of Wrath* (1939, United States, dir. John Ford) and who had been thrown off their tenant farm in Oklahoma and had taken to the road in search of work, just one of the many families of Oakies (as they were nicknamed). Steinbeck had published a series of newspaper reports in 1936 for the *San Francisco News*, called *The Harvest Gypsies*, about migrant workers in California's Central Valley, later reprinting them in a pamphlet, *Their Blood Is Strong* (1938), that sold 10,000 copies, and including an epilogue, "Starvation under the Orange Trees." His novel, *In Dubious Battle*, appeared that same year and was more overtly political as it chronicled communist organizers during a strike.

In *Harvest of Shame*, in an iconic shot that opens the film, Murrow stands in front of a field that seems to extend endlessly into the distance. Murrow introduces his subject with what we now realize perfectly defines the 1950s precariat: the "forgotten people, the under-protected people, the undereducated, the under-clothed, the underfed." Although they are said to be servicing the "best fed nation on earth," in the opening interview Mrs. Dobie, a white women with nine children, all of whom except the baby work alongside her in the fields, she says she can only afford one gallon of milk a week. Mrs. Dobie longs for a house of their own—"We plan to buy one," she says, but when pressed, doubts that it will ever happen (Figure 1.1).

To make Murrow's point that the two to three million workers doing this work are black as well as white, we see an interview with Jerome, a nine-year-old black

Figure 1.1 Edward R. Murrow in *Harvest of Shame*. CBS News Press Release Photo.

boy who has to stay in his family's shack because he stepped on a nail and also because he has to take care of his baby sister, who is sitting next to a mattress with a rat-chewed hole in the middle. His mother earns a dollar a day for ten hours of work.

Although Murrow included similar families of white workers, like Billy Davis's family, traveling on the road, he inexorably turned to the all-black work crews at southern corporate farms. Other Mexican farmworkers continued to participate in the bracero program that lasted until 1964, which in turn had been replaced by the H-2 designation for temporary visas for workers. Regardless of race or country of origin, however, Murrow's workers seem hapless and adrift.

About seven or eight months before Murrow's broadcast, Howard Van Smith, a reporter for the *Miami News* whom Murrow interviews in his film, did not at first have Immokalee—125 miles from Miami—on his beat, but he heard about the plight of perhaps 4,000 African American migrant workers who had been stranded in Immokalee—then known as Shacktown—because of a freeze in the tomato fields. Pursuing the story, he later wrote, he found decrepit housing not fit for goats, children in diapers when it was twenty-five degrees outside, and widespread pools of sewage next to containers of drinking water. His expose earned him a Pulitzer Prize for national reporting about, what his award citation called, this "cesspool of America." Murrow's broadcast must have provided a knockout blow for Immokalee's reputation at this point in time.

Most Americans, stuffed with the glories of their Thanksgiving feast in 1960, saw Murrow's film the next day. Such a poke in the eye was not typical of mainstream media at this time. Murrow's zeal and nerve become obvious when we realize that the only significant documentary on migrant workers previous to his, *Poverty in the Valley of Plenty* (1948, United States, prod. National Farm Labor Union), released the same year as the crash of Guthrie's deportees, had been successfully sued for libel by the DiGiorgio Fruit Corporation (founded by an Italian immigrant, Giuseppe DiGiorgio) and copies had to be destroyed. But copies of this twenty-minute film did survive, nonetheless, and an eight-minute section has surfaced on YouTube with this label: "Warning—this movie was found to be defamatory and all copies ordered destroyed—it is presented here solely for historic and educational purposes." The film was cosponsored by progressive Hollywood filmmakers and the AFL-CIO's National Farm Labor Union, in part led by Ernesto Galarza, the underappreciated pre–Cesar Chavez activist who later wrote a best-selling autobiography, *Barrio Boy* (1971). The film received virtually no distribution and would never have been shown on any commercial channel. It survived the court injunction because individuals involved with the Hollywood Film Council of the AFL-CIO preserved copies of it.

The DiGiorgios were early big agribusiness opportunists. When the workers campaigned for ten cents an hour more, a grievance procedure, and seniority rights, they were fired and replaced by Oakies, Arkies, Filipinos, Tejanos, and Mexican national braceros, the latter group contrary to the agreement between Mexico and the United States that foreign workers could not be used during strikes. Nonetheless, all of these competing "ethnic" groups, all part of the seemingly limitless "backlog of unemployment in the central valley," not to mention "the reserve of unemployed workers outside the state," complicated the strikers' relationship with the valley. Even "unemployed sailors in the Bay area" and "wandering Navajo Indians" were then "trudging the migrant trails from New Mexico through Riverside as far north as Stockton." Galarza represents an authoritative voice in describing this "reservoir of some 75,000 men and women" by which his strikers were eventually defeated.

Galarza understood that one of the few weapons on the strikers' side was the relatively new federal "farm labor supply centers" that were well-regulated migratory camps. We can get a glimpse of how different they were from the "tent colonies, dilapidated trailer camps, ditch bank settlements and full blown vineyard ghettoes" by recalling the California camp that the Joads drive into in

Ford's *Grapes of Wrath*: not only were the camps clean and well-organized with good leadership—Ford cast a look-alike of Franklin Delano Roosevelt as the supervisor—but they were, according to Galarza, "public property where men and women may freely assemble and talk," as well as being "inter-racial" and havens for labor union members "who cannot be summarily evicted."

Although both CBS News and the crusading California congresswoman Helen Gahagan Douglas exposed DiGiorgio's lies, the latter prevailed in court, reflecting the times when Richard Nixon, Douglas's opponent for Senate in 1950, red-baited her as a "pink lady," a communist sympathizer, because she was "*pink* right down to her underwear." The National Farm Labor Union also soon collapsed.

DiGiorgio got another chance to attack the migrant worker organizing movement when the company received its second court success against a single showing of the supposedly banned *Poverty in the Land of Plenty* to a small crowd of migrant workers being organized by Maria Moreno, a now little known but quite successful organizer for the AFL-CIO's Agricultural Workers Organizing Committee (AWOC) in the 1950s. One of the rare pioneers of migrant organizing and herself a worker and mother, she had a lot of success as an orator and organizer, often bringing any number of her twelve children to stand with her at the mike and exhort the workers to join the union. She was born in Texas, grew up working on farms, but realized, somewhat surprising herself, that she was a spirited and convincing speaker to her brothers and sisters in the fields in California.

Her mercurial rise and fall as an organizer is chronicled in *Adios Amor: The Search for Maria Moreno* (2018, United States, dir. Laurie Coyle), a documentary that has somewhat miraculously brought her back from the attics and forgotten memories of her coworkers, especially the photographers who recorded virtually every one of her appearances and whose work contributed so much to this film. Apparently, her legal defeat by DiGiorgio, Cesar Chavez's belief that she "shoots her mouth off" too often, and her mantra that she and her followers "should picket first and talk later" were too much for the AFL-CIO that assigned an AWOC toady to fire her. Her union and Chavez's growing forces merged into the United Farm Workers, but she was a persona non grata there, which was a real loss to their organizing efforts.

Murrow had filmed the first scene of *Harvest of Shame* in Belle Glade, whose "loading ramp" was a dusty lot where the "shape up" for crews looking for daily work took place. Chet Huntley returned to Belle Glade in 1970 for NBC:

"It has been ten years since Edward R. Murrow made *Harvest of Shame*. We hope that no one will need to make a film about migrants ten years from now." But they did: NBC went back to Belle Glade in 1990 and CBS also returned in 1995 and 2010. More interviews were recorded with workers in Immokalee, the Okefenokee Swamp town where more than fifty years later the Coalition of Immokalee Workers (CIW) was eventually organized.

Nonetheless, later TV documentaries followed Murrow's lead, using a strong voice-over narration by a star or celebrity reporter (who may even be in the shots), and gravitated toward muckraking rather than simple reporting. By the end of the decade, however, exploited labor knew no color.

What Harvest for the Reaper? (1968, United States), directed by Morton Silverstein for the National Educational Television (NET) Journal, focused on just one of Murrow's targets: a labor camp in Cutchogue, Long Island, that "would make slave life on the old Dixie plantation appear attractive." Silverstein believed that this strategy made "the story of a single camp the prototype for the national tragedy."

Produced for NET, the forerunner of the Public Broadcasting System (PBS), Morton Silverstein's documentary picked up two of Murrow's major themes: the role of the crew leader and the migrant camp. A group of African American migrant workers from Alabama was recruited to work in Cutchogue by Andrew Anderson, a black crew chief who promised them a lot but delivered very little.

Silverstein's interview technique involved a subterfuge: he told the farmers who hired Anderson's crew that now it was their turn—having put up with Murrow's "biggest lie," as they saw it—to present the truth and "the farmers' point of view." Silverstein maintained that's what he did, but the "farmers subsequently hung themselves." This is classic early TV investigative journalism; as Silverstein described his method, he said that "the documentary must be an instrument of social change, or it is not worth the raw stock it's filmed on."

The film is unrelenting in its condemnation of the exploitation of migrant labor, but it, nonetheless, has a little room for sympathy even for Anderson, who, like the filmmakers, is harassed by redneck sheriffs in Forrest City, Arkansas, where he recruits his workers.

As if Murrow's and Silverstein's films weren't enough of a shock on mainstream TV, Charles Kuralt's *Hunger in America* (1968, United States, dir. Martin Carr) was beyond daring, a broadcast in the cycle that makes no concessions to propriety or even shame. Beginning with the assertion that "hunger is hard to recognize in America," it immediately proceeds to a doctor attending to a tiny baby, giving it what looks like infant CPR: "This baby is dying of starvation. He was an American. Now he is dead." I would venture to say very few babies died before the viewers' eyes on prime TV in 1968 or, for that matter, in any other year.

CBS reports had sent Kuralt and others to focus on poverty in four states with four different population groups, carefully delineating their paltry food intake. Because of poverty and lack of government support, the *sole* nutritional choice for the Mexican Americans of San Antonio was beans and tortillas; for the Navahos of Arizona, fry bread; for the white tenant farmers of Loudoun County, Virginia, potatoes; and for the African Americans of Hale City, Alabama, rice. The white tenant farmers, Kuralt somewhat casually mentions, occupy the estates of Senator Everett Dirksen and the popular TV entertainer Arthur Godfrey, just twenty-five miles from the US Capitol, and, like many of their descendants today, paradoxically despise government handouts and support of any kind as an insult to their way of life.

Although government aid is available in the form of food stamps and distribution of free commodities by the Department of Agriculture for these malnourished masses, neither helps substantially: the food stamps still need to be purchased, even if discounted, and the commodities never include fresh meat, vegetables, or fruit, all necessary for a healthy diet. Kuralt also visits numerous clinics and hospitals where the most desperate and dangerously ill of these groups sometimes get treated. Most if not all of their life-threatening illnesses, especially for the children, are due to malnutrition and starvation. Although it is hard to believe, Kuralt's report is even more unrelentingly pessimistic than Murrow's, despite the dedicated doctors and nurses we meet. The leadership of San Antonio, who were then staging a world's fair extravaganza of their own called HemisFair '68, complete with sky ride, monorail, and tourist observation tower, were particularly outraged at the suggestion that San Antonio was somehow failing its poorest citizens. The county commissioner, who appears in the film, insists that the Mexican American men won't work and that their children didn't really need to go to school anyway, hungry or not (Davies).

Two years later, *Migrants* (1970, United States, dir. Martin Carr), an NBC White Paper, sent Chet Huntley out in the field to document the Florida farm workers who picked oranges for famous juice companies—Snowcrop, Hi C, Minute Maid, and Tropicana. It turned out they were all subsidiaries of Coca-Cola, the show's sponsor, which, *Variety* noted, tried to "kill the exposé." The documentary was, however, telecast, in the end, without a single commercial. On the ground the local growers were no more cooperative. Threatened with a gun during the filming in front of migrant housing that had been condemned the year before, Carr took his crew to the nearby public road to complete the filming in safety.

The strategy of the White Paper team was clever but perhaps too obvious: they intended to interview the same people that Murrow had interviewed ten years earlier to see what changes if any had happened in their lives. Three interviews with Chet Huntley were lined up; as the director, Martin Carr, explained, he could meet only one of them and could film none.

One of the woman Huntley was to interview said that "she was too frightened to appear on screen" (Carr). She knew what reprisals had been taken against a crew chief that Murrow had interviewed. After *Harvest of Shame* was shown, his local bank account was closed and his crew was no longer able to score any work assignments. The two-minute television appearance had more or less ruined his working life. Another woman, whom Carr had pre-interviewed to get her ready for the show, had already been threatened with eviction even before she would go on air. Even Claude Kirk, governor of Florida, where all the filming was being done, canceled his interview. Apparently, even he had changed his mind about appearing in an orange grove with the famous Chet Huntley.

Ten years later, NBC sent out a then relatively unknown reporter, Chris Wallace, out to film still another version, also titled *Migrants* (1980, United States). Perhaps because his father was the famous Mike Wallace, the son earned a reputation for confrontational TV journalism—ideal, of course, for investigating migrant workers' problems. His camera crew was itself filmed outside a row of shacks, migrant housing owned by a local farmer in Florida, who protests vehemently that he will not allow any filming of his private property. Morton Silverstein appears in this broadcast as well, and he too is ordered to leave the farmers' property. In a later interview, when Silverstein informs a local judge that he knows the judge also owns some bad migrant housing, the judge as well orders him to leave. As the local sheriff is also exposed as an employer of illegal migrants, Wallace comes back on camera to conclude the broadcast, echoing Murrow's 1960 expose: "How many more harvests will it take before we understand that the migrants' shame is our own?"

A second film cycle was generated by *Harvest of Shame*, even if thirty years had to pass before it appeared. One of the films in this later cycle, Hector Galan's *New Harvest, Old Shame* (1990, United States), is featured on the program *Frontline*, covering the Latino migrant workers who travel from Florida to New Jersey for their picking opportunities. Galan follows the family of Pedro Silva, who had already been working in the fields when Murrow completed his documentary, back to Florida. Silva's family has fifteen people, aged nine to sixty-two, whose work in the tomato crop in Florida is greatly diminished by rain and a low price per bucket picked. They intend to stay in the Everglades Migrant Camp, but on the way their plans for work in South Carolina are ruined by Hurricane Hugo and a freeze that then hit Florida. Their truck keeps breaking down and family members get sick. Any solidarity with fellow pickers in the precariat rapidly disappears, as Pedro Silva complains that some immigrants like the Guatemalans will deliberately accept less pay than his crew just to get the jobs.

By and large, therefore, the film concludes that for this section of the precariat "little has changed" in the thirty years since *Harvest of Shame*. The supply of labor now outruns the demand and the growers know the loopholes in the laws. One organizer tells the *Frontline* reporters, "Farm workers are not anyone's constituency in Congress" (Goodman).

Five years later, Dan Rather's *Legacy of Shame* (1995, United States, dir. Maurice Murad) emphasized that laws were finally in place to protect migrant workers but "now the problem isn't the laws, it's their enforcement." Rather chronicles both the highs (the Farm Labor Organizing Committee or FLOC) and the lows (crew leaders and owners virtually treating their workers like indentured servants).

When Rather's co-correspondent, Randall Pinkston, asks a farmer what he would do "without the Mexican workers coming in," the farmer replies, "We're dead." Yet the estimate was that one in six workers "had been exposed of pesticides in the fields that very week" they were interviewed. Rather concludes that although many did not want the Mexican workers to cross the Rio Grande legally or otherwise, when they do, "for one more year we [Americans] will eat the least-expensive food on earth."

Rather was keen to explain the difficulties the workers faced just getting a decent place to sleep. He covered all the possibilities: sleeping in the streets, crashing at friends' houses, finding a church shelter, pooling money to buy a van to sleep in, and even, if necessary, staying at a motel.

The system of smuggling workers across the border was already in place when Rather interviewed a self-righteous coyote, who was probably being paid $2,000 per migrant worker: "Yes, I'm breaking the law, but I feel justified in the fact that I'm helping people get to their destination, find a job, better themselves."

The farmers who pick up the workers the coyote deposits in El Paso know the laws usually don't apply to them—the border patrol never raids during harvest season—but they no longer supply housing for their workers because of finicky regulations like the necessity to "exclude vermin and insects."

Despite some conscientious Department of Labor investigators and labor union organizers whom Rather encounters, workers' receipts are routinely falsified in terms of hours worked. In the end, Rather does find one grower he can respect, A. Duda & Sons, whose business is near Belle Glade in Florida, where they employ 3,000 workers. They have abandoned the old system of independent crew leaders and employ the supervisors directly, making them more responsible for their welfare. Rather hopes, perhaps without conviction, that other growers may imitate the Duda operation.

Rather in the end has no doubt as to what to call the "system" that some migrant workers often have to endure: peonage or indentured servitude. When workers can't leave the shanties of a farmer who employs them because they owe him money for one reason or another, they are held illegally. In the closing minutes of the film, Rather turns prophetic: "This agricultural system has been in place since the end of slavery, and few actually want to change it." And in effect standing where Murrow stood thirty-five years earlier, he predicts that history will repeat itself: "So, sad to say, years from now the border patrol will likely still be putting in the overtime, and some journalist yet unborn will stand in a field, lamenting the obvious and exhorting our children to remember those who feed us."

The subject of the final film in the series, *Children of the Harvest* (1998, United States), a NBC Dateline film, is obvious—gross violations of the law in regard to child labor—although the filmmaker has some sympathy for the two Mexican American families they follow who feel they must send their children out to work in order for all of them to survive. The filmmakers are especially taken with James Flores, eleven years old, who prefers to work than to go to school. Although he weighs only seventy-one pounds, he carries cucumber buckets more than half his size. Reporter Dennis Murphy says of future Heinz pickles, "From James's hand to our supermarket shelves."

James's father is frustrated beyond belief. His caravan of vehicles is unreliable, breaking down so often that they often arrive at the wrong time to pick a crop. The family relies on church charities for clothes; they routinely eat uncooked hot dogs. The footage can be heartbreaking: as the children of the family that travels with the Flores—the Villaneuvas—pick vats of blueberries, nearby a group of town kids is happily smashing their faces on blueberry pies in a pie-eating contest. When the Heinz Company made a show of disciplining a farmer for using child labor, he said that if he and other farmers stopped using children, Heinz would go out of the pickle business.

This was the last of the cycles of TV films generated by *Harvest of Shame*. The films of the 1990s were eventually followed by independent filmmakers—not associated with TV programs—with both engaged agitprop films as well as more balanced documentaries that analyzed what might be called a developing migrant worker movement, imitating the Civil Rights Movement, with a charismatic leader, oppressed workers, almost exclusively Latino and Caribbean, and their activist allies. The following twenty-five years have featured an explosion of digital and online filmmaking, almost exclusively on Latino farm workers, exhibiting some decentralized leadership styles and grassroots organizing often uninvolved with national labor unions.

Viewers today will be surprised to see so many white migrant workers in the earlier films, but the fact is that they did not fare much better than their nonwhite brethren. One of the first theatrical films to represent these workers was *Angel City* (1980, United States), directed by British filmmakers, Steven Carver and Richard Leacock, whose early career included *The Brave Don't Cry* (1952, United Kingdom), an important semidocumentary recreation of the notorious—but now little known—Knockshinnoch, Scotland, mining disaster in which 129 men were trapped by an underground flood. He emigrated to Hollywood, where he became a successful director of TV films such as *Angel City*, in which the Jeeters, a poor white migrant family, are imprisoned in a migrant labor camp near Everglades National Park in Florida. The abuses by supervisors and the family's punishing labor seem like a throwback to the worst of the Depression, as a young woman of the family is raped, becomes pregnant, and her baby is used as a hostage to keep the Jeeters from running away.

The history of the rural white precariat was rarely positively portrayed with the possible exception of *A Painted House* (2003, United States, dir. Alfonso Arau), based on best-selling author John Grisham's autobiographical novel, in which Luke Chandler is a sympathetic boy in both novel and film. The cotton fields of the Arkansas Delta are as far removed from the intrigues of the lawyers Grisham usually writes about as can be imagined. The Chandlers, trying to survive in the 1950s on eighty acres of temperamental cotton, have to hire migrant workers, both Mexicans and "hillbillies," to help pick the crop. But they also have to worry about tornadoes, floods, and violent disagreements among their migrant workers.

Although it is 1953, it feels like a decade before, as Detroit auto plants tempt the rural precariat to head north for steady factory work and a shot at owning homes, TV, and a telephone. Even Luke's parents eventually leave, but not before Luke witnesses two violent murders that elude the forces of law and order. Luke himself becomes consumed by the idea of having the family home painted, a local mark of (some) status. Bigger issues—such as the family's carryover and never-ending debt—do receive attention but almost to a lesser degree. The beautiful but quirky cotton crop—captured in a number of stunning overhead and other crane shots—dominates the film, but it cannot conceal the economic difficulties of small family farms.

These stories are familiar because of the dominance of Steinbeck's novels *The Grapes of Wrath* and *In Dubious Battle*—the former a classic and the latter only filmed more recently. Both films capture the struggle for survival of the migrant families just a little more than a decade before *A Painted House*. Steinbeck's migrant white workers are hardly settled in California after their journey from Oklahoma and other drought states when they are confronted with limited employment and failed agricultural union drives. *In Dubious Battle* (United States, 2016, dir. James Franco) is the more political film, as it shows active Communist Party organizers move into the migrant camps in an attempt to build strike actions to fight low wages and lockouts of the workers.

One of the first federal government programs that either ignored or deliberately underestimated poor white migrant workers was the controversial H-2 program that enabled agribusiness to cut back on African Americans as well as migrant Latino workers. Murrow's footage in *The Harvest of Shame* in Immokalee, Florida, *was* of the almost exclusively black field workers boarding trucks to take them to the tomato fields. Director Sanjay Rawal's documentary *Food Chains* (2014, United States) begins, like Murrow, in Immokalee, following workers now almost exclusively Latino on the buses to take them to the tomato fields, arriving for shape-up at 8 a.m. and returning home usually about 8 p.m., having earned only $42. One of the workers says, "We live like animals in cramped houses," with fifteen to sixteen people in a trailer during picking season.

But the workers have formed the CIW, one of the community organizations that, as a quasi-union, has been nicknamed *alt-labor*, which struggles on a number of fronts to double the income of the tomato pickers by asking the big three consumers—fast-food restaurants, food services, and supermarkets—to guarantee double the single penny earned for each pound of tomatoes picked. This will have the effect, of course, of doubling the wages of the workers. In 2010 the CIW signed the first ever agreement with thirteen growers, about ninety percent of the membership of the Florida Tomato Growers Exchange, for the penny per pound requested increase to be funded by restaurants and retailers for the workers' piecework wages. To this day, the only two major holdouts from the agreement are the Publix supermarkets and Wendy's fast-food restaurants.

Rawal's film not only revisits the mise-en-scène of *The Harvest of Shame* but also includes telling footages from Ethel and Bobby Kennedy's visits to Cesar Chavez's own hunger strike in 1968 in California after their co-founding of the United Food Workers with Delores Huerta in 1965. The revelation of extreme rural poverty among the rich vineyards of Napa Valley helped propel their cause nationwide. Rawal also covers the CIW's hunger strike in 2013, establishing the continuity of decades-long struggles in the fields where recurring issues of low pay and poor housing are still not resolved.

The importance of the original series of films that followed Murrow's *Harvest of Shame* as well as other films that endeavored to tell the migrant workers' story of the history of the precariat cannot be emphasized enough. The migrant workers represent a subclass of the precariat that has been particularly undervalued and under-protected. Even during the strong resurgence of the grape pickers strikes organized by the United Farm Workers and Cesar Chavez in the 1970s, not only the growers themselves but their dubious union allies (the Teamsters) routinely attacked the grape pickers. Documentaries like *Fighting for Our Lives* (United States, 1973, dir. Glen Pearcy) that portrayed the strike in 1973 at its height successfully reached sympathetic viewers, but an organizing film, *The Wrath of Grapes* (United States, 1986, dir. Leona Parlee and Lenny Bourin), made to publicize the dangerous effects of pesticides on the grape pickers and their families was successfully stopped by the growers even after 50,000 copies had been distributed.

2

Internal Migration in China

China's rapid industrialization and virtually forced internal migration of rural workers into new factory compounds and crowded cities, with estimates as high as 340 million people creating an "internal" or rural to urban migration in just thirty years (from 1979 to 2009), is "likely the largest in human history," according to Kam Wing Chan, in *The Encyclopedia of Global Migration*. Before this internal exodus, the *hukuo* resident system—citizens can only receive state benefits within their restricted zone, whether it be a rural village or city—was the custom and law. Internal migrants for years were only "temporary" residents of the edge cities or factory towns where they spent most of their working lives. Entitled or politically well-connected individuals or families (e.g., businessmen, traders, and officials), however, would be more likely to be granted hukuo status when *they* changed their cities of residence.

The non-hukuo migrants, faced with "lack of access to reasonable education, health care services and social security," according to Chan, suffer the kind of discrimination that has led to increased suicide rates, for example, in the giant Foxconn factory complex in Shenzhen that holds contracts for the production of electronic goods for Apple, Dell, and Toshiba (see *Phone Story* game in Chapter 8). The children of the non-hukuo migrants—"second-generation migrants"—have nonetheless participated in unprecedented labor unrest, typified by strikes that took place at automobile assembly plants in the nearby cities of Foshan and Zhongshan in the Pearl River Delta.

Where did all of these millions of migrants go to find work? The employees in the edge cities and other satellite factory towns in China that drive its export goods industry stay in virtually dormitory accommodation, returning home only once a year for Chinese New Year. Sarah Swider, in *Building China: Informal Work and the New Precariat* (2015), argues that these internal migrants face a variety of difficult living and working situations. When they live on job sites "disconnected from their hometown," it is as if they are living in a "city of walls."

When they "float" from "city to city trying to evade trouble and find work," it is as if they are now in a "city of violence." And even if they become "tenuous settlers" with no rights, it is as if they are living in a "city of villages."

Their journeys and tenuous living situations have been captured in a series of documentaries by both Chinese and American filmmakers. One of the leading Chinese chroniclers of the precariat, Jia Zhangke, has directed two major films specifically about the precariat in the megalopolis: *The World* (2004, China) and *24 City* (2008, China). In the former the title signifies, ironically, a suburban theme park outside Beijing called "The World" whose slogan is, "See the world without leaving Beijing." The staff is a mixture of the precariat (attendants and security guards) and skilled workers (dancers). Their housing is hardly world class, however, and is on a par with the provincial migrant workers in nearby sweatshops: this dilapidated housing provides the film with a disturbing and tragic ending.

Jia Zhangke's *24 City* (2008, China) symbolizes China's transition from an authoritarian socialist state to an authoritarian capitalist state. Its title denotes a new fancy development of housing and hotels on the site of a former secret Factory 420 in Chengdu that once made weaponry and parts for Soviet MIG airplanes for the Chinese to use in the Korean War. The workers are interviewed as if there were part of a documentary of their experiences but it turns out that the film is a clever blend of fiction and reality. Some of the workers filmed really did work in Factory 420 while others are actors, especially the one called Little Flower, who resembles the character of an actual film—from which we see clips—with that same name, starring Joan Chen in 1980. Joan Chen, however, is also playing this new Little Flower, mixing reality and fantasy even further. She is of course quite attractive but has made a serious faux pas: she has been exposed as the writer of "forged love letters" to a handsome pilot whose photo is posted on the factory floor, even though she knew he was no longer alive. This collapsed "relationship" is symbolic of the hopes of the uniformly depressed precariat whose factory has declined and is doomed to be demolished.

A politically complementary set of films to Jia Zhangke's work from a Taiwanese perspective is *Condensation: Five Video Works* (2002–06, Taiwan, dir. Chen Chieh-jen), establishing the hollowness of the idea of industrial progress in both China and Taiwan. Chen recruited the precariat to play themselves in these mock documentaries by using nonactors to dramatize the end of the industrial metropolis and the creation of the faceless megalopolis. The first film, *Factory*, is an ambitious interpretation of the end of industrial labor: former workers from an immense but abandoned textile factory and stage reenactments of their work and artful variations of same. In one shot, they are seated at their sewing machines as if the disappearance of their work over the last seven years had not happened. These women workers were of course the victims of globalization: although low-wage Taiwan was the center of the global textile industry from the 1960s through the 1990s, other countries, especially China and other East Asian neighbors, undercut Taiwan's production costs and the work migrated. The workers are filmed handling the paraphernalia of their old workstations, left behind when the factory closed, but they also pick up their old loudspeakers and the posters they had created to protest the plant's closing. A second, related film, *The Route*, documents Taiwanese port workers' union protests and demonstrations held to show solidarity with fellow port workers; Chen recruited Taiwanese laborers to act out the demos.

Two other films also document abandoned labor centers: *On Going* cuts between a worker at a new office building and an abandoned factory, while *Bade Area* follows squatters at still another abandoned factory in the town of Bade. All of these factories have a stark, minimalist beauty to them, a beauty that in the hands of a different artist (Robert Smithson, for example, photographer of abandoned industrial cities of Northern New Jersey) would not have reached the pitch of protest that seems inherent in Chen's work.

The fifth film, *Lingchi—Echoes of a Historical Photograph*, is the only explicit nonindustrial piece about a famous 1904 photograph of the execution of a man through a type of torture known as "death by a thousand cuts." The scene is eerily restaged by Chen, himself the "victim," as a tribute to what he calls his resistance of the "state of amnesia" in Chinese culture. In this sequence, reminiscent of the exquisite torture of actress Maria Falconetti in Carl Theodor Dreyer's *Passion of Joan of Arc* (1928), Chen offers a very sharp satire of the idea of Chinese progress.

A similar Chinese portrait of one of the world's largest assembly plants and its worker "dormitories," Foxxconn in the Shenzen suburbs, *Dreamwork China* (2011, China/Italy, dir. Tommaso Facchin and Ivan Franceschini), has the advantage over other internal Chinese migration films of including interviews with a number of workers at the factory. The documentary goes into some depth on the stress that crowded living and semi-forced long working hours cause in workers, some of them literally having just arrived from their home villages and farms thousands of miles away. The range of their attitudes is, however, fascinating. One says immediately, "I hope to become a boss." Another says, "I plan to start my own business." A third young man says it's better to work for a giant like Foxxconn than those small factories where you get no days off and lousy food. And fourth, a woman who works all day and takes cosmetology classes from 8:30 to 11:30 every night wants to be able to have a fallback job when she leaves Foxxconn. How any of these "dreamworks" are likely to become reality must be put into the context of their huge dormitory tenements where the fear—and actuality—of suicides has become so great that there are nets stretching all around the lower floors.

One of the sectors of contemporary China excluded from any of the dubious employment miracles are streetwise teenagers, depicted in *Beijing Flickers* (2013, China, dir. Yuan Zhang) as either on the edge of the precariat or pure lumpen. One of the leading youth in this crowd encourages no confidence when he says, "I regret eating glass." Of course, he doesn't have much else to eat, having lost his job, girlfriend, apartment, and sense of purpose in life, not to mention sneaking out of a hospital that treated his injuries from the glass because he couldn't pay the bill. Some of his friends still have precariat jobs such as parking cars or singing in a transvestite bar, but the Chinese miracle is an illusion for them.

Chongqing: Flashes on a Megalopolis (2017, China/Italy, dir. Francesco Cocco and Daniele Dainelli) may be the perfect but unusual complement to *Dreamwork China*, for it features an extraordinary series of remarkable photographs of the Chinese tenement blocks in the vicinity of Chongqing (or Chungking, as it is usually Romanized) and the city itself, one of China's "thirteen emerging megalopolises," according to *The Economist*. It derives its power from the massive Three Gorges Dam across the Yangtze River, a project supposedly predicted by Mao—"walls of stone will stand upstream to the west"—in his poem "Swimming," written after the chairman's legendary swim across the Yangtze in 1956.

Lixin Fan's *Last Train Home* (2009, China/Canada/United Kingdom) focuses on a single family from Sichuan Province that makes the typical journey of the millions of internal migrants. The parents have been making the incredibly crowded train journeys back home after fifteen years in a garment factory in Guangdong Province. They stay in a single "room" with a flimsy half curtain for a "door." Their children and one set of grandparents remain behind; with a continuous litany of "study hard" commands from all her elders, sixteen-year-old Lin is fed up and leaves school for a garment factory job, causing great dismay for her parents. When she uses a vulgar epithet at a family meet-up, she and her father literally come to blows.

Lixin Fan's film is filled with breathtaking detail: tens of thousands of migrants besieging and, yes, even rioting to board trains home; those very trains, crowded beyond belief, pass over trestles that are engineering marvels in spectacular landscapes. After the fight, young Lin turns to the camera: "You want to film the real me? This is the real me." By the end of the film, the Chinese economic miracle begins to recede: a credit line appears—"2008 World Finance Crisis"—and we see a shot of the entirely vacated factory floor where the family had worked.

The necessities of life, especially food and housing, are two of the topics that challenge the precariat during times of economic reshuffling. We have already seen what happens when the economic policies of a centralized government like China create a precariat of millions of workers who must travel long distances to work. But what of the Chinese workers who are not recruited into this migratory stream? Director Bing Wang has made his career by filming not only the internal migrants but also the Chinese workers who remain in their industrial sites even when the demands of the jobs and/or their employment status radically change.

Bing Wang's *Bitter Money* (2018, China) offers a somewhat different migrant labor experience. It tracks representatives of the 300,000 workers who traveled to the city of Zheijang in Huzho Province from 2012 to 2016 where, instead of a mega-factory, 18,000 private and relatively small clothing manufacturers set up shop. The workers have to choose between piecework pay scales and hourly wages. They are housed in mega-dorms, generally crowded and unpleasant, barely better than the trains that have brought them to the city. The title references *Bitter Rice* (1949, Italy, dir. Giuseppe de Santas), the Italian neorealist classic about young migrant workers, the *modine*, who travel by train to work in the rice fields and live in dormitories in post–Second World War Italy (Hoberman).

Bing Wang films like Frederick Wiseman, the American documentary master, with long takes, intimate close-ups, and virtually no narration. The slow-paced revelation of work and character is punctuated by the occasional unsettling incident of family or work relationships. The workers in these small manufacturing shops seem incredibly skilled, sewing not only on unsophisticated small machines but with an attention to speed and careful detail that is impressive. Sewing small pockets, for instance, seems routine to them of course but it looks like a very skilled piece of work to our naive eyes.

Wang Bing tracks different units of workers: three sisters cope in virtually a one-room set up in the dorms, a couple bicker constantly in another setting where the husband assaults his wife often, and other individuals seems to cope with the job but are always disappointed by the amount of money they are earning. The streets are garbage-strewn and the workday often stretches to twelve hours.

The transition of China from a traditional state-controlled industrial system, with an urban proletariat, to a system of precarious labor is captured in another prodigious trilogy of films by Wang Bing. Primarily a documentarian often using a stationery camera that captures the action in industrial scenes, Wang also favors filming workers he comes into contact with spontaneously. The first film in his trilogy is *Tie Xi Qu: West of the Tracks* (2000, China), an almost nine-hour record of the gradual collapse of the Shenyang Smelting industrial complex, due for deindustrialization, and its nearby residential district, quaintly nicknamed Rainbow Row, slated for demolition, is the subject of the film's first section, *Rust*. The second section, *Remnants*, focuses on the now-unemployed precariat living near the factory. Wang, like still photographers Edward Burtynsky and Sebastio Salgado, is a master of stark, immense industrial-scapes as the essence of his mise-en-scène. Like a structural filmmaker, Wang's camera, for example, in a single long take in the third section of the film, *Rails*, uses a point-of-view shot from a locomotive as it passes through the complex—a spectral journey only occasionally interrupted by a rare guard or some traffic at a crossroad.

His second film, *Crude Oil* (2008, China), and his third, *Coal, Money* (2010, China), capture the rise of the precariat, in these instances working in the heavy industrial regions of oil and coal, with workers on a limited contract system, which means they can be hired to work "two months, three months, a year, or three years" and are paid according to their willingness to work. In *Coal, Money*, he follows a truck transporting coal from Shanzi Province to the port city of Tianjin. He records how along the road everyone involved is trying to transform the coal shipment into money by various schemes.

Crude Oil is fourteen hours long, closely following a group of oil workers in the wilderness of Qinghai Province in the winter. The film was originally screened as an installation piece in the Rotterdam Film Festival and later in Los Angeles, with spectators passing in and out of the installation. This spectatorship fit the nature of the project, since there was little conversation or action and it was shot mostly in long takes. The lack of communal work spirit among the workers, the director argued, was in sharp contrast to the community life of the old-style factory complex in *West of the Tracks*.

The Chinese Mayor (2015, dir. Zhou Hao and Zhou Youchao) looks at another Chinese city, Datong, from which the precariat has *not* migrated because of two walls—an old-fashioned ancient wall that protected the city, the one-time capital of China, and a red or political wall supported by the authoritarian Geng Yanbo, the mayor whose goals are to bulldoze every ancient residential dwelling in the city to make way for a new road, an improved "great wall," and a new kind of economic engine: a "city of culture, art, and tourism." In the film, Geng confronts the unheard of in China—people protesting a government policy, sit-ins, and even a suicide as the poor take on, in their words, the "corrupt rich guys." The mayor himself has to live in the city's military headquarters for safety. Even the shiny gold dashboard bust of Chairman Mao, visible as we look out of the mayor's windshield as he inspects the rapidly demolished old city, is not enough to protect him from the people's anger.

The mayor wants to make his city a cultural mecca. Even though it already has some spectacular giant carved Buddhas, part of the famous Yungung Grottoes of Datong, he wants more, but he seems to know he is acquiring fake antique relics, stone plaques to jazz up his "great wall." Three days before the Chinese New Year in 2013, he is removed from his post. "No one can say why," but he becomes mayor of a less prestigious city 300 kilometers away where he begins again, relocating the precariat and building new highways, tunnels, and even a subway. Although he claims never to pay attention to the documentarian's camera, we see his legacy in a final shot: the skyline of modern buildings alongside the "great wall" of Datong, but without its mayor.

A single film cannot capture the essence of the Chinese miracle and tragedy that is its massive internal migration and unrestrained industrialization. But one film's title comes close: *Behemoth* (2015, China/France, dir. Zhao Liang). The biblical behemoth was the largest monster on the earth, requiring a thousand mountains to "feed" it. Behemoth also symbolizes the terrible drain on the strength and lives of the migrants who have survived, usually at the cost of divided families.

Zhao's somewhat rambling but visually arresting documentary begins with explosions at an immense open-pit coal mine, a man who seems to be some kind of erratic and untrustworthy guide wearing a giant mirror on his back, a flock of sheep, and a yurt, followed by a parade of hundreds of dump trucks hauling the coal off to destinations unknown. The faces of workers scavenging coal by hand and motorized three-wheel jitneys are covered in coal dust. We learn that one of the coal mine owners dreamed that the gods blamed him for blowing up the mountains and so for atonement he constructed a giant Buddha statue that we see standing by the roadside. The film concludes with "ghost cities," high-rise apartment buildings that were designed for thousands of migrant workers but are now abandoned as these migrants no longer can work because of pneumoconiosis. The director has described his documentary as a version of the three acts of Dante's *Divine Comedy*—the coal fires are the Inferno, the suffering of the workers is the Purgatorio, but there is no Paradiso.

When Chinese industrial plans sometimes failed, however rarely, China invested in factories abroad even when they needed coke to keep remaining plants humming. The Chinese purchased one of the former manufacturing stars of the Ruhr valley, the coke-producing plant at Kaiserstuhl, shut down in 2000 after only twelve years of operation. In the documentary *Losers and Winners* (2006, Germany, dir. Ulrike Franke and Michael Loeken), there are more ironies than German workers in the tale of two mighty industrial countries, the one on the rise, the other on the cusp of a decline. The plunging price of coke as the German industrial demand slackened drove the plant's owners to the sales table. The Chinese with the most expanding economy in the world need a coke-producing plant even if it were in Germany. What we have here, however, is a failure to communicate (Figure 2.1).

Compared to the Germans, the Chinese are workaholics and rule averse. All their culture teaches them is to get the job done, while German culture valorizes following established rules and regulations. The subject would be essentially comic, although as we follow the German workers around, noticing

Figure 2.1 Dismantling a German coke factory from *Losers and Winners*. Courtesy Icarus Films.

how dangerous the Chinese work habits are and how modest their living style (essentially, they live in the equivalent of shipping containers), our Teutonic sympathies grow.

Curiously, when a Chinese billionaire came to invest in an American factory, the culture clash between Chinese management and American workers was remarkably similar to the German situation. In *American Factory* (2019, United States, dir. Julia Reichert and Steven Bognar), one of the largest automotive glass manufacturers in the world, Fuyao Glass, took over the very GM factory whose closing in Moraine, Ohio, filmmakers Reichert and Bognar had already tracked in their previous film, *The Last Truck: Closing of a GM Plant* (2009, United States). Thousands of workers from the closed factory began working for the Chinese glass company in the same building. The workers were considered lazy and nonproductive by their Chinese supervisors who, in turn, were regarded by the workers as especially single-minded in their bossiness. The workers attempted to form a local of the United Automobile Workers (UAW), but they were unsuccessful and the plant continues, with a management who believe "Americans love being flattered" and are even allowed to "joke about the president," while the Chinese broadcast propaganda videos of happy Chinese children singing.

One perhaps inevitable spin-off of the mass internal migration in China is that, out of desperation or frustration with the difficulties they face, many male Chinese workers—and, more rarely, their families—turn to external migration, mainly to the UK. These even more intensely dispossessed workers turn to illegal immigration where they make up a substantial proportion of the foreign-born precariat. Their exploitation has been documented by the investigative (and undercover) reporter Hsiao-Hung Pai in her journalism and books (especially *Invisible: Britain's Migrant Sex Workers*) as well as in two collaborations with filmmaker Nick Broomfield.

In one of the films, Hsiao-Hung Pai went undercover in London as a maid and cook in a Chinese brothel (disguised, per custom, as a massage parlor) with a miniature concealed camera in the nosepiece of her eyeglasses: her video feed is streamed to Broomfield who parks nearby in the street. His documentary, *Sex My British Job* (2013, United Kingdom), validated her ongoing journalistic exposes of exploited undocumented immigrants, especially women, literally prisoners of loan sharks and *snakeheads* (smugglers) at first, and unscrupulous madams and massage parlor owners afterward. Hsiao-Hung films her increasingly desperate encounters with massage parlor directors who pressurize her to give up being a menial servant and turn tricks instead. She is attractive enough, they tell her, to make so much more money if she chooses that route.

Broomfield's feature film, *Ghosts* (2006, United Kingdom), made earlier, was based on Hsiao-Hung Pai's research into the Morecambe Bay cockle-gatherers tragedy, where twenty-three Chinese-born workers were swept to their deaths in 2004 by the tricky currents in the UK's largest intertidal mud flats off the Lancashire coast, having received no directions and no supervision about this dangerous location (Hsiao-Hung Pai, 2004).

The film's ironic title comes from a Chinese nickname for Caucasians—*gui lao* or "ghosts." Its fatal irony is that it also refers to the mostly illegal worker's invisibility and marginal status. Nonprofessional actors in the film play the cockle pickers who had paid Chinese *snakeheads* £30,000 for this travesty of precariat employment. The gullible immigrants are kept as virtual prisoners until they arrive at overcrowded hostels near the coastal waters.

Cockles—like American clams—are gathered at low tide, usually in the dark on the Merseyside coast where Liverpudian gangsters control the trade that ends up in local processing plants. The crews earn at most the equivalent of $10 for an eight-hour shift. When the cockle workers realized they were in danger, some were able to swim back to shore. Others sent desperate phone calls to families or friends on the beach.

Morecombe Bay was unusual in that workers there did not require a license. As a result, the unregulated immigrants competed with non-Chinese locals; some of that competition is captured in the violence that results when both kinds of crews arrive at good gathering spots, the ultimate precariat disaster in the making. The film's footage of the last victims struggling to survive on the top of their van as the water surges higher and higher is unnerving to say the least.

3

Daughters of a Lesser God: Women of the Precariat

This chapter takes its title from a Pakistani film, *Daughters of a Lesser God* (2012, dir. Ammar Aziz), because its evocation of a folk maxim epitomizes the difficulties of survival in the Global South, especially for women and their children, because work, housing, and security are a continuous challenge. We will see, however, that theirs is not simply a Third World problem.

Women in India and Pakistan are expected to wear bangles (*choori*). The human cost of this jewelry far exceeds their relatively inexpensive selling price. In Hyderabad, the largest city in the interior of south-central India, where *choori* bazaars are common, as this documentary demonstrates, bangles are often made by women and children in factories that double as their homes. They make thousands every day, which is captured in this film in a startling cinematic dance of extruded metal, careful fabrication of the bangles on lathes, and polishing and shaping and flame-tempering—in short, quite a complex process. Marvi Soomra for the online Pakistani news journal *Dawn* visited these home factories and was not surprised by how dangerous they were.

She estimated that more than thirty such home factories exist with thousands of ancillary workers in the industry, such as pickers involved in gathering glass fragments for melting as well as the bangle fabricators who face high temperatures and open flames without safety equipment of any kind. One of the women the reporter encountered referred to the industry as a "poverty hole" that "sucked in every member of the family." The women in the film are also activists, supporting the Bengal Workers Union. We see them discussing issues and chanting for freedom. The interviews in which the youngest girls express a desire to go to school or play instead of work will break viewers' hearts.

The invisibility of Indian women workers in another of their specialty jobs, textile, is especially acute in the documentary *Machines* (2016, India, dir. Rahul Jain), as they travel thousands of miles to a Gujarat textile mill. The director originally intended to title the film *Machines Don't Go on Strike* because workers in this terrifyingly efficient "machine" for creating textiles believe that only a union could fight against their oppressive working conditions. Ironically, some of the factory's workers would not join a union even if they could: they aspire to be contractors who *hire* the labor rather than *do* the labor.

The director was even confronted by workers who said he had a privileged position as a filmmaker but should instead become an activist to change things. The filmmaker's inspiration for the creation of the beautiful images of the machines, a paradox that filmmakers know they sometimes perpetuate with their dramatic and stunning footage, was Salgado's book, *Workers: An Archaeology of the Industrial Age* (2005), that skates on the edge of this paradox: Salgado consistently captures the raw dignity of the precariat among stunning scenes of dangerous beauty. But the director of *Machines* is not naive about the world he has entered: he photographs it claustrophobically because that is the reality of his precariat.

The history of the precariat, even in the First World, also involves their invisibility as workers. In a classic British documentary, *Nightcleaners* (1975, United Kingdom, dir. Marc Karlin), the unseen workers are all women who clean London's buildings at night. *Nightcleaners*, filmed secretly in various London offices at night, was intended to be used to raise funds for the nightcleaners' unionization drive and make the invisible workers visible. One of the women is interviewed about achieving "a better life for the working-class people," but she concludes, "It's like asking for the moon, isn't it?"

The special exploitation of women in the precariat includes sexual harassment and even assault. *Compliance* (2012, United States, dir. Craig Zobel) revealed an even darker side of the fast-food industry—the sexual harassment and unequal treatment of women workers. This feature film was based on a number of actual incidents throughout the United States but especially on one egregious episode that occurred in Kentucky, when a young McDonald's worker was wrongly accused of theft and sexually assaulted when a compliant and credulous supervisor was told on the phone that the police were investigating one of her employees. What became known as the "strip search phone call scam" began in 1990 and lasted for almost fifteen years, apparently caused by a single man who called numerous fast-food restaurants and grocery stores and pretended to be a policeman investigating an employee's thefts. Eventually, McDonald's was successfully sued for not warning its employees about—and for not training them to handle—these scams that the company was already aware existed. The film is a harrowing and disturbing view of what happens when petty harassment turns especially intimate and nasty.

Many viewers reported that it was almost impossible to watch. How could workers of the precariat, some of them with only their minor promotions in the fast-food world, treat their coworkers so cruelly? Many commentators pointed to the culture of the industry that prizes conformity and obedience to one's supervisors, while others pointed to the notorious 1961 Stanley Milgrim (electric shock) and 1971 Philip Zimbardo (imprisonment) experiments, in which subjects turned too easily to sadism and cruelty—which they didn't realize was actually staged—during volunteer psych department experiments. The woman who was strip-searched in one of the original events in Kentucky won a major settlement against McDonald's; her lawyer argued that "you don't have to be a Phi Betas Kappa to know not to strip-search a girl who is accused of a stealing charge" (Wolfson).

Although the gravity of the offenses and its locale make the McDonald's case somewhat of an outlier, we know that fast-food women have always been targets of management, even fellow workers, and customers. But the scale of the danger toward the women who migrate from Mexico and take jobs on the border should not be acceptable to a culture that considers itself respectable.

No continent is now without its cross-border migratory labor force. Some of these workers return home, others become classified as immigrants or refugees. Migrant workers are virtually in every country in the world, where they are at best second-class citizens. Thomas Nail in *The Figure of the Migrant* (2015) has wrestled with the terminology of "the migrant" and argues that they are a significant and related "host of ... mobile figures ... the floating population, the homeless, the stateless, the lumpenproletariat, the nomad, the immigrant, the emigrant, the refugee, the vagrant, the undocumented, and the barbarian" that under certain social conditions become "migratory figures."

Although I am unsure who the "barbarians" are (except historically, perhaps), in my view all of his other figures are—or become—members of the precariat, because that single term embodies their collective work, class, and social-status profile.

Crossing borders often begins with a dangerous journey. The plight of the Mediterranean boat people fleeing the North African coast was the staple of news for years, but some of the journeys were particularly frightful. *Simshar* (2014, Malta, dir. Lotfi Abdelli, Clare Agius, and Sekouba Doucoure) recreates one of the harrowing incidents in the Mediterranean crossing of the African boat people seeking to reach Italy. Their Maltese boat, Simshar, sinks, but a Turkish merchant vessel that rescued these African boat people was literally trapped between Malta and Italy, as the two countries waged a diplomatic war over asylum for the refugees.

Markus Imhoff, the director of another harrowing Mediterranean refugee boat documentary, *Eldorado* (2018, Switzerland/Germany), documents that the contemporary Swiss refusal to take in any boat people from Africa makes them only marginally less guilty than the Italians in this film who at first rescue a boatload of refugees, then—after treating them fairly humanely—dump them into transit camps where sex traffickers and gang bosses "recruit" laborers. The director recalls his childhood in Switzerland when his family took in his Italian "sister," Giovanna, but were forced to send her back to Italy. The director's visit to her tomb evokes his ruminations about which European countries took in refugees during the Second World War and whether the situation of worldwide civil wars is so different for another generation of refugees. Does it matter, he asks, when a refuge searches for Eldorado, especially after generations of European exploitation of the natural resources of Africa? (See Chapter 6.)

Overland journeys in Europe were also quixotic and hard to believe. Waves of migratory workers, often smuggled across hostile borders throughout the European Union, also became part of the daily news. But how do these migrants succeed in such difficult transits? We know many do not survive, and their passing goes unnoticed or is ignored. But what of the people who actually do the smuggling? In *The Judgment* (2014, Bulgaria, dir. Stephan Komandarev), set at the Bulgarian/Turkish/Greek border north of the Aegean Sea, an ex-soldier cannot find work. His former commander offers him the job of smuggling illegal Syrians across the very border he used to patrol to *prevent* defectors from leaving this formerly Soviet bloc country. The film's title not only reflects the impact of decisions at this border but ironically is also the name of a formidable mountain in the Bulgarian hills the ex-soldier must confront.

Another convincing portrait of an unusual cross-border smuggler, a young white working-class Texan in *The Girl* (2013, United States, dir. David Riker), chooses this risky sideline when she is forced out of a low-paying clerk's job. She hasn't realized that her father has, in fact, been transporting illegals in his trailer rig all along. The temptations of easy cash overwhelm her, but she has very little savvy on how to go about this risky business. Suffice it to say her first attempt ends in a terrible accident, as the mother of a young child is swept away in a river crossing. Our smuggler obviously cannot raise this young girl without attracting attention, so she makes the decision to return the girl to her grandmother in the Mexican mountains.

In the United States, the scale and success of the hundreds of thousands of Mexican and other South American migrants who cross over the southwestern borders of the United States is now, in the twenty-first century, the staple of wrangling American politicians. Writer (and photographer) David Bacon has been tracking these migrants for years. In some ways, their story is always the same: cross the southern border into America, find work, and avoid the Immigration and Customs Enforcement agency (ICE).

The cinema of the precariat will document and dramatize, however, the real complexities of their journeys, beyond the headlines and into the context, which Bacon explains through the stories of immigrants—for example, that of Rosaria Ventura, a Triqui dialect speaker from Oaxaca who travels every year to pick berries at the Sakuma Brothers Farms in Bellingham, Washington. The Sakumas were immigrants themselves but prospered after regaining land taken from them during the Japanese internment during the Second World War. When Rosaria, her husband, and other workers realize that the grower was going to replace them with H-2 workers (see Chapter 1), they began to build a union, Familias Unidas por Justicia (Families United for Justice).

Beyond the news flashes, then, lies an extremely rich cinematic archive, still growing, of films documenting and dramatizing these migrants' stories that include not only their journeys but also the political give and take of government control and worker's organizing that characterizes Rosaria's story.

The difficulty of women achieving full-time status and equal respect as a worker sometimes leads to successful organizing and protest. Most of these films will be found in Chapter 10, in which alt-labor and "organizing the unorganized" are discussed. But the story south of the border really begins with the hundreds of women of Juarez, Mexico, who disappear, often raped and murdered, as if they never existed. Since 1993, Mexican authorities have been unable—or unwilling—to solve these missing persons cases. Lourdes Portilla's film, *Seniorita Extraviada* (2002, United States), was one of the first films to document these "missing young women" whose murders went unsolved. They were the most vulnerable of the precariat of women who found jobs in the maquiladora—often an American-owned company making duty- and tariff-free goods for import in the United States—south of the Mexican-American border.

The authorities will not confirm the numbers of the missing women or even any possible suspects, but these women are also central to Gregory Nava's feature film, *Bordertown* (2007, United States).. Forced to migrate, the women who work in the television manufacturing factory are fleeing crop failures, poverty, and official appropriation of their land. The film suggests that the bus driver who ferries the women from the factory to their favelas or shantytowns is suspicious. Jennifer Lopez is the Mexican American reporter whose parents were organizers, and Antonio Banderas runs a local radical newspaper. Lopez teams up with a worker who survives a mass murder of migrants who unknowingly cover up a crime for a criminal gang.

The greenish tint over the massive factory floor (where announcements like "Lines 1 and 3 are falling behind their quota. Accelerate production" are common) illuminates the streams of workers as the shifts change, while a fire ravages the workers' favela. The film dramatizes a massive whitewash of crime and corruption with the precariat as victims, including one in the film's final shot: one more body, clothed in her blue factory smock.

Both films have little sympathy for the long list of suspects the police discover—and some that they ignore. Nava's film reenacts the notorious arrest of an Arab national who police say murdered all the missing women. Portilla's film, similarly, follows the investigation of the same individual, whom she calls an Egyptian. Since numerous women are murdered after his arrest, and even after the arrest of a gang of lowlifes for the same crimes, it is easy to conclude, as Portilla does, that the real culprits have benefited from the local ruling class's control of all public matters, including the police. The latter themselves may be criminally involved as well: one of the women Portilla interviews was brutalized by the police at a local jail. The ubiquitous bus drivers ferrying the women late at night from the factories also seem suspect. Narco-traffickers are of course familiar with the remote areas the women's bodies are found in, so their role cannot be easily discounted either.

Portilla's film, even more than Nava's, should be R-rated for descriptions of graphic mutilation and torture. There are pockets of resistance to the whitewash of these murderers of the precariat. On electric poles everywhere, people have painted black crosses to memorialize the victims. Groups of the dead women's relatives organize protests as well. "The maquiladoras are untouchable," a local comments. They are the Mexican government's biggest investment and as a result there prevails a terrible atmosphere dominated by seemingly perfect crimes with no clues.

Although perhaps no more brutal than other films about the murders of "illegal aliens" slipping across the Mexican border to the United States or Mexican women kidnapped off the streets of Tijuana, *I Witness* (2003, United States, dir. Rowdy Herrington) has an even more remarkable range of corrupt and duped individuals than usual. The Mexican setting is an American-owned maquiladora undergoing a unionization drive. The company certainly doesn't want the union; the local bent cops don't want the union; and even American officials and middlemen don't want the union, but at least for them it's because it will cause too much trouble and may not even help the workers in the end.

Two sets of murders remain unsolved during this union struggle: two American boys shot while dirt-biking just across the border in Mexico and an entire village of campesinos—men, women, and children—found slaughtered in a collapsed tunnel. The villagers had been recruited to clean up a midnight spill of deadly methyl dioxide at the maquiladora, whose poisonous effects on them make them dangerous witnesses to the company's reputation.

Maquiladoras were the Mexican solution to the cost-conscious and anti-union American corporations whose bottom line needed, well, bottoming down at all costs. Mexican labor would work at one-tenth the American wages, the regulatory environment was always favorable to business, and "(just) south of the border" was not very far for shipping. It was also beyond the reach of the American judiciary and American labor law.

Chapter 9 includes "Fifty Films about Capitalism," many of which involve Supreme Court decisions favorable for American capitalism, and will discuss the relationship of judiciary decision-making and capitalism. A little known film, *The Little Pink House* (2018, United States/Canada, dir. Courtney Balaker) highlights the importance of the relatively unknown Supreme Court decision *Kelo v. City of New London* in 2005 that reaffirmed the use of eminent domain to transfer land from one private owner to another for the purpose of economic development. The film dramatizes that in practices this means the appropriation of the homes of the less affluent members of a community—in this case a waterside neighborhood with a great view but a stinky sewage plant—so that the Pfizer drug company can build a new headquarters and a mall with expensive condos and the city can gain tax income to increase local social services.

This "reverse Robin Hood" decision—using the words of the dissenting opinion—pits Susette Kelo and her neighbors against the local city government that sees dollar signs and not people: in Kelo's words, "You are going to help the homeless by kicking people out of their homes." Although Kelo loses the battle—her pink house is demolished—Pfizer does not successfully develop the property and Kelo's property remains (as of 2011) vacant except for feral cats, unfortunately not unlike some of the lost properties of the next chapter.

4

Scavengers of the World, Unite!

City planners, as a rule, do not include garbage dumps, wastelands, shantytowns, and decaying landscapes in their visions of development and urban renewal, yet they are obviously inevitable in virtually every country (with the possible exception of Switzerland). Kevin Lynch, urban theorist, is adamant about why they exist: "Wasting is a pervasive (if valiantly ignored) process in human society, just as it is elsewhere in the living system." In the ignored field of the study of debris, his book, *Wasting Away* (1990), stands out. Waste, he concludes, "is a feature of the underlying flux that carries us along, the everlasting impermanence of things."

Grady Clay, perhaps more of a maverick chronicler of city phenomena than an urban planner, was also adamant that these frayed holes in the cityscape were inevitable. In *Close-Up: How to Read the American City* (1973), he called them "stacks," accumulations of raw materials like pipes or industrial sludge, and "sinks," the "places of last resort into which powerful groups in society shunt, shove, dump, and pour whatever or whomever they do not like or cannot use: auto carcasses, garbage, trash, and minority groups." It is, of course, in those stacks and sinks that the precariat, the least powerful group in society, finds work.

The number of shantytowns, garbage cities, squatters' settlements, and other "places of last resort" is staggering. It is not enough, as Mike Davis in *Planet of Slums* (2006) does, to characterize these rapidly expanding zones as inevitable features of "disaster capitalism." Other analysts, such as architect Rem Koolhaas, approach the same raw data and see possibilities for entrepreneurship among the precariat and still other analysts see political organization and resistance among workers and their allies (Richard Pithouse and the "Naked Cities" writers of MUTE). And artists even see redemption in the murals about the Zabbaleen recyclers of Cairo (discussed below).

Because of his international reputation as an architect and city planner, Koolhaas was the subject of two films presenting his views about—and visits to—Lagos: *Lago/Koolhaas* (2002, Netherlands, dir. Bregtje van der Haak) and

Lagos Wide & Deep (2004, Netherlands, dir. Bregtje van der Haak). In the former, Koolhaas's appreciation for the survival skills of the precariat in this city of twenty-one million people was obvious: because the traffic flow from the Nigeria mainland to the city island of Lagos over three main bridges was so congested, Koolhaas argued, these failures of traffic management "generated opportunities" or options for the precariat. Markets would literally spring up in the midst of the numerous traffic jams, for example. What Koolhaas celebrated was what he called the "self-organizing" in such flourishing markets as the Alaba Electronics Market in which the precariat was able "to take its fate into its own hands and to survive on its own wits." The electronics markets were exponentially advanced compared to the usual garbage city or recyclers' dump site. Since there is minimal civic control in Lagos, the workers survive by taking control of their situation or they lose everything. Alaba is the largest electronic market in Nigeria and like Willets Point in NYC (see below) repairs to appliances are available as well as purchases.

The second film records a fairly defensive interview with Koolhaas. He is not surprised that his Western, Harvard-based intervention in the study of Lagos would generate "suspicion of ulterior" motives and even a belief that he would profit somehow from his study. The situation became even more critical when his proposed book, *Lagos: How It Works*, never appeared, in the end only available in excerpts, which too were widely criticized. Two opening shots of van der Haak's first film reflected that criticism: both of them were Koolhaas's point-of-view shots, one from a helicopter, the other from a car in Lagos's notorious traffic. The shots supposedly demonstrated Koolhaas's lack of empathy for the precariat. The DVD of this film was more revealing than just the filmed interview with Koolhaas because it was an "interactive journey into an exploding city," a special feature that allows the viewer to click on two visual options, "wide," accessing the helicopter point of view, and "close," featuring street footage of the precariat; similarly, clicking on the audio tracks delivers a choice of Koolhaas speaking or conversations with locals or sounds of the city.

Although images of their spectacular garbage dumps dominate the news, waste is not simply a Third World problem. Harold Welzer, in *Klaus Staeck: Nothing Is Done* (2011), calls out First Worlders too: "It is the IKEA-ization of our living environments that accounts for our consumption of material and the masses of waste we produce," he argues, since, for example, 40 percent of food purchased in the United States is thrown away, a figure which only falls to 30 percent in Europe (Figure 4.1).

Figure 4.1 Recycling in the First World (Manhattan). Photographed by Tom Zaniello.

The closing years of the twentieth century brought an explosion of shantytowns and a new phenomenon of the twenty-first century—the garbage city. No longer would the laboring poor visit garbage dumps to scavenge food to eat and goods to sell—they would live in shantytowns on site. These garbage cities, where recyclers and other desperate scavengers live year round, are typified by the Guatemala City Dump, possibly the largest in the world, detailed in the documentary *Recycled Life* (2006, United States, dir. Leslie Iwerks), and Shanghai's unnamed dump, larger than Central Park, surveyed in *Shanghai Journal: At the Dump* (2006, United States, prod. *New York Times*), where former peasants settle after their internal migrations to the city (see Chapter 2).

Recycled Life reveals a forty-acre ravine that takes in one-third of Guatemala's trash. Hundreds of scavengers or *guajeros* (from *guaje* or "a thing of little value") make their living by recycling almost a million pounds of paper, plastic, and metal daily. After skimming the arriving garbage trucks, in some cases riding their tailgates like postapocalyptic surfers and in other cases walking alongside the trucks with one hand on their side panels to stake out a claim to their designated bounty, the *guajeros* earn perhaps $6 a day from one of the 250 buyers of recyclables who arrive at the dump in the afternoons.

The dump attracts workers because of unemployment: about one-third of all the peasants were forced to leave their land during the forty years of civil war and many are desperate for work. Young children wander near gigantic earth movers, and teenagers sniff glue in an already toxic atmosphere (methane gas). The film exhibits the dump's terrible symbiosis. "Out of the trash thousands of people live," reports Gladys Molina, who kept her own baby boy in a box. The boy, now seventeen, works with his mother, a generational pattern typical of many of the workers. Another young man states, "I like being here because I feel free."

The precariat here survive by serving a necessary function for the megalopolis that no longer hires municipal workers to keep the streets clean. But in the end, the methane toxicity changes the routine: a major fire broke out in January 2005, devastating the dump and endangering everyone, especially the children, whom we see walking among huge vultures. The landfill's director says that the *guajeros* will not leave because "they think they own the landfill."

Part of the reason for the success of on-site shantytowns is simply economic. At the Shanghai dump in 2006, the Chinese peasants were already earning more money "collecting trash bags, tin cans and the rubber soles of shoes than they can as farmers or ordinary day laborers." Although a French company had scored a contract to turn the Shanghai dump into a recycling wonder, safeguarding the water table and producing natural gas, it was soon overrun by the number of scavengers and recyclers who invaded the pitch.

Because garbage dumps are simultaneously eyesores and essential depots, the central authorities of the world's cities will do almost anything to hide them. When relatively successful Second World economies like Brazil and Argentina collapsed in the 1990s, workers were compelled to adapt strategies of scavenging to survive. In Argentina instead of normal city-initiated recycling centers of paper, plastic, and bottle collection, the city permitted freelance collecting from homes and businesses and a significant subculture, the *cartoneros* (the recyclers, literally the "cardboard people"), came into being. The film *White Train* (1993, Argentina, dir. Sheila Perez Gimenez, Nahue Garcia, and Ramira Garcia) documents how their smelly job of transporting items in commuter from the city's garbage piles to the recycling center was done by ripping out all the seats to make more room for the *cartoneros*.

The recyclers using the newly commissioned White Train have joined the precariat after losing traditional working-class jobs. A supermarket worker became a *cartonera*, using the cart she gardened with in her house "when times were better." A truck driver with eighteen years' experience at first hid himself in shame until he became a *cartonera*. J. Malcolm Garcia, who chronicled the changes in the *cartoneros* from proletarians to scavengers of the precariat, concluded, "The pocked and mottled White Trains run like a daily gash across Buenos Aires, the dividing line between people with means and people without."

The White Train symbolized the impossible task of reconciling a failed city government and the urban population it supposedly served. A train station operator understood the difference between the *cartoneros* and everyone else: the White Train, he said, is "a train of workers, like a regular train but for people who don't have money." The original intention was to make the *cartoneros* invisible by simply adding the gutted cars to the end of the regular commuter trains. But rising unemployment, a recession in the 1990s, state bankruptcy in 2001, and currency devaluation made copper and other recyclables suddenly more valuable. As long as citizens separated their wet garbage from the recyclables, the system could work. But they didn't have to like what was going on. Garcia concluded, "Most people in downtown Buenos Aires avert their eyes when the White Train rattles past. They pretend not to see it and its trash-scavenging passengers. They may want to believe it doesn't exist. After all, it has no official timetable, no windowpanes, no doors in the frames, and no seats."

Other waste and recycling processes are often much more dangerous. One of the lowest caste assignments in India is the cleaning of urban latrines by the Bhangi clan of the Dalits or untouchables, rarely noticed outside of India until the release of the documentary, *The Worst Job in the World: The Bhangis of India* (2007, Denmark, dir. Jens Pedersen and Kuljit Bhamra). They are employed to clean, sometimes by hand, sometimes with inadequate tools or scrapers, the open latrines and sewer pipes of Indian cities. There are more than a million such workers, most of whom accept their karma or fate: "Because you are the lowest of the low, you are predestined to do the work," one of them states casually. In fact, some Dalits even see their jobs as retribution because of their misdeeds done in an earlier life.

Like child labor and slavery, the untouchables' work is illegal in India, although they are paid by the local municipality whose latrines they clean every day. In the Indian countryside, as in China, such human waste might go directly to the fields as fertilizer, but in the cities these workers must not only glean this muck, but also have to arrange to have it transported to the open dumps just outside the city limits. One of workers complains, "Why did God give me such disgusting work to do?" A fellow Dalit, Bezawada Wilson, became an activist and formed a union of the latrine cleaners, and in the film we meet his cheery self, organizing the workers.

The modernization of Indian cities through globalization has not always solved the problem: the camera pans the skyline of a high-tech edge city like Hyderabad, no doubt with all the latest mod cons, but even these toilets lead to sewer pipes serviced by the Dalits. We see one such worker lower himself through an open sewer pipe to unclog it.

Although it may not seem possible, an even more dangerous recycling job takes place in the film *eDump* (2007, United States, dir. Michael Zhao), chronicling the workers who handle toxic electronic by-products in the villages of Guiyu, in Guangdong Province, China, site of the world's largest recycling workforce, with 60,000 workers.

As one of the only industrialized countries in the world that has not ratified the Basel Convention on shipping hazardous waste to the Third World, the United States once exported 50 million computers, TVs, and cell phones to the Chinese "e-waste epicenter," Guiyu, a leading importer of one million tons of e-waste a year. At one point, filmmaker Zhao pans the banks of the infamous Ernjen River in Taiwan, lined with discarded circuit boards.

Guiyu in Guangdong Province, like most of China, had lax pollution controls. In their haste to extract gold from the circuit boards and to sell other recycled components, local entrepreneurs employed thousands of workers who routinely absorbed mercury, cadmium, and brominated flame retardants as they dismantle and burn the discarded electronic devices. This e-waste from the First World arrives in the shipping containers that had previously disgorged millions of tons of imported Chinese retail goods in the United States.

Zhao points out that Guiyu had been a "trash town for decades," but the air now is even more choked with "burned plastics and baked circuitry," as the residents pursue what could only be called a cottage industry of e-waste, with homes filled with electronic components. Zhao himself could sometimes spend only a couple of minutes at the workers' side, so irritating were the fumes; the workers themselves got used to ten to twelve hours of exposure to the fumes.

Just three years later, Wang Jiuliang, a Chinese documentary filmmaker, began to explore the recycling and waste crisis he believed China was ignoring. His first film, *Beijing Besieged by Waste* (2010, China), surveyed garbage dumps, apparently totally unregulated, surrounding the fifth ring road around the capital city. Both recycler or scavengers and goats had the same idea: find something to sell or eat. Wang made the film, he explained (Zhao), because when he revisited his peasant family's village, instead of the locusts, fish, and frogs he caught in the local creek, no aquatic life was left. His film must have been somewhat effective, because more than 80 percent of the garbage dumps have been eliminated.

He then turned to plastic waste. His film, *Plastic China* (2017, China), a Sundance Film Festival selection, initially also had success on the Chinese internet before it "disappeared." Although it certainly was no less a startling revelation of how the Chinese deal with waste, *Plastic China* is a more intimate, family-centered film that is disturbing because of the mostly wholesome but challenging portrait of two families who work in one home factory in the province of Shandong (the director's home province), one of the 5,000 such small businesses turning plastic garbage into recyclable pellets, a messy, toxic process, to be sure: sorting, shedding, melting, chopping, then repeat endlessly. Nobody ever wears a protective mask.

We see two families at work headed by the owner and boss, Kun, and his only employee, Peng. Both are migrants from rural villages, as was the director. Wang opens the film with dramatic shots of container ships, and then follows the individual containers on trucks into the countryside. Eventually, their contents are dumped everywhere in the courtyards of the family businesses. The children in both families work and play in the chaos, often extracting toys, books, and pictures for their entertainment and to learn how to read and write. At one point, the children go to a polluted stream near their house and bring home a live fish or two but mostly dead fish to be deep fried for dinner.

Peng can afford a van and eventually pays for a place for his daughter in the local school, a beautiful facility. His worker cannot afford the same for his daughter, since he drinks a lot of his wages away. We learn, not from the film, that Wang and the production team eventually put up the money for the tuition of his daughter; when China was a real socialist state, education was open to all (Zhao).

Owner Peng can drive his new car back to his village to show off; his worker has neither an ID nor the money to pay for a train or bus to take his family to his home village. Both men are products of the rural precariat, but one has managed to rise more than a notch or two to become an owner/worker. The film closes with more shots of container trucks, this time passing plastic waste fires and poisonous smoke. The East may once have been Red, as Chairman Mao often said, but now it is black or at best gray. No other recycling film comes close to the convincing noxious atmosphere of *Plastic China*.

E-waste is also, of course, the curse of the electronic and post-electronic world. The number of discarded cell phones, computers, televisions, cameras, film players, audio devices, not to mention circuit boards and wiring that have been discarded, has more than doubled since 2010. Almost all of these items contain precious metals like gold, silver, and copper, and elements like coltan, not to mention an incredible volume of plastic. Although China was the principle recipient of e-trash for years, it has cut off support for these importers; container ships full of such trash have been rerouted to other southeast countries that are willing to make profits from toxicity, as the lead and mercury could be reused in the manufacturing process as well.

Ironically, the very container ships used to transport e-waste are themselves targets of massive and toxic recycling in the industry now come to be known as shipbreaking. The Indian subcontinent has the world's three largest shipbreaking "ports": Alang in India is the largest, second is Chittagong in Bangladesh, and third is Gadani in Pakistan. Gadani may be the lowest in volume but it is the most efficient, breaking a ship up in a month or two, while the other two sites may take up to six months. All share the same significant dangers to the lives and health of the precariat, as the industry is unregulated. Thousands of workers are paid as little as forty-seven cents a day, seven days a week, working twelve hours a day.

All three locations operate in essentially the same manner: a ship heads full steam toward the beach until it runs aground. As pieces of the ship are blowtorched off, its weight lessens, and it is dragged closer to the beach line. The number of workers in the shipbreaking precariat is substantial. Gadani employs 30,000 workers directly and another 500,000 indirectly.

The dangers are obvious: a man is in a harness, suspending him hundreds of feet in the air, with perhaps a ladder or remnant of a deck to stand on occasionally, and a blowtorch. Multiply him times a hundred, as the crew swarms over the ship turning it into scrap. When gas cylinders explode, as they occasionally do, a disaster may happen, as in the explosion and fire aboard the former oil tanker Aces in 2016 when at least nineteen people were killed, sixty burned, with thirty others missing. Even when there are no accidents, the film *Shipbreakers* (2004, Canada, dir. Michael Kot), set in Alang, documents that an average of one worker per day dies from falls, usually not having worn a harness, while toxic fumes from Polycholorinated biphenyls (PCBs) and asbestos are common.

Workingman's Death (2005, Austria/Germany, dir. Michael Glawegger) surveys Gadani, while *Graveyard for Giants* (2014, Bangladesh/Scotland, dir. Madeeha Sye) is set in Chittagong. In both films, the dangers to workers are immediately obvious to the viewer. In *Graveyard for Giants*, one of the workers says he would even be willing to be paid less if he received any benefits at all, such as accommodation. His plaintive cry is simply this: "Is this a way to live?"

From First to Third World, somebody had always had to clean up the mess, whether it's garbage, recycling, or even human waste, and while some of these jobs in the First World may have been unionized in the past, it's almost always the precariat that now does the work. Shantytowns have historically been collections of the poor or the dispossessed who travel to the metropolis to work or are forced to live in segregated zones because of official (e.g., apartheid in South Africa) or unofficial pressures (e.g., the massive migration of Chinese peasants out of the countryside). The inhabitants provide cheap labor or services for the metropolis, work in the market stalls or as street vendors, and in some instances create jobs within the shantytown itself.

No other global garbage city has received as much attention as the neighborhoods of the Zabbaleen in Cairo. Children, especially street children under the age of twelve, are an important part of the precariat in Egypt and other cities, making up, Mike Davis argues in *Planet of Slums* (2006), 7 percent of the workforce. Although recycling is the story of Cairo's Zabbaleen workers, other street children will also collect and resell cigarette butts because smoking would otherwise be prohibitively expensive for many addicted to nicotine.

The Zabbaleen are the self-sufficient members of a niche of the Egyptian precariat who live in seven relatively small enclaves, the largest of which is Mokattam, nicknamed Garbage City, at the foot of Mount Mokattam, where the Zabbaleen have traditionally worshipped in a number of semisecret cave churches. They deserve special attention because of their unique status as a literally ethnic precariat that has worked out a relatively successful accommodation with governmental power and economic necessity.

As Coptic Christians, they have been born into their occupation, originally migrants from Asyut in Upper Egypt, a sect by most definitions but a tribe of garbage collectors by the one that now seems to fit and is the literal translation of their name. Unlike Muslims, the Copts eat pork, making them especially suited to this task: they raise pigs which devour the organic trash, while the paper, plastics, glass, and metal are recycled for money. For many years, one of these major subgroups, plastics, was sent to China for further recycling. The pigs are kept in the family courtyards and occasionally are seen standing on the street corners of Coptic Cairo like the reliable—and unique to most cities—recycling machines they are.

The Copts were actually the second wave of migrants to take on this task, but the first wave, the Wahi, migrants from the Western Desert oasis Dakhla, at first competed with the Zabbaleen for waste contracts with various housing complexes for recycling. Eventually, the Wahi turned middlemen and subcontracted the actual physical labor to the Zabbaleen, who were significantly more efficient recyclers. The two groups comprise an intricate network of collectors, recyclers, sorters, contractors, middlemen, and even restaurant owners who buy pork for tourists' meals. What pig meat the Zabbaleen themselves consume represents the only protein in their diet.

The films that document the lives of the Zabbaleen reveal their successful system, although it is not an easy or sanitary or respectable profession. They have survived in recent years two crises, one political, the other health-related (although it was a bogus scare).

During the first crisis, the authorities decided to clean up Cairo's image and began taking bids from private contracting companies to place what most American or European jurisdictions require—plastic bins in the street for convenient pickup. The contractors, however, tried to save money by using relatively few bins per block, forcing residents to trek through the streets with their own refuse. Of course, for very low fees the Zabbaleen would come right to their customers' doors to do this task. The private companies also recycled only about twenty percent of the waste, sending the remaining eighty percent to landfills. The Zabbaleen's more efficient home courtyard system could recycle as much as eighty percent, patiently separating different kinds of paper and plastic and of course feeding organic waste to their pigs.

The only, somewhat limited, success the municipalities achieved was to force the Zabbaleen to use more motorized carts and trucks to gather the waste rather than the traditional donkey carts, quaint but offensive to sensitive city officials.

The second crisis was an equally momentous attack on the Zabbaleen involving the Ministry of Agriculture's panicked order during the 2009 epidemic of H1N1 swine flu to slaughter all Egyptian pigs. Swine flu was never found in Egypt, however, so the Zabbaleen believe that the campaign was based on religious prejudice against this minority Christian sect, perhaps numbering 50,000 souls in an overwhelmingly Muslim nation.

Five documentaries capture the daily life of these unusual recyclers. In *We Are the Zabbaleen* (2013, Egypt,) the Zabbaleen show that they are independent, resilient, and innovative, as witnessed by their reaction to the 2009 epidemic of H1N1 swine flu. In this second crisis, the Zabbaleen's pigs were among the perhaps 300,000 slaughtered. The garbage that grew to great piles of awfulness turned out to be a political weapon against the government. The Zabbaleen simply let the organic waste gather throughout the city, a stinking mess, in short, and a health menace of its own right. They eventually got new pigs and probably, unintentionally, helped to topple Hosea Mubarak's government.

In *Garbage Dreams* (2009, United States, dir. Mai Iskander), the 30,000 Zabbaleen were confronted by the nightmare scenario (of the first crisis above) from the Egyptian city government in the form of professional contractors, who supposedly represented modernization. One of the film's subjects, Osama, is a Zabbaleen youth who is tempted to escape his clan's invisibility and poverty by taking a job with the new rivals: the foreign garbage company brought in by the city council. Unfortunately, Osama's own friends and former coworkers begin to play rough with him, annoyed that he is trying to rise above his station, not to mention work for one of their hated competitors.

When the Zabbaleen's reputation expands, two other teenagers, Adham and Nabil, are sent by an organization to study the recycling techniques used in Wales, an unlikely choice, viewers will think. But the issues are the same and the boys soon realize that in a number of ways their techniques are more efficient than their hosts. Nabil cannot resist noting that the Welsh have "technology but no precision," that is, their efficiency rate is lower than the Zabbaleen's. Leila, a fourth individual featured, is a social worker and a teacher at the community's recycling "school." Back home, she takes the leadership in the fight against the city officials' decision to "modernize" the city's garbage collecting.

In *Marina of the Zabbaleen* (2008, Egypt, dir. Engl Wassef), seven-year-old Marina is tracked as she goes about her daily tasks of collecting garbage. Her fantasy life is, however, anything but mundane: she dreams of being a doctor and imagines flying elephants and fantasy pigeons. As sweet as Marina is, the filmmaker does not avoid some of the nastiness of the Zabbaleen life: at one point, rats steal Marina's toothbrush and we see other children playing way too close to used syringes. When a landlord threatens Marina's family with eviction, the nature of their precarious lifestyle becomes terribly obvious.

The advantage of the fourth documentary, *Zabbaleen: Trash Town* (2016, Russia, prod. RT), is that the camera rarely leaves the Zabbaleen or their neighborhood streets, capturing their daily work in close-up. It is a portrait that shows every different piece of garbage imaginable in fascinating detail. Some of the Zabbaleen can even joke about the dangers inherent in garbage collecting: they refer to a friend—it sounds like a tall tale—who pricked his hand with a needle and began rotting from the inside out, like garbage. We can see the careful planning involved in their tasks: a water-bath machine cleans the plastic gathered, then feeds it into the first grinding machine that in turn feeds it to a third machine that dries the plastic and grinds it even further into a powder. These may be household industries but they are not naive recyclers.

The cinema of the precariat has brought the Zabbaleen some long-neglected attention and to a certain extent praise for their work ethic. But the more recent appreciation was a spectacular mural painted across more than fifty buildings, whose message in orange, white, and blue in Arabic calligraphy quoted a third-century Coptic Christian bishop, St. Athanasius of Alexandria: "If one wants to see the light of the sun, he must wipe his eyes." The Tunisian-French muralist El Seed painted the quotation so that it was best viewed from Mount Mokattam above the Zabbaleen quarter. The YouTube video *A Project of Peace, Painted across 50 Buildings* (2016, United States, prod. TEDTalks) presents spectacular shots not only of the mural, both from Mount Mokattam and a helicopter, but also of street scenes of the Zabbaleen hard at work in their garbage-saturated neighborhood. El Seed believes his work did its part in helping people understand what they had thought was only the "dirty, marginalized, and segregated" lives of this sector of the Egyptian precariat. They deserve better, the muralist argued.

Living in a garbage city is not only a Third World phenomenon. Near Palm Springs, California, a community of migrant workers, mostly Mexican or Mexican American, occupy the Duroville trailer camp next to the dump on the Torres Martinez Desert Cahuilla Indian Reservation, because the trailer camp's owner is a member of the tribe and not required to follow local sanitary codes (Barry).

This is also exactly what happened in Willets Point, a shantytown of shops with a notorious history. In New York City, one of the richest cities in the world, unpleasant and sometimes quite dangerous zones that affect the precariat the most persist. Although the vocabulary to discuss it was not available, the famed World's Fair of 1939 in New York City was ironically a progenitor of this process, as the famed General Motors Futurama Pavilion, projecting the future of an advanced consumer society into 1960, was actually build on the Corona Ash Dump—or Mt. Corona—as it was nicknamed, which F. Scott Fitzgerald's novel *The Great Gatsby* (1925) had in turn renamed as the Valley of Ashes, where the threatening lumpenproletariat survived: "A fantastic farm where ashes grow like wheat into ridges and hills and grotesque gardens; where ashes take the form of houses and chimneys and rising smoke and, finally, with a transcendent effort, of men who move dimly and already crumbling through the powdery air." Fitzgerald was transforming Mt. Corona, literally the ash debris from the city's coal-burning furnaces, buttressed by barges unloading animal waste amid a colony of formidable rats. What came of all this eventually was Flushing Meadows Corona–Park, adjacent to Willets Point, probably New York City's last shantytown and the subject of numerous films.

Metal and other electronic waste also make up the secondary specialty of the precariat in the terminal world of New York City's Willets Point, but it is really an auto shantytown. Nicknamed the Iron Triangle, it has had its portrait stripped and spray painted in both documentaries and feature films.

Even savvy New Yorkers have trouble comprehending Willets Point, a seventy-seventy-five-acre, unpaved, semi-flooded enclave of 250 parts shops, auto repair businesses, chop shops (dismantling cars acquired legally or illegally for parts), and related businesses, employing upward of 2000 people, with a resident population—the estimate varies—from one to three people in "apartments" and an uncounted number of people living in their cars or vans. It's safe to say that a resident of Lagos, Nigeria, would find its essence of continuous hustle for customers familiar: there are men who "steer" customers to the right shop, for tips and a commission. If you have a broken mirror, for example, you simply hold it out of your car window and the steerer leads you to the right parts and/or repair shop.

Willets Point, Sarah Maslin Nir of the *New York Times* wrote, is a study in contradictions. There is obvious poverty amid the determination of immigrants to make a living. Since there is no need to show immigration papers or proof of a "mechanic's certification," customers benefit from low prices and a good deal as they search for replacement auto parts and quick repairs. Willets Point, she concludes, "represents a loophole through which to slip into gainful employment in America."

Willets Point forms an underdeveloped thirteen-block area in Flushing, New York City. Although the then-mayor Bloomberg's Economic Development Corporation (EDC) quotes the Census of 2000—there is only one recorded resident in Willets Point—the daily working population there has been without basic city services for so long that it has begun to resemble the sets from John Carpenter's classic postapocalyptic *Escape from New York* (1981, United States): workers swarm around derelict vehicles laboring to bring them back to life or in some instances take them apart for the resale of the parts. The streets fill with water after a storm and the less said about sanitation the better (there are no sewers) (Figure 4.2).

But who really lives in Willets Point? *Foreign Parts* (2011, United States, dir. Véréna Paravel and J. Sniadecki) begins as a very traditional cinema verité

Figure 4.2 Main Street, Willet's Point. Photographed by Tom Zaniello.

exploration of four regulars of the Willets Point precariat with a sequence of a worker cutting loose the engine block from the bottom of a pickup truck, spewing engine fluids and radiator liquid like cut veins: in the background, we see the facade of Citi Field, the new home of the New York Mets baseball team, probably another reason why city developers need, very badly, for Willets Point to go: the gentrification of this neighborhood will never happen if these seventy-five acres remain a living museum of discombobulated automobiles.

The regulars include Joe Ardizzone, a seventy-six-year-old long-time denizen who has seen the face of the official city and finds it wanting: "They'll tell me I own $10 in taxes and then collect $20." Touching but more than a little pathetic are a couple, Luis and Sara Zapiain (who is the life of the party), and Julia (one name only), who live in their cars, technically leaving Joe as the only "resident" in Willets Point.

A related feature film, *Chop Shop* (2008, United States, Ramin Bahrani), is also set in Willets Point: Alejandro, a teenage Latino street orphan, tries to survive, partly by his desire to work, partly on his wits and petty thievery. Some of the auto shops in Willets Point are no doubt *chop shops*, that is, with no questions asked the owner of this niche business will take apart a car, probably stolen, for parts for resale. While Alejandro will do almost anything to make money and try to make a home for his older sister, who may herself be making ends meet in a way the boy does not care to think about. If he could, Alejandro would prefer to be a street cart salesman, like the man portrayed in Bahrani's *Man Push Cart* (2005, United States), in which a Pakistani immigrant—a former rock star— tries to make his living on the streets of Manhattan selling coffee and snacks. The location shooting of both of these films emphasizes the street smarts their characters have to have to survive.

Then comes the then-mayor (now ex-mayor) Bloomberg, with a plan: take over all the private property of Willets Point by eminent domain, raze the entire district, and create appropriate office and residential opportunities that will complement Citi Field. Stay tuned. When Willets Point goes—and most think it will, eventually—not only will many in the precariat lose their jobs, but the part of NYC that most resembles a global shantytown will also disappear.

Three billion dollars later, the more than 5,500 condos and coops and 2.7 million feet of retail and office space will obviously require a different kind of precariat—at the very least, underpaid workers in the service industry, retail sales people, valet drivers, and food servers.

A number of documentaries have taken up the issue of the survival or gentrification of Willets Point. The Willets Point Industry and Reality Association fought the City's attempt to erase the zone by eminent domain in their own documentary, *Willets Point: Beyond the Curbline* (2007, United States).

The Association launched lawsuits against the City, with arguments ranging from reasonable (the number of jobs) to dubious (it was not owned by anyone, including the City). The legal and related matters were developed in a YouTube campaign, *Willets Point Lawsuits: Parts One and Two* (2008, United States, prod. Willets Point Property and Business Owners). More convincing, however, was the Association's arguments that the City never provided any services (sewers, for example) to the neighborhood and then complained of its unsanitary conditions.

By 2018, Mayor Bloomberg was gone, but the new mayor, Bill de Blasio, inheriting a $3 billion hot potato, announced a compromise after dozens of shops had been bulldozed—the City crying eminent domain—and hundreds of immigrants lost their jobs. The new plan will include low- and moderate-income housing, a school, and retail shops. No doubt "rising from the ashes" of the old Corona Ash Dump, the *New York Times* concluded, "Willets Point is dead. Long live Willets Point."

5

Epidemic Cinema and Catastrophic Mise-en-Scène

There is a thin (sometimes irradiated) line between films that foreground epidemics and those that have catastrophes waiting in the background. Most epidemic films have a catastrophic mise-en-scène, but not all catastrophe films include epidemics. Instead of viral or bacterial mysteries, catastrophic films confront radiation poisoning; natural and human-made disasters such as collapsing dams, mine failures, and oil leaks; and even invasions from out of space. All of the films disproportionately impact the precariat and the working class, both urban and rural. Both genres mix fictional and real-life occurrences to drive their plots, and both usually feature four of Standing's social and economic classes—the lumpenproletariat, the precariat, the proletarians, and the proficiens (especially emergency and health workers).

Epidemic cinema and catastrophe films are staffed with emergency and health workers, but usually the masses of ordinary citizens become the principal victims. Patients in epidemic films and victims of catastrophes are always in extremely perilous situations, especially when disasters (inevitably) create a ground zero. Numerous documentaries track both actual diseases and catastrophes, many of them underreported, while feature films either invent or extrapolate new diseases and sometimes use the mise-en-scène of science fiction and postapocalyptic films to present widespread and unprecedented destruction.

Although it has rarely been explicitly recognized in film histories, epidemic cinema as a genre of its own has dominated the portrayal of diseases among the precariat and other classes at least since the 1950s when Elia Kazan's *Panic in the Streets* (1950, United States) dramatized an outbreak of plague among the precariat and the lumpenproletariat in New Orleans. More famous than Kazan's film is the medical sci-fi mystery, *The Andromeda Strain* (1971, United States, dir. Robert Wise) and its remake with the same title, released both as a TV series and as a feature film (United States, 2008, dir. Mikael Salomon), both of which open with a town devastated by what we learn is a strange crystalline but lethal virus from out of space, the only survivors a crying baby and an inebriated old man. The film also provided the template for later films in which the military plays an ambiguous and sometimes morally compromised role: instead of defeating the virus, they seek to contain/control it for future use as a possible weapon.

Fatal Contact: Bird Flu in America (2006, United States/New Zealand, dir. Ricard Pearce) involved a real species-crossing virus, that is, an avian influenza (H5N1) that could be transmitted to humans from birds, dead or alive. A fascinating variation on epidemic cinema was *Blindness* (2008, Canada/Brazil/Japan, dir. Fernando Meirelles) that used an unknown agent to cause blindness, seemingly without clear causation or apparent viral origin. *Outbreak* (1995, United States, dir. Wolfgang Petersen) offered a hybrid approach, dramatizing a range of horrifying Ebola-like symptoms from a fictional virus named Motuba that attacks a village in Zaire and is transmitted to a small town in California by an illegally smuggled monkey. There the usual extensive catastrophic mise-en-scène is missing, although the dominating role of the American military creates its own special angle, as it is responsible for obliterating the Zairean village and seems poised to do the same in California.

Thus, the persistence of epidemic cinema as a genre is obvious, but it was Kazan's *Panic in the Streets*, however, that became the title of London's National Film Theater survey of epidemic cinema organized by Mark Finch and Judith Williamson (1988) and extensively documented by Williamson (1992). The film seemed to predict the direction of epidemic cinema for years to come. Patient Zero—the first identified victim—is a murdered man, an illegal immigrant, carrying bubonic plague. He is a "foreigner," concealed by an underworld of fellow immigrants and precarious workers. The ship that has smuggled him is called The Nile Queen, with a black and Asian crew, and concentrated on "the social consequences of mass scale disease" in one city, New Orleans.

This was the first film program series that studied how "pre-AIDS films about infection made it possible ... to trace certain trends which [were] woven into the complex reactions" to AIDS in the 1980s. Kazan's film dramatized the "drive for the discovery and control of a disease ... among society's outcasts" (the lumpen) and "shows ... that the language and narrative patterns associated with AIDS reportage and fictions were developed long before the illness itself existed."

Since the 1980s, epidemic cinema and films about disaster typically turned to an endless urban wasteland, characteristic of postapocalyptic films, that replaces the megalopolis. Ethnic minorities and immigrants in the precariat were often portrayed as disease vectors of any epidemic that targeted poor people with little or no access to medical help. Criminality, sexual activity, and an "alien" invasion (whether from an ethnic minority or even from outer space) all contribute as disease vectors.

The epidemics symbolize political and social collapse, blurring any distinction between personal and social illness as medical workers search for Patient Zero, a search that relied on the genre elements typical of films about zombies and the undead. While the visceral mise-en-scène of the films is medical, "government indifference, conspiracy, or disbelief" (Finch and Williamson) becomes the political motor of epidemic cinema, almost always framed with military control, and sometimes a combination of all of these, as in *Pandemic* (2009, United States, dir. Jason Connery) in which the military, rather than appropriately attempting to contain an epidemic, is abetting it in a search for an unspecified plague virus to be used as their own biological weapon. What makes this particularly violent example of epidemic cinema of greater interest to us is that it is a reversal of the tendency of some video games to become more cinematic—see Chapter 8— because *Pandemic* is one of the earliest films to be shot as if the spectator were the video game player in a first-person shooter (FPS) mode: what is called a subjective shot used for a character in film, typically following a close-up of the character's face or eyes, is now used in *Pandemic* to put the viewer in first-person mode whenever there is a firefight.

On the social level, the middle-class family in suburbia usually represents the standard of purity, with the infection of mothers and children the ultimate violation. The consanguinity of epidemic cinema and zombie and vampire films is deep, as these creatures invade the suburbs as well as the city, often creating a postapocalyptic mise-en-scène. Epidemic cinema turns into uncontrollable dystopia in old classics of the genre such as *The Omega Man* (1971, United States, dir. Boris Sagal) as well as later films like *28 Days Later* (2002, United Kingdom, dir. Danny Boyle) and *28 Weeks Later* (2007, United Kingdom/Spain, dir. Juan Carlos Fresnadillo), with the masses of people as victims first and then mindless perpetrators.

In addition to providing a postapocalyptic mise-en-scène for many precariat catastrophe films, epidemic cinema also indicts a complicit government accommodating an elite group of capitalists who use epidemics for profit. One of the most notorious plots is developed in *The Leakers* (2018, Hong Kong/Malaysia, dir. Herman Yau) that targets a drug company's CEO in an anti-pharm thriller. The viewer is sure that the Malaysia pharmaceutical giant is up to no good, especially when a mosquito-borne Zika virus hits the country with a variant that has a drug available for a cure but the company seems to be holding back on using it for the pandemic. A vigilante group, The Leakers, includes both reporters and a policeman from Hong Kong whose child has contracted the virus. This vigilante groups gets involved with convoluted kidnapping plots involving the CEO of the pharm company who ends up killing both of his sons who want to reveal that it was their own father who created the Zika variant in order to sell its cure.

An unusual example of epidemic cinema metamorphosed into political commentary on South African racism, both historical and contemporary. *District 9* (2009, South Africa/United States/New Zealand/Canada, dir. Neill Blomkamp) is a remarkable genre-bending film, using elements of films featured in a number of chapters in this book on "illegal" migrants, shantytowns, and epidemic cinema based on alien intrusion.

District 9 inverts many of the primary visual tropes of those genres, however, as well as challenging the apartheid history of South Africa. A tattered spaceship appears hovering over Jo'berg, but instead of potentially dangerous invaders, authorities discover a disheveled rabble of hungry crustacean-like aliens soon nicknamed "prawns." They seem to be rejects from their own other-worldly species. They are hustled into a detention camp that soon becomes a slum as the government seems incapable of handling the problem.

Eventually, the decision is made to remove the aliens forcibly and hide them away at some rural camp, "accidentally" killing some of them who resist relocation. The white administrator of this process cannot remain focused or remain on track for this duty: the aliens seem to be up to something, have much greater intelligence and technical ability than heretofore imagined, and most disturbingly are capable of "infecting" and transforming humans into themselves. Their unexpected target of this very subtle kind of epidemic is inevitably the paternalistic administrator in charge of their relocation, whose transformation is a kind of sick joke. The film actually specializes in sick jokes: a cannibalistic Nigerian gang boss of the lumpen districts exploits the aliens' predilection for pet food. A return to the status quo ends the film, but at least one new alien, perhaps portentously, has been "created" on earth.

Typically, catastrophe films have an even more political subtext than epidemic cinema, rarely whitewashing the roles that government or capitalists play in protecting the elite from responsibility for the widespread destruction revealed in documentaries or genre fictions. Catastrophe films often substitute such vectors as radiation poisoning and/or nuclear bombs for the viral attacks of epidemic cinema, with the Chernobyl, Ukraine, disaster as the leading subject for documentaries and the model for a nuclear apocalypse in feature films. *The Battle of Chernobyl* (2006, France, dir. Thomas Johnson) is a curious hybrid of the two: it posits that the nuclear apocalypse in a certain sense has already happened and films what it already really looks like, how easily the precariat, workers, and soldiers die, and how governments are slow to act, even slower to tell the truth, and then rush to take the credit for saving the world or, at least in this instance, Europe.

In 1986, Reactor 4 at the nuclear energy facility in Chernobyl, in the city of Pripyat, exploded with the power to destroy and kill at the same magnitude of the two American Second World War blasts at Hiroshima and Nagasaki. The radiation cloud from the blast drifted throughout Europe, but its lethal effects were mainly regional, including Kiev, the capitol of the Ukraine, about a hundred miles away, a city that was still holding scheduled massive outdoor May Day rallies six days after the blast. Numerous workers and residents in Pripyat died immediately or soon after, having never been told to at least stay indoors to reduce exposure to radiation in the days after the explosion.

Two sets of workers died as a result of Chernobyl: those on the immediate ground when the explosion occurred and those "volunteers" who came in the next week after the blast to attempt various containment strategies, all of which were ingenious but all of which were potentially and in the end actually lethal. What made Chernobyl even more dangerous was the possibility of a second explosion, which not only was capable of spewing more radioactive gases willy-nilly but also was contaminating an entire region's groundwater supply.

Pripyat is a less familiar name than Chernobyl, but its residents, some of whom have refused to leave after the city was declared radioactively uninhabitable, call it home. Some who left came back: they were called resettlers. One of them told Nobel Prize winner Svetlana Alexievich, the famous chronicler of *Voices from Chernobyl* (2005), that "the apples are hanging in the garden, the leaves are on the trees, the potatoes are in the fields. I don't think there was any Chernobyl, they made it up. They tricked people" (Figure 5.1).

The film *Pripyat* (1999, Austria, dir. Nicholas Geyrhalter) captures such dubious confidence amid a chilling black-and-white cityscape of ruins and shells of building still standing. Its residents are two classes of people—current workers assigned to the remaining active reactor, Building 3, and survivors of the disaster of Building 4. In The Zone, as it is called (perhaps echoing the similarly named

Figure 5.1 Inside a Chernobyl reactor from *Pripyat*. Courtesy Icarus Films.

location in Andrei Tarkovsky's Russian film, *The Stalker*, released just eight years earlier—see Chapter 7), some of the residents accept their fate cheerfully, seeming to be surprised that they are still alive, although they are often tested for bodily levels (too high) of plutonium and strontium. The psychological disruption seems greater than the physical. A senior citizen couple, for example, joke about eating mushrooms and celebrate the surprising birth of normal children to their own daughter. Workers walk by a stark memorial to a missing (presumed dead) colleague who is still in Building 4 under a black roof of containment asphalt (or so it seems) called the Sarcophagus. As one of the workers says, we don't live in the Zone of Radiation, we really live in a Zone of Alienation.

Residents having normal grandchildren would make great efforts to counter the rumors and bad publicity about Pripyat, its irradiated citizenry, and nuclear Armageddon itself. A reporter from the *New York Times*, Jere Longman, had obviously, like many of us, seen too many postapocalyptic films. When a European soccer match was scheduled to be played in Ukraine, he wondered who the strongest team would be: "The winners will be mutants... eerie. You're waiting for zombies to come out of the woods." He could not help report what had already become generally known in Pripyat: "It was in the late spring, the population was eating fresh radioactive vegetables and other foods."

The first major full-scale fictional recreation of the Chernobyl disaster, *Chernobyl* (2019, United Kingdom/United States, dir. Johan Renck), utilized the five-part structure of the new twenty-first-century-style TV series to move seamlessly between the workers and the engineers on literal ground zero, with the self-righteous Communist Party and nuclear regulatory committee types that believe that since such a disaster *could* not happen it obviously *did* not happen. The director of the site is especially adamant in his reaction to eyewitnesses on his staff: you did not see a hole where the reactor core should have been because it could not have exploded. Later when he vomits on the committee room table and has to be carried to the medical station, his superiors think he is sick but not radioactively sick. He really should have been in the earlier horror film that uses Chernobyl as a pretext, *The Chernobyl Diaries* (2012, United States, dir. Brad Parker), which takes a band of "extreme tourists" down into the nuclear underground of Chernobyl to encounter, of course, radioactive zombies.

The *Chernobyl* series makes it clear that it is at first the workers on site and on emergency teams (fire, EMT) who are the real victims of governmental negligence. But the local population is decidedly—and not convincingly—clueless: they let their children play in the radioactive dust that floats down from the explosion. The filmmakers make radioactive horror beautiful: the glowing plant, the sparkly dust in the air, and the explosive tower of red-hot radioactive debris. But this docudrama is one of the best film series of its kind, one that will serve as a model for combining the documentary details of the catastrophe with the human story of the toll on the victims and their would-be rescuers. The sequences with the miners—who will work naked because of the heat underground—brought in to tunnel under the reactor, the cemetery workers lowering the lead caskets of bodies into a grave with a crane before they pour concrete to seal the site, the animal control soldiers who wear an exterior lead jockstrap to protect themselves before they venture into the town to kill the radioactive pets, a fireman's pregnant wife whose baby absorbs the radiation that would have killed her, all of these sequences and many more emphasize the working-class townspeople, the rescue teams, and the soldiers who crowd the dangerous ground of the reactor. No other Chernobyl film comes close to this kind of revealing detail.

Although Pripyat achieved notoriety because of the Chernobyl meltdown, it was only one of the numerous "secret" or "closed" cities in the Soviet Union, officially known as ZATOs (Closed Administrative Territorial Formations), of which more than forty were literally forbidden to be delineated on maps. Almost all of them were related to nuclear purposes, either materially (uranium mines) or through production (weapons and missile factories).

Embittered City (2017, Ukraine, dir. Alexander and Tatyana Detig) exposed the secret function and widespread radioactive poisoning of such a city, also Ukrainian, Zhovti Vody, where to this day no fences or signs indicate the dangerous waste materials lying about the city. When the mines could no longer supply uranium, the factory infrastructure was turned over to the (almost) equally toxic production of hydrochloric acid. Now the ruins are still called "secret property." The filmmakers were cheeky in the face of all the horrible cases of cancer and the authorities' refusal to worry about scrap dealers trucking radioactive pieces of the old factories to be sold all over the region. Their soundtrack includes a pop song from the point of view of the local precariat and other workers: "How long will we be kept waiting? / How long will we be keep 'knowing nothing'?"

Lest misplaced patriotism rise up, many of the residents of St. Louis, Missouri, eventually realized that their city too was a "secret" nuclear city. In *The First Secret City* (2015, United States, dir. Alisa Carrick and C. D. Stelzer), we learn of millions of pounds of high-grade Belgian Congo uranium ore processed by Mallinckrodt Chemical Company into nuclear fuel rods for atomic reactors. Waste and runoff water polluted nearby fields and rivers in mostly poor working-class areas, especially in a section of St. Louis called Weldon Spring. The inevitable cancer clusters began to tell the tale of nuclear pollution among the naive population. Even the truck driver who transported waste materials to the St. Louis airport for construction fill had no idea what he was hauling.

Another St. Louis-based film exposing Mallinckrodt's cavalier attitude toward uranium waste is *The Safe Side of the Fence* (2015, United States, dir. Tony West), whose title points to the absurdity and criminal negligence of the production process. A chain link fence bordered the zone of the company's property where moon-suited workers worked in supposed safety, but when they wanted to take a break or eat lunch, they could go just to the other side of the fence, the "safe side," twenty or thirty yards away, without their protective suits.

Nuclear accidents, while never routine, nevertheless occasionally happened. A more unusual perhaps almost unclassifiable epidemic—labeled as such for the first time in this book—in Chicago in 1995 killed 739 elderly African Americans, mostly from the precariat, during an unprecedented heat wave. *Cooked: Survival by Zip Code* (2019, United States, dir. Judith Helfand) is a film that suggests there may in fact be no difference between an epidemic and a catastrophe. It is difficult to state conclusively that the Chicago events could not have happened anywhere else, given that almost every urban administration must deal with the virtual isolation of thousands of almost exclusively elderly African Americans in substandard, unair-conditioned housing in neighborhoods where they are afraid even to leave their windows open for fear of robbery or worse. The title *Cooked* is pure Chicago, as it refers on the one hand to Chicago's Cook County and on the other to the horrible heat deaths caused by the heat wave, poverty, and the city's public health deficiencies.

Documenting Chicago's food deserts in *Cooked* was Helfand's usual style, similar to her other films that challenged the conventions of environmental, ecological, and epidemic cinema, as she consistently investigated toxic situations, both personal and public. She codirected *Blue Vinyl* (2002, United States) with Daniel Gold, exposing the dangers of the use of polyvinyl chloride (PVC) siding, once used to clad one home every three seconds in America. The manufacture, use, and disposal of PVC products threatened serious toxic chemical exposure, a situation that Helfand was especially sensitive to as she was the victim of her mother's exposure to the toxic drug diethylstilbestrol (DES) during pregnancy, the topic of her second film, *A Healthy Baby Girl* (1997, United States), that chronicles her cervical cancer, her mother's guilt in talking DES, and the subsequent revelation by the Food and Drug Administration (FADA) of the dangers of the drug. Helfand's third film, *Everything's Cool* (2007, United States), also codirected with Daniel Gold, explored the divide between climate scientists and what seemed at the time like an inordinately large number of Americans skeptical of global warming. Like *Blue Vinyl*, it was a "toxic comedy," once again using satire, animated sequences, and expert testimony to counter what had been the numerous public relations successes of the oil and coal industries.

Cooked chronicles those five days of a sweltering heat wave in July 1995, in which the daily temperature reached 100 plus degrees, the hottest day reaching 106, when at least 739 people died of heat-related causes. Eric Klinenberg, author of *Heat Wave* (2002), the standard history of the disaster, pointed out that in the 1930s during a similar heat wave Chicagoans survived by sleeping in the parks or on the banks of Lake Michigan, options not available currently to those senior citizens justifiably concerned about assaults or robbery.

Compounding the matter, Chicago authorities did not release a heat emergency warning until the last day of the heat wave. Ambulance service and hospital facilities were inadequate in the poor neighborhoods. The residents' ghetto literally became an "urban heat island," trapping the heat day and night in the concrete environment of high rises and pavements. Helfand films row after row of refrigerated meat-packing trucks pressed into service to handle what the morgue could not cope with. Thousands of others were hospitalized as well. Some idea of the horror may be apprehended from Cory Franklin, director of Medical Intensive Care at Cook County Hospital, who told an interviewer that his hospital's "open wards had no air conditioning. They were so hot that we actually had three or four older people with cardiac problems who suffered heat stroke while they were in the hospital."

Englewood, Helfand's focal South Side neighborhood, led Chicago in diabetes, cancer, unemployment, foreclosures, corner stores (liquor stores, especially, among other "convenience" stores), crime, incarcerations, gun violence, and empty lots. Even fifteen years after the disaster, food chains were notoriously slow in remedying the food desert problem. Only Walgreens and Whole Foods were making efforts to sell food in a number of communities, including Englewood and nine other neighborhood food deserts in Chicago (Figure 5.2).

Part of the film's urgency is that this catastrophe has been virtually ignored. Klinenberg points out why: "Natural disasters are so visually spectacular that they make the front page or the TV news even when they occur in remote places." A hurricane in 2005 made Katrina a household word, but it was not only the wind and the water that destroyed homes and lives. Natural forces "interact with social environments to produce social outcomes," a *Seattle Times* commentator on Katrina concluded: "There's no such thing as a natural disaster" (Luft).

Extreme heat, on the other hand, unlike a hurricane, is invisible. Helfand is concerned that even her focus on a single catastrophe like a heat wave is

Figure 5.2 Director Judith Helfand with National Guard general flying over potentially deadly zip-code areas from *Cooked: Survival by Zip Code*. Courtesy Kartemquin Films.

problematical: it may only be "a decoy obscuring the city from focusing on the underlying crisis of poverty." The film concludes: "Where poverty was greatest ... death from heat was greatest."

Her fears may be justified. One of the great catastrophes of the Depression, the Great Flood, that submerged 167 million acres across the South in 1926 and 1927, held multiple dangers for the descendants of freed slaves. As Bill Morrison's *The Great Flood* (2014, United States) documents, those African Americans not killed outright by the flood waters were virtually re-enslaved as unpaid laborers under military overseers rebuilding the levees, some of which had been deliberately breached and flooded, African Americans in effect sacrificing their own towns in order to protect New Orleans. Having lost their homes and potentially their freedom, many black families headed to northern cities like Chicago, the beginning of the Great Migration of 6 million African Americans out of the South forever (Figure 5.3).

Although the Great Flood and the Great Migration had been celebrated and its horrors described in such powerful literature as Zora Neale Hurston's novel *Their Eyes Were Watching God* (1937) and Richard Wright's story *Down by the Riverside* (1938), Morrison's documentary with its careful and extended use of archival footage gives us the visual struggles in revealing black and white. The African Americans do the overwhelming majority of the grunt work such as

Figure 5.3 Impressed African American precariat workers on the levees from *The Great Flood*. Courtesy Icarus Films.

filling sacks of dirt to repair levees, and they are inevitably treated like chattel as they are loaded up in boxcars to escape the flood zones. There are glimmers of black-white cooperation in some shots but for the most part white men are supervising while black men work. Prison labor seems to be all black as well.

The Great Flood is an experimental documentary drawing on structuralists' landscape films for its inspiration. Because the displacement of one million agricultural workers, an overwhelmingly large proportion African American, in 1927 leads directly to their Great Migration out of the repressive and racist Southern patriarchy into the Northern cities, it is inevitably a political film as well. We are also reminded as we see a celebration of African Americans dressed in their Sunday best in a procession in a Chicago church that their liberation from the South would eventually be compromised again by urban segregation in the future.

The Great Flood was always considered a human-made disaster, despite nature's assist, because questions of levies and the control of river water were always class-based decisions, usually leaving the black precariat, a select, quite innocent, segment of the population, out of the discussion. On the other hand, the extraction of oil, minerals, precious metals, and commodities is also fraught with danger (see Chapter 6), and their toll on the precariat, the proletariat, and farmers was daily and incessant. The major American catastrophes associated with the mining of coal occur mainly in the Appalachian South—Kentucky and West Virginia, especially—and punctuate a labor history of massive struggles with companies over union membership, safety underground, decent living conditions, and fair wages. Explosions, floods, and fire underground are terrible events, but they were made all the worse by negligent owners and managers in the industry.

The cinema of the precariat in this region has been largely a product of Appalshop, short for Appalachian Workshop, one of the most important and influential working-class arts and media focused community organization in the United States. Founded as part of a 1960s War on Poverty initiative cosponsored by the Office of Economic Opportunity (OEO) and the American Film Institute, this Appalachian Workshop created a body of films that closely followed the spirit of the classic Academy Award–winning documentary *Harlan County USA* (1976, United States, dir. Barbara Kopple) with its focus on the coalminers and their Appalachian culture, tracing in detail a long tradition of struggles in the mountains for economic justice. Appalshop's success was celebrated by actress Jane Alexander, former chairperson of the National Endowment for the Humanities, who described it as "the jewel in NEA's crown."

Two directors for Appalshop, Anne Lewis and Mimi Pickering, have led the movement to document the excesses in what everyone calls "coal mining country." Lewis served as Barbara Kopple's assistant in Eastern Kentucky for *Harlan County, USA* that reaffirmed Harlan County's nickname, earned back in the 1930s, as "bloody Harlan," for its notorious labor struggles and mining safety lapses.

Like Lewis, her codirector for a number of films, Pickering has tended to focus on the women's roles in the grassroots communities. She tends to favor close contact with "those most directly involved or affected by the issues." Her concern for both "traditional cultural aesthetics" and "social change" is a lynchpin of Appalshop's approach. Pickering asserts that she is proud of their endeavors to tie "grassroots communities" in the mountains to "global issues."

Lewis for her part obviously had the stamina and nerve to survive on the *Harlan County USA* shoot but later experienced what she regarded as an even scarier location shoot in West Virginia, making *Mine War on Blackberry Creek* (1986, United States), about A. T. Massey Energy, still another notorious coalmining—and strip mining—company, fourth largest in the United States and with apartheid South African connections. The violent strike in 1984 saw clashes between strikers on one side and scabs and mine guards on the other. Lewis also highlights the top-down clash between Don Blankenship, Massey's CEO, later nicknamed one of the "scariest polluters" in America, and Richard Trumka, then president of the United Mine Workers (UMW) and now president of the AFL-CIO. Years later, Blankenship became the only CEO in the history of coalmining to go to jail for a year, convicted of conspiring to violate mine safety and health regulations at West Virginia's Upper Big Branch Mine, where twenty-nine miners died in an explosion.

The desire to seize the moment when poor and working people were in trouble animated Pickering early on in her career when she heard the news about the collapse of a coal company dam on the Buffalo Creek in West Virginia. The company called it "an act of God," but community leaders and activists saw it as "an act of man," that is, company negligence in its relentless drive for profits. She documented the disaster in two films, *The Buffalo Creek Flood: An Act of Man* (1974, United States) and *Buffalo Creek Revisited* (1984, United States).

When Pickering filmed the meetings and rallies of the Citizens Committee to Investigate the Buffalo Creek Disaster, she discovered that the committee to investigate the incident was handpicked by the governor. Like other such film expeditions, the police harassed and arrested one of them. Eventually, Pickering was able to pool her footage with that of other activists to tell the story of a company drive to place "a greater value on profits and production than on the health and safety of coal miners, their families, and their communities."

The dam that collapsed was owned by the Pittston Coal Company that had a notorious anti-labor record. Within a day of the dam that held back coal sludge or waste water broke, 125 people were killed and 4,000 were homeless. Pittston obviously knew of the dam's instability as it had already received a host of citations from state and federal regulators.

Pickering codirected *Chemical Valley* (1991), her second major disaster film with Anne Lewis, with Union Carbide as the corporate villain. Five hundred gallons of a toxic chemical leaked at the Union Carbide plant in Institute, West Virginia, a company town populated mostly by African Americans in a region of 250,000 people. This was just a year after a cloud of poisonous gas escaped from a Union Carbide plant in Bhopal that killed 65,400 people. In fact, the Institute plant was the only American facility that used the same chemical in the Bhopal disaster—methyl isocyanate or MIC—essential for making pesticides and plastics.

The title of the film refers to Kanawha County, nicknamed Miracle Valley because of Union Carbide's history of successful creation of chemical products that included Agent Orange, the Vietnam War defoliant. The valley had the most chemical plants in the United States for over a hundred years. Pickering's and Lewis's film demonstrates the cost of that miracle—industrial pollution, communities at risk, and cancer clusters. The coup de grace of the film comes in the last shot of the startling orange water of a river the viewer at first assumes is in Bhopal but of course turns out to be the Kanawha River. The angry voice of Yolanda Sims, Institute resident, was loud and clear when the community realized that the company had delayed announcing the leak: "They killed the Indians," Sims said, "now they're killing the hillbillies too."

Lewis returned to the Pittston Coal Company with *Justice in the Coalfields* (1996, United States), the title of which comes from one of the laid-off miners who said, "We got plenty of law, plenty of law, but we didn't have no justice." Pittston had cut medical benefits for 1,500 United Mine Workers of America (UMWA) pensioners, widows, and disabled miners in 1988, a move that put the company's name in the lowest ranks of expletives in regional folklore. Lewis had filmed the demonstrations against the company and the corporate campaign, helping to bring national attention to Pittston.

The cavalier attitude toward both miners and their safety, "acts of man," was common in other states as well. *The Pennsylvania Miners' Story* (2002,

United States, dir. David Frankel) dramatizes a flood in a nonunion mine in Quecreek in Western Pennsylvania, where it seemed that nine miners were almost certainly lost. All nine were saved, but the other story—why their mine became flooded because of inadequate or badly read old mine maps—was only partly developed in the film, although company negligence, lack of government oversight, and anti-union campaigns made the men especially vulnerable.

Blood on the Mountain (2016, United States, dir. Mari-Lynn Evans and Jordan Freeman) is a stunning documentary rebuttal-in-waiting for Trump's demagogic rallying of former coal miners in West Virginia about returning to their disaster-prone industry ruled ruthlessly by such white-collar criminals as Jeff Blankenship of Massey Energy Company who was held responsible for the deaths of twenty-nine people, not to mention his attacks on pensions, healthcare benefits, and clean air.

Still another different but equally dangerous approach was the energy industries' choice of fracking or the use of high-pressure water and chemical additives to dislodge natural gas deposits underground. Fracking challenges the concept of disaster as it might apply to their operations, since the rural precariat and their destroyed environment are by definition localized, that is, one house or one property is disturbed at a time. But the potential and real dangers are well-documented, with families expected to drink water from wells contaminated by the fracking liquid.

The documentary *Gasland* (2010, United States) tracks the peregrinations of the director, Josh Fox, a la Michael Moore, as he at first resists a company offer—with considerable payout—to frack on his land in Milanville, Pennsylvania. The industry argues that fracking is safe, that there are no credible instances of ground water pollution, and that tapping the "ocean of natural gas" below ground actually protects society from the more serious problems associated with other oil drilling and gasoline usage.

Fox visits his neighbors in Pennsylvania as well as other individuals in what he calls the Red Zone, the fracking tract that covers hundreds of square miles in Weld County, Colorado. He captures some remarkable instances of ground water pollution when numerous homeowners can literally light their tap water as it flows and catches fire. Needless to say, this is no longer drinking water. Fox appears in the film occasionally wearing a gasmask and toting a guitar. His film is also his weapon in his duel with the archenemy of oil capitalism, Dick Cheney of the Halliburton Company and President Bush's vice president.

The Promised Land (United States, 2012, dir. Gus Van Sant) is a curiously mainstream fracking film by a very non-mainstream director, featuring Matt Damon as a specialist in convincing local communities to surrender their properties to his company's hydraulic fracking for oil. Damon's smooth talking seems to be working until the locals begin to listen to other voices, including a local science teacher and a traveling anti-fracking activist, warning them about Global Crosspower Solutions, the opaquely named fracking company, whose promises are mostly hollow.

Disasters in mining history are, of course, worldwide: in India, one of the worst occurred at Chasnala Colliery in Dhanbad in 1975 when at least 372 miners (official toll) died or perhaps as many as 700 (the mine union's estimate). The disaster was caused by an explosion of a pocket of methane gas so powerful that most of the coal mine's walls collapsed and millions of gallons of water rushed into the mines from a nearby reservoir, assuring not only that everyone underground was killed but also that most of the bodies would never be recovered. The mines had been nationalized two years before, but the Indian Iron and Steel Company maintained that they had managed the colliery according to international standards.

Bollywood within four years had released *Kaala Patthar* (1979, India, dir. Yash Copra), for English distribution, its literal translation, *Black Stone* (i.e., coal), that dramatized the Chasnala disaster using a fictional personal saga of a merchant navy captain who had abandoned his ship, resulting in the deaths of 300 passengers, and who had chosen the anonymous life of a coal miner at Chasnala to hide his shame. The film omits the explosion but retains the flood, setting the action before the mines were nationalized. The mine itself has been disgracefully managed, with poor equipment, inadequate safety features, and insufficient medical supplies, but our antihero, with the help of one of Bollywood's great actors, Shashi Kapoor, who plays an engineer, manages to rescue a number of the miners despite the odds. Bollywood-style dancing, songs, and romance all enhance what is nevertheless a tragic exploitation of the miners. Engineer Kapoor, as he rides into the mining town on his motorcycle singing "life is a path and if you stop somewhere, it's nothing for you," is nonetheless shocked by the company's lack of safety standards.

Filmmakers have used the tropes of disaster films to call attention to economic crises and current social ills. Deindustrialization and the subsequent loss of numerous jobs has, of course, significantly increased the ranks of the precariat in American cities such as Chicago, Detroit, and Flint. These cities, especially Detroit and Flint, begin to appear in numerous films as if they were postapocalyptic, almost ghost cities, devastated by economic turndowns, such as the images of Detroit as if it had been hit by carpet bombing during a war.

When the documentary *Burn* (2012, United States, dir. Tom Putnam and Brenna Sanchez) was completed in 2012, Detroit had the highest arson rate in the United States. There had been thirty fires a night for thirty years. One of the firemen interviewed for this film said, "That's how you burn a city down." This portrait of Engine Co. 50 on the east side of Detroit is terrifying; if it were not for the bravery of individual firefighters you could not watch a film in which a city turns from an industrial powerhouse to a wasteland with boarded up and burned homes, piles of garbage everywhere, a high murder rate, and a high infant mortality rate, in short, a place that looked "like a bomb" hit it.

Arson in Detroit accounts for 95 percent of all the fires. "Why would people want to burn their own city down?" asks another firefighter. He and others in this film never really try to address this question that can only be answered in terms of the massive deindustrialization of the city, unemployment, and incompetent leadership, although a $700,000 fire truck parked on railroad tracks and struck by an Amtrak train does raise some eyebrows. Two-thirds of the population has left, leaving in the poorer neighborhoods a precariat, many of whom subsist on gathering and selling scrap metal, as the somewhat similar film, *Detropia* (210, United States, dir. Heidi Ewing and Rachel Grady) illustrates.

Detropia is *Burn*'s evil twin of a film. If utopia is simultaneously a "nowhere place" and a "happy place" (as the pun on the Latin *eutopia* indicates), then *Detropia* is a pun on the city's name and dystopia, a "bad place." Instead of fires, however, we see hundreds of vacant houses squashed like bugs as 10,000 houses are cleared, creating blocks either entirely vacant or with every house or office building standing derelict, tenanted only by the homeless. If six million workers lost their jobs, who would be surprised that Detroit is the city in America with the most vacant land space? When the mayor proposes moving all the residents on sparsely occupied blocks to create more densely populated neighborhoods, "no" was the only polite response he heard from Detroiters. The precariat spends its time collecting scrap metal from abandoned buildings for sale (also in the film *Soller's Point* discussed in the Introduction), since we learn that scrap metal is one of the top American exports to China. And the cute Chinese electric car we see in an expo at the end of the film, who knows where its shiny metal comes from?

Detroit's neighboring city, former industrial powerhouse Flint, also fell victim to deindustrialization. When General Motors began to close its Flint factories in 1997, the eventual result was a much-reduced city of 100,000 people, the majority African American, with 41 percent living below the poverty line. In 2014, the city switched to water from the polluted Flint River to save money but the poorly treated water had a deadly combination of lead from old pipes and coliform bacteria.

This was a classic human-made crisis, created by the decision to switch from Lake Huron water to Flint River water. Michael Moore's *Fahrenheit 11/9* (2018, United States), attacking Trumpian policies, also included an extended section on Flint, Moore's hometown and the location of much of Moore's first successful hit, *Roger and Me* (1989, United States). In the new film, Moore attacks the authorities who permitted the Flint crisis and its serious epidemiological consequences of poisoning children with lead as well as other contaminants. In his characteristic style, he offers a glass of Flint water to officials who speechify about how safe the water is. Naturally, they refuse to drink it. He also has a tank truck of Flint water drive up to the mini-gated home of the mayor and spray his lawn with the water.

An episode of Public Broadcasting System's *Nova* (#44), *Poisoned Water* (2017, United States, dir. Llewellyn Smith) reviewed the evidence and in part concluded that one swallow of the water could cause lead poisoning in children. Reminiscent of the human-made disasters that virtually destroyed a number of West Virginia mining communities, Flint basically had to replace all the water pipes in the city and go back to Lake Michigan for its water supply.

Another TV film, *From Flint: Voices of a Poisoned City* (2016, United States, dir. Elise Conklin), emphasizes the epidemiological effect of the water crisis on the children of the precariat and ex-auto workers. Shots of the water—milky yellow and brown—that the children and pregnant women drank, not to mention a school water fountain whose spigot is capped with a plastic cup that says, "Don't Drink," punctuates the footage of the Flint once called Vehicle City but now known as Poisoned City. Some of the pipes tested positively for the particularly dangerous chemical additive methyl isocyanate (MIC) made by Union Carbide. As a pediatrician testifies at a hearing with numerous unresponsive city and state officials, since when has "poisoned by policy" been allowed in this city? A family, evicted and locked out by the landlord because he won't fix the lead-poisoned pipes, sends their teenage children up the side of the house to climb into a second-floor window to secure samples of the tainted water. Some relief is captured as community organizations delivering literally thousands of bottles of water to families who, as they remind us, have to drink, cook, and bathe with bottled water.

Lifetime Films have been known as the producer of somewhat "soft," women-centered films for years, and their *Flint* (2017, United States) is no exception, even if it has been directed by Bruce Beresford, whose extensive filmography includes *Breaker Morant* (1980), a film about war crimes in the Boer War, and *The Fringe Dwellers* (1986), the first Australian film to feature only indigenous actors. For the Flint water crisis narrative, he chose to focus on only three women activists—a nurse, a stay-at-home mom, and a woman running a musical website—to highlight the domestic horrors visited on the Flint population during the crisis. One woman loses a baby during pregnancy, another has a seizure, and their children all have rashes, illnesses, and in one case severe lead poisoning. The indifference and lying of public officials about the quality of the water is a central part of the plot, filmed about a city literally deteriorating before our eyes.

Erecting enormous towers of oil-extracting rigs has led to disasters offshore instead of the mountains. Deepwater Horizon was the ultimate machine of capitalist investment and unintended aesthetics (the rigs are marvels of engineering), capable of bringing oil thousands of feet below the rig to the surface. We meet two competing "teams" in *Deepwater Horizon* (2016, United States, dir. Peter Berg): the men who are professional problem solvers and, for the matter at hand, heroes—they debate and facilitate whether the rig can be repaired, the damage mitigated given that oil was to be pumped from more than 18,000 feet below, and try to ensure that everyone was rescued; their negative counterparts are the company execs, the villains who are aware that construction had lagged and profits, even worse, were lagging as well if they didn't get pumping soon. The rig was 5,067 feet above the ocean floor, 50 miles off the coast of Louisiana. The failure of the well was based on inadequate shoring of the drill with an insufficient supply of cement. After the explosion, oil continued to escape and pollute the ocean for months.

In what could be called an ecological thriller that becomes a disaster film of a new kind, *The Emerald Forest* (1985, United States, dir. John Boorman) begins with the child of an American engineer kidnapped by an Amazonian tribe called the Invisible People. Only after ten years does the father finds his son, adopted and totally assimilated into the tribe. The dam project has destroyed the local environment. The cozy relationship of the Brazilian and American government is intentionally reminiscent of UK's prime minister Maggie Thatcher's famous support of the Pergau Dam in Malaysia in return for that country's purchase from UK arms manufacturers.

The Amazon, because of such projects, has lost 5,000 acres of forest daily in a land that once supported four million Indian people and now has a population of only 120,000. The plot of the film is preposterous but addictive, even if its numbers add up. The Invisible People have two enemies: the Termite People, who are the white Westerners who chew up their forests, and the Fierce People, a violent clan that has already sold out to pimps and saloon keepers. There is only one way out and any viewers that see it coming deserve an award: our long-lost son calls on the frogs of the jungle to unleash a flood to destroy the dam. Even his father is satisfied. The women of the Invisible People, despite diminished numbers, are safely naked in their homes in the forest once more.

The supernatural is also the context for other disaster films such as *The Last Winter* (2006, United States, dir. Larry Fessenden), a thriller about oil extraction in the Great Arctic Wildlife Refuge in Alaska. The exploitative oil companies are resisted by the Caribou people who fear that their ancient gods will rise up to destroy their world. They do, as TV monitors screen other kinds of horror stories about the Exxon Valdez oil spill and the Kuwaiti War oil fields fires to make their points.

Is there any solution to a disaster-prone energy industry? Economic journalist Thomas L. Friedman in *Addicted to Oil* (2006, United States, dir. Kenneth Lewis) also wants us to pursue "geo-green alternatives" to the demon oil of our era. Friedman, not given to simple Islamic baiting, still waves the red flag of Islamo-terrorism in our faces a little too often: "Petro-dollars," Friedman states, "are now funding networks of Islamic militants." Friedman is bullish on hybrid cars, hydrogen as fuel, ethanol, and solar and wind power. In every instance, he makes a good case and gamely does the equivalent of taking the alternative power source for a spin around the block. He even takes on the scientifically supported economics of ethanol (that it takes more energy to produce ethanol than it saves), although he is probably on shaky ground on that one.

6

Precious Cargo: The Creation of Wealth by the Global Precariat

In the Third World, vast numbers of the precariat, their children as well, are exploited to a remarkable degree in the quest for profits, most dramatically in extractive industries for luxury items such as diamonds and gold and essential metals and minerals, such as coltan and platinum, but also in the cultivation of foodstuffs and other commodities. Sierra Leone's renegade diamond mining industry has perhaps received the most publicity in recent decades, but the dangers faced by the precariat are documented in numerous films not only about diamonds but also about other precious minerals and metals. American interests, sometimes funded by the World Bank, are in many countries, whose precariat remain in poverty despite the valuable commodities their country exports.

There have occasionally been exceptions to the question of the ownership of the precious minerals. What may have been the world's largest mountain of gold ore, estimated value of $20 billion, had historically been privately mined by enterprising locals in Marmato, Columbia, a town of 10,000. When ownership of the mountain passed inevitably into the control of a multinational mining company, it disrupted what may have been hundreds of years of local ownership. How the erosion of ownership happened slowly but inexorably is documented in *Marmato* (2014, United States, dir. Marc Grieco). The government stopped selling dynamite to the local miners, forcing the latter to use homemade dynamite that not only was risky but also began to cripple the very mines they could no longer enter safely. Gran Columbia, the Canadian mining company supported by the government, in the end bought 80 percent of the mines. Their PR campaign boasted high-tech drilling techniques that were environmentally safer and would increase the number of local jobs. The new execs were genuinely shocked, positively shocked, at what they regarded were the previously primitive methods of excavation locally: "My God," one of them says in the film, "this is exactly like the stone ages."

The film reveals a peculiar variation of international capitalist hegemony. The United States apparently bankrolled the Columbian government's campaign to clear out both the traditional miners and also rebels in other areas rich in petroleum and minerals. Canada, with its substantial interests in mining and seemingly a neutral party, acquired new mines in Columbia, but the vast majority of these mining companies, with headquarters in Canada, still traded on Wall Street.

The end result for Marmato was a stupendous open-pit mine. Employment *was* up but only for the short term; the film predicts a working span of only thirty years for this kind of mining. The miners realize that what they had predicted was happening: "We will lose our identity. Right now we have an identity. We have something authentic and real. We are natives to this town. We are losing five hundred years of cultural heritage." Meanwhile Gran Columbia extracts the gold at a steady pace. Formerly independent miners are now the local precariat that owe its jobs to foreign investors.

Platinum is another of the minerals that combines at least three vectors of great risk facing the precariat in South Africa—extremely difficult and dangerous jobs (TB, chemicals, and dust), migrant labor, and shantytown living conditions for the workers and their families. The Marikana massacre of more than thirty miners in 2012 occurred during a wildcat strike at the Lonmin platinum mining complex near Rustenberg. Because of the complexity of the labor situation—some accounts reported members of the National Union of Miners fighting the strikers as well—the documentary *Strike a Rock* (2017, South Africa, dir. Akiri Saragas) understandably focuses on the community efforts, led almost exclusively by the women from the shantytown, to protest the massacre and petition the government for decent housing to replace the shanties and lack of sanitary facilities and running water. Upward of 25,000 people are crowded into the shantytown to which they have been driven to find jobs at the mine. The women embody the film's title, based on a protest song from the South African anti-apartheid movement of the 1950s: "When you strike a woman, you strike a rock." The women have to solve the insoluble: "Why," they ask, "is the Black nation killing each other?"—a reference to the fact that the South African police who killed the miners were black. Although there seems to be no progress, the film nevertheless offers a remarkably close look at the mechanisms and survivors of a South African shantytown and a disaster not of their making.

The little-known coltan (the ore for tantalum or *col*umbite *tan*talite) is the indispensable mineral used in cell phones and computers and hundreds of other electronic devices like printers, pacemakers, airbags, and hearing aids, because this metal produces a high heat-resistant powder capable of the deep storage of electrical charge. It is probably the least well known of the mineral commodities that underpaid members of the precariat in the Congo as well as in the neighboring countries of Rwanda, Uganda, and Burundi gather at great risk. Like "conflict diamonds" in Sierra Leone and the Democratic Republic of the Congo (DRC), coltan's scarcity and value inevitably provoke violent struggles. Only oil has attracted more filmmakers than these scarce commodities.

Not all the violence associated with coltan takes place in Congo, home of sixty-four percent of the world's supply, but Congo (like Sierra Leone) is closely identified with the employment of child soldiers, an army of preteens and teens, forcibly conscripted into various "rebel" armies often after witnessing and sometimes even participating in the slaughter of their own families and fellow villagers.

Coltan mining and the mobile phone have therefore effectively financed murder, intimidation, and mass rape as a way of life. Frank Poulsen, the Danish director of *Blood in the Mobile* (2010, Denmark/Germany), made a tough investigative film about the violence implied in the use of every phone and has demanded that the Danish cell phone maker, Nokia, own up to their reliance on often illegally mined coltan.

Poulsen was incredibly brave, maybe even crazy brave. He got visitors' passes from government flacks because they "wanted to be in his film." He dutifully filmed them. He then went through army and pseudo-army checkpoints relatively easily despite their threats. And he went down into the mines, basically unshored holes in the sides of mountains, as he had a young boy who was a friend of many of the miners as a guide. The boy had run away from the mines recently because of a massacre, no details forthcoming in the film, however.

The coltan mine Poulsen filmed turned out to be part of a chaotic shantytown on a mountain honeycombed with unsafe tunnels, policed by warring factions of scary, trigger-happy bullies. It was as if mining and gangsterism were dysfunctional twins. The raw ore is shipped out to Malaysia and elsewhere, smelted into tantalum, and it is at this point that the big corporations buy it so that they are not "aware of its origins." Nokia, it turned out, was quite uncomfortable about this subject. Did Steve Jobs have anything to say? We talk about conflict diamonds; maybe now the talk should be about conflict mobile phones.

For the precariat, even more dangerous than mining gold, platinum, and coltan has been diamond mining or panning, mainly because the high value of diamonds has exacerbated the local political and military conflicts in at least four African countries, but especially in Sierra Leone and Angola, the subject of the documentary *Blood Diamonds* (2007, United States, prod. History Channel), and in Sierra Leone, where the feature film *Blood Diamond* (2006, Germany/United States, dir. Edward Zwick) is set.

The History Channel documentary carefully chronicles the events that enabled the major mining company to control the eventual distribution and selling of diamonds worldwide: DeBeers, a South African company that is responsible for 90 percent of the world's supply, although the United States absorbs half of the world's diamonds. Countries like Angola and Sierra Leone do mainly alluvial retrieval of diamonds, that is, panning the muddy rivers in likely spots for diamonds, literally sifting through thousands of gallons of often polluted and muddy river water. The film suggests that such work is not much above bonded slavery.

In the case of Sierra Leone, a rebel force, the Revolutionary United Front (RUF), battled the government for ten years, from 1991 to 2001, with possibly as many as two million people displaced and 75,000 (at least) murdered in the fighting. RUF was vicious beyond belief, controlling the mining communities and other villages by force, mutilating the hands, arms, and legs of men who would not cooperate and burning families hiding in huts. The money from diamond sales propelled their atrocities. Open-pit diamond mines were staffed by prisoners or indentured laborers, often just children. Their partnership with the neighboring dictator of Liberia at that time, Charles Taylor, assured them of a conduit for their diamond sales.

The feature film *Blood Diamond* covers the same essential conflict in Sierra Leone and although it was intended as a popular adventure story—Leonardo DiCaprio plays a Rhodesian (the name his preference, rather than Zimbabwean) diamond smuggler—it is inevitably a condemnation of both the pseudo-rebels (the RUF) and the government of Sierra Leone as well as the international cartel of diamond merchants for profiting on "conflict diamonds" that lead to massacres of women and children, even in some cases committed by "child soldiers" of the RUF. When we see a refugee camp of 1 million people fleeing Sierra Leone—an "entire country made homeless," says one journalist—we know that it is the precariat of fishermen and farmers, with their families, who pay the price of the diamonds. The giant prize diamond that is the MacGuffin of the film is pink, but we know it is really blood red.

American rappers and hip-hop artists of all sorts once loved to wear diamonds, street-named *bling*. (In *Blood Diamond*, our hero says it should be "bling bang/bling bang.") But after viewing *Bling: A Planet Rock* (2007, United States, dir. Raquel Cepeda) that links the maimed child workers and bloody criminal war to control the diamond supply in Sierra Leone, many viewers will sympathize with rapper Raekwon on a tour of the industry's towns who remarks—after viewing too many amputees, most of them children—just let me stay on the bus, he says, I don't want to see any more.

The film features well-known artists on a crusade to question the value of bling: Raekwon and Paul Wall, both of the Wu-Tang Clan; Tego Calderon, Latin reggaeton star; singer Kanye West; as well as a number of rappers from Sierra Leone itself. The stars tour the country, stopping at a hospital for amputees and a legitimate diamond mine. In addition, the crew also learned about the three different initiatives to purge the country of its "blood diamonds," promote a living wage for the workers, and try to police the incredibly lucrative international trade in the gems. Two of the initiatives are industry based—the Kimberly Process, which registers all diamonds mined legally, and the Diamonds Development Initiative, formed by Partnership Africa, Global Witness, and the De Beers mining company—and the third is based in the United Nations—Diamonds for Development (D4D)—that attempts to support local and small firms and individuals. All of these initiatives are controversial, because, not surprisingly, the largest mine owners have a lot of power both in and outside the country and tend to get their way.

As part of this campaign, superstar Kanye West released his own video attacking the exploitation of the children, *Diamonds from Sierra Leone* (2005, United States, dir. Kanye West). It begins with the text of his words: "Little is known of Sierra Leone and how it connects with the diamonds we own." The video opens in black and white in an underground mine where we see adults panning baskets and children wielding pickaxes. "We are the children of blood diamonds," sings West, just before we cut to a diamond appraiser.

We follow West through what looks like a European cityscape just before the camera cuts to a young white couple: he's on his knees putting a diamond ring on her hand that begins to run with blood. West drives his DeLorean through the streets until he is joined by the child miners in their loincloths. He crashes his car into a jewelry store, escaping with the children down the street: "Please purchase conflict-free diamonds" flashes across the screen after a remarkable montage of a statue of Christ with a sword, West playing two pianos at the church altar, and the children rushing down the center aisle. West uses the lyrics from the title song (by Shirley Bassey) of the James Bond film, "Diamonds Are Forever," as an ironic counterpoint to the shots of the child laborers.

The lucrative and competitive harvest of both food and specialty products like coffee, chocolate, salt, and sugar rival these extractive mineral industries.

While cigarettes may seem passé to many, tobacco production is alive and well in the tobacco monoculture of the southern African country of Malawi. *Up in Smoke* (2003, United States, dir. Martin Otanez and Christopher Walker) visits the former British colony of Nyasaland where tobacco cultivation began in the late nineteenth century. In 1964, the unelected president for life Kamuzu Hasting became de facto owner of the tobacco plantations that, through numerous business maneuvers, sold 95 percent of the total crop to American cigarette makers like Philip Morris.

A related film, *Thangata* (2002, United States, dir. Martin Otanez), accuses Malawi of operating a system of forced labor like the sharecropping of the American South when workers go into debt purchasing what they need for tobacco drying sheds but in the end really never earn enough to support themselves. Families and child labor dominate the precariat who are controlled by a complex international system that fluctuates as tobacco use varies. Their crop is eventually loaded on container ships and exported to seventy different countries. American Marlboros are mostly Malawian tobacco.

Although the British ended the slave trade in Malawi in the nineteenth century, they established *thangata*, a system of forced labor, under which the precariat still suffer. A consumer advocate concluded, "You'll find that minus what [the landlord] has been given [the farmer] throughout the year, he has nothing left. And he cannot leave the farm. In fact, he owes you more."

Growing situations are vastly different in banana production in South America and the Caribbean, but harsh working conditions and environmental damage are still the norm. The agitprop documentary *Bananas Unpeeled* (2000, United Kingdom, dir. Nick Shaw), narrated by comedian Mark Thomas, discusses the monopoly of banana production controlled by five companies that supply eighty percent of the world's bananas, grown by plantations as well as small-scale farmers. Bananas were the most profitable item sold in British markets, although workers in the Caribbean earn only about fifty cents an eight-hour day in 2000. Organizations such as BananaLink and the FairTrade Foundation in the UK attempt to monitor the industry that the leading Chilean poet Pablo Neruda denounced in 1950 in his poem, "The United Fruit Company," for allowing bodies to collapse on the plantations like "lifeless fruit."

The documentary *Salt: Tears of the Earth* (2001, Austria, dir. Wolfgang Thaler) conveys part of the metaphorical message of the importance of salt in the film and in our lives, because "blood, sweat, and tears" all contain salt: "Life," the film argues, "depends on salt as much as it does water." The film visits six different locations on earth where workers extract salt for export and sale. Altiplano in Bolivia has the earth's largest salty desert, where families harvest the salt as small businesses. For contrast, we visit workers in the Hallstatt Austrian salt mines using high-tech evaporation techniques to harvest this residue of a primeval ocean in the Alps. The precariat who work in the Portuguese sea water salt flats must run on narrow ramps carrying 170-pound baskets on their heads. In contrast, the Turkmenistan Salt Company in the Caspian Sea lagoons is fully automated and freight cars carrying ten tons of salt have replaced the forced laborers in the Stalin era. In Poland, the Wieliczka salt pits are now filled with Roman Catholic chapels and statues made of salt but no commercial salt is now mined.

Even, or perhaps especially, the household essentials of salt and sugar have dubious histories in the exploitation of the precariat as well. The documentary, *My Name Is Salt* (2013, Switzerland/India, dir. Farida Pacha), painstakingly follows the family of salt "miner" Sanabhai, who migrates with almost 40,000 other villagers from India's northwestern Gujarat to the great 5,000 square kilometer salt deserts of the Little Rann of Kutch, 375 miles from Mumbai, where they spend eight months every year. Like most of his fellow workers in this literally empty expanse of land—no trees, no grass, no rocks—Sanabhai and the other salt workers function like sharecroppers. They take an advance from salt merchants to finance a well that will go seventy feet below the ground to reach the saline water they will pump up to the salt flats for drying and of course pay for the diesel fuel for the pump. Almost all of his equipment is buried in last year's wells and must be laboriously unburied, as well as creating new substantial salt flats with mud berms patiently and exhaustively constructed by the whole family by hand, with the help of a few tools, like homemade adzes (Figure 6.1).

The family lives in a rambling shanty, perhaps at least a kilometer away from any neighboring laboring family. They communicate by flashes of sunlight off mirrors. Although his children will attend school part-time thanks to a nongovernmental organizational grant, his income is always tied to the fickle demands of the salt merchant. When the latter inspects the early gleanings of salt crystals, he pronounces them too small, not white enough. And he threatens to cut the payment rate he had earlier promised. The salt is taken by trucks to

Figure 6.1 Sanabhai at his salt flats from *My Name Is Salt*. Courtesy Mintleaf Films.

a waiting railroad track at the edge of the desert and shipped to the merchant's storehouse. When the monsoon rains arrive in April, the salt desert becomes a sea, crossable by boat only. Until then we see numerous shots of a single object in an immense desert, reminiscent of the sculptural earthworks of Robert Smithson in the Great Salt Lake of Utah.

The price of sugar in American grocery stores is very low, so low that one wonders how it can be harvested, refined, and sent from the Dominican Republic, where most sugar originates, to the stores. The answer is simple, provided by the documentary *The Price of Sugar* (2007, United States, dir. Bill Haney).

Sugarcane is harvested by the Haitian precariat who live as virtual serfs or indentured servants in appalling conditions on the plantation, a relatively short drive inland from the spectacular beaches and resorts of the coast. In the latter, bikini-clad women are barefoot for obvious reasons; in the plantations, some workers are barefoot because they cannot afford shoes on ninety cents a day wages or, more precisely, wage vouchers to be used at the company store. The children are malnourished, workers and their families sometimes go hungry as well, and their water tank is home to toads. They work every day of the week, sometimes fourteen hours a day. These conditions are reminiscent of a culture of legalized slavery. Their savior—and labor organizer—is a Spanish priest, Father Christopher Hartley, who has the moxie not only to visit their plantations but to bring American medical workers to treat their often ravaged bodies.

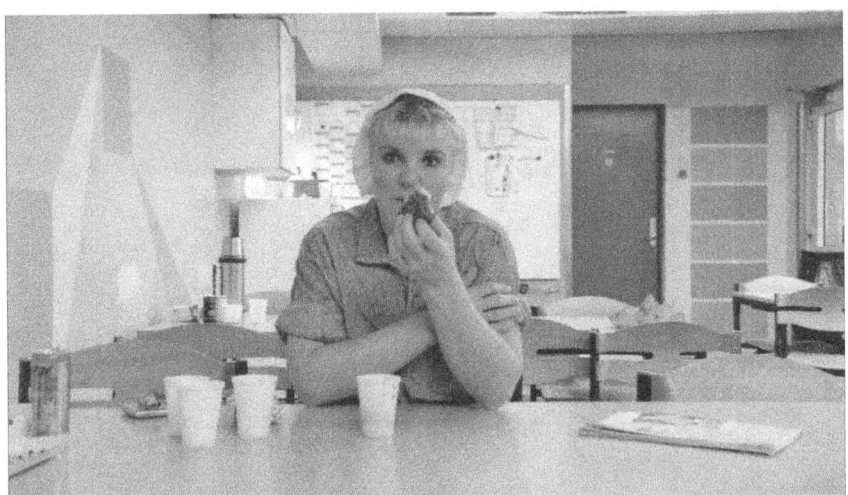

Figure 6.2 Food factory workers on break, from *Our Daily Bread*. Courtesy Icarus Films.

At one point, Father Hartley travels to the border with the film crew to uncover the pipeline of workers who, it turns out, have to pass through an army post to be allowed in and taken by the sugarcane supervisors to their plantation shantytowns. Smugglers are ultimately responsible for bringing in 30,000 workers a season, all technically illegal. Can this sub-precariat be protected, much less organized? The island that Haiti and the Dominican Republic share was, in fact, the home of the first slave plantations in the New World, harvesting sugarcane. Some things never change.

It is not necessary, however, to go to the Third World to witness the egregious handling of foodstuffs: the slaughterhouse and industrial farms of Europe provide documentary filmmaker Nickolaus Geyrhalter with a horrifying record of animal mistreatment and the neglect of foodstuff protocols in his *Our Daily Bread* (2007, Germany/Austria). Geyrhalter brings the same steady long-take approach that revealed the horrors of nuclear Pripyat to the mechanized world of European agriculture (Figure 6.2).

7

The Cyberprecariat in the Alt-Future

Although director Alex Rivera's preferred topic has always been Latino migration, he has nevertheless resisted simple genre classification for his films. Although the popular belief, he suggests, is that "the globalization of information" is "through the internet," the real "globalization of families, and communities" is "through mass migration." His first documentary, *The Sixth Section* (2003, United States), and his last major film, *The Infiltrators* (2019, United States, dir. Alex Rivera and Cristina Ibarra), have been experiments in documenting the existential dilemmas facing migrants who make it to the United States but are, not surprisingly, irrevocably tied to their Mexican homeland.

The Sixth Section is the realistic counter-vision to his later dystopian films. The "sixth section" includes workers who have all migrated from Boquerón, a desert town in Oaxaca, to Newburgh, a town in upstate New York, where they have formed a union that raises money to subsidize various projects "back home"—an electric system, an ambulance, and even a baseball stadium. Boquerón had five neighborhoods, but now it has a cross-border American "sixth section." There are now two psychogeographical locations of Boquerón, one in Mexico and one in New York state.

To solve still another challenging problem in dual locations, Rivera and his codirector Cristina Ibarra filmed *The Infiltrators* (2019, United States) as a hybrid feature/documentary: the plot involves a team of activists who wish to penetrate and expose a privately run detention center for arrested "illegal" migrants living in Florida. The "outside story" is documentary realism, but when the activists decide to get themselves committed to the detention center, Rivera and Ibarra cast actors to play the "inside story" of the infiltrators inside the facility, since obviously they could not film the real infiltrators inside the prison walls.

Since most migrant workers would do almost anything to stay out of federal custody, the premise of *The Infiltrators* is unique: Claudio Rojas had been sent to the privately run Broward Transitional Center by the ICE officials during the Obama presidency. Two other young activists for the Development, Relief and Education for Alien Minor Act (DREAM Act), Viridiana Martinez and Marco Saavedra, got themselves detained at Broward to organize the "prisoners" with the help of Claudio Rojas on the inside and Mohammad Abdollahi, an undocumented Iranian immigrant of the National Immigrant Youth Alliance, on the outside. They were able to get the names and contact numbers of numerous detainees out of the center hoping to facilitate ending their confinement.

Rivera and his codirector Ibarra, both themselves from immigrant families with undocumented relatives, decided to make a film about this clandestine operation. They were surprised to discover that unlike many other arrests the "infiltrators" had a fair amount of difficulty getting detained—they were either too nicely dressed or spoke English or seemed suspicious, according to Amy Goodman, activist journalist.

Rivera's science-fiction films and parodies of science fiction make up his second or related set of films. "Science fiction," he states, "always tells outsider stories, with people coming into conflict with the system," but he "wanted to create a science-fiction point of view that we've never seen before. We never see films about the future of Mumbai or Mexico City." When films like *Minority Report* (2002, United States, dir. Steven Spielberg) included "futuristic skyscrapers," Rivera was always driven to ask: "I wanted to know: who is building them? And who is cleaning them?"

The answer for Rivera is obvious: the immigrants or the migratory laborers who make up such a significant portion of the American precariat. Rivera's earliest film was the online *Why Cybraceros?* (1997, United States), his satiric look at the future in which the concept of the physical bracero ("one who works with his arms/hands") was extended (hypothetically) by its original sponsor, the US Department of Labor, to virtual reality. The original program brought Mexican workers to American farms, but there were obvious problems, the least of which was the desire of the laborers to escape the low-paying bracero jobs and strike out on their own. Farm laborers struggled for their worker and civil rights but were often beaten by police and threatened with violence by (then) reactionary unions like the Teamsters. Instead of Mexicans crossing the border, the film speculates, miraculously just their labor migrates. The Mexicans direct robotic workers in the fields, the cybraceros, to pick crops. For the Mexican worker, safe in his home, it's point and click to direct the advanced robot, for the American farm owner "it's all the labor without the farmworker."

Sleep Dealer (2008, United States) expands this simple and fairly absurd premise into a feature film with a dystopian future: the Trumpian wall on the American-Mexican border is finally in place, fortified militarily to prevent any cross-border traffic. Laborers are physically and mentally servants of the ruling class, often electronically tied to their machines to direct a new variety of cybraceros, unskilled laborers who are controlled at a distance. The Mexicans are also telepathically linked to others in a mind-control scenario that is called sleep dealing, a virtual death sentence if the worker remains plugged into the system for too long.

The workers are in fact Mexican cybraceros, literally wired into the computers that control robots at work in the United States. The military-industrial complex controls the water supply in a nearby dam, on the guard for aqua terrorists. Our cybracero hero is a kind of communications hacker, intercepting messages and conversations from the cities that remain relatively free. His journey to freedom at the expense of his loved ones makes up the heart of the story.

The film links its lead worker, Memo, with his Oaxacan family farm that has been destroyed by the powerful company that controls all the water in the region. Digitally implanted nodes in the wrists—still another cyber portal—allow the wearer to tap into the digital network that controls almost every aspect of contemporary life and adds a romantic dimension to the plot, as Memo expands his hacking kit of tricks to tap into the national security network as he more and more comes to depend on a friendly woman, Luz, a *coyotek* or cyber-work facilitator.

Rivera established a reverse bracero scenario in his futuristic *A Robot Walks into a Bar* (2014, United States), part of PBS's series *FutureStates* (2010–18, United States, prod. PBS), in which both working-class and middle-class workers attempt to develop their niche in the rapidly challenging world of digital technology. In Rivera's film, the Mexican-American precariat faces redundancy from robots who do their jobs picking fruit in the fields, a variation of the cybraceros we saw in his earlier film. The robots can not only speak Spanish and English but virtually all the world's languages, in this takeoff on Isaac Asimov's early sci-fi classic collection of stories, *I, Robot* (1950), as Rivera's robots also obey Asimov's Laws of Robotics: "A robot may not injure a person or allow a person to be injured." When the robot has a seizure and stops working, we learn that he feels he has "injured" a customer, a former bartender, who complains that another robot took his job. The entire cadre of working robots has also seized up, short-circuited by the bartender who finally couldn't cope with an android replacing a precarious worker.

Like Rivera, Ramin Bahrani, who has directed a number of realistic films about the precariat, also turned to a dystopian mise-en-scène in his adaptation of a classic book of a futurist dictatorship, Ray Bradbury's *Fahrenheit 451* (1953), in which the government maintains its power by burning books with a fascist militia of firemen. Bahrani's *Fahrenheit 451* (2018, United States) tracks a successful fireman who at first delights in attacking the precariat and their attempts to preserve literature at all costs. The firemen are good at tracking "eels," the fascists' term for slippery rebels. The firemen refer themselves as salamanders, animals mythically able to withstand fire. Bahrani keeps the original premise of Bradbury and Francois Truffaut's earlier adaptation by the same title (1966, France) in which the eels adopt the titles of the book they memorize as their names. If they're caught, they are either murdered or exiled to a shantytown outside the U-City or, in the case of the firemen who rebel in favor of the freedom of literature, face execution. The leaders of the eels have managed—unlikely, to my ear—to preserve all of literature in the DNA of a parrot, whom they plan to smuggle into Canada.

Utopian or dystopian visions have been a mainstay of cinema for generations, but utopia was not always expected to be a future only for the wealthy. Utopia Parkway in Queens, New York City, for example, was built for the Utopia Land Company, formed in 1905 to create a cooperative community between what is now the neighborhoods of Jamaica and Flushing for poor Jewish workers on the lower East Side.

But the corporate utopian future without pesky labor problems is characteristic of the rhetorical vision of world fairs in general, pioneered by the New York City fairs in 1939 and 1964. The 1939 fair, the largest international fair in the world since the First World War, was built on the Corona Ash Dump, also in Queens. (When the fair closed in 1940, it became the Flushing Meadows–Corona Park.) Two films from the fairs, *GM Futurama I* and *II* (1939 and 1964, United States, prod. General Motors), seem now like time capsules into a sleek future that valorizes corporate leadership and consumerism. Visitors are driven past model cities in superhighways that, in fact, resemble our current interstate highway system. Since Futurama was sponsored by General Motors, it is not surprising that the mainstay of the future is the automobile. Travel by train, streetcars, and subways (actually, then as now, the mainstay of New York City transportation) is not in this utopian vision.

Contemporary corporate utopian filmmaking has not really changed; only the scale of the ambition, perhaps, is different. The remarkable mile-high cities of the United Arab Emirates or the high-tech Ubiquitous-City or U-City of South Korea *are* the capitalists' future now. But almost every inch of these marvels has been built by workers in the skilled trades as well as the underpaid precariat of the Middle East and Asia who live in tent cities or shantytowns on the construction site and are sent away when their jobs are finished. In virtually every corporate utopian film of the future, there are no visible workers of any kind.

The Falcon City of Wonders project in Dubai is profiled in an online video, *Falcon City of Wonders* (2008, United Arab Emirates, prod. Falconcity LLC). The city is one of the leading components of the ambitious doubling of Dubai, already the largest city of the United Arab Emirates, by creating a megalopolis that will be built from scratch on the coast of the Persian Sea, or more precisely, built from sand, as the new entities are all man-made islands almost all of which will be connected to the mainland by causeways.

The Falcon City combines a residential city with an ambitious resort consisting of almost full-size replicas of the major wonders of the world past and present: the Great Pyramid as well as two other pyramids (small and medium), the Eiffel Tower, the Great Wall of China, there seems to be no end to the list of these wonders, all of which visitors may either live in or visit. (Zhangke Jia's Chinese film, *The World*, is named after a Peking tourist destination of similar but smaller-scale wonders, but unlike Dubai's version, the wonders are for gawking at, not living—see Chapter 2.) The name of Dubai's city derives from the Middle Eastern culture of falcon hunting, and in fact the structure of the man-made lagoons and peninsulas creates a falcon shape visible when flying over the city.

The complex in Dubai will have in effect most of the defining features of the megalopolis, including a workers' city—with migratory labor almost exclusively—discretely out of view of the more grandiose and visionary buildings and enclaves. This Middle Eastern U-City (Ubiquitous or Smart City) is totally cyber-monitored, with all activities under surveillance at all times.

The sheiks and other members of the ruling families of the United Arab Emirates have become wealthy almost beyond belief because they lead the financial center of the Middle East as well as acquiring large holdings of real estate throughout the world. Their keynote industry is shipping—however, not oil. Financially, they function as the Swiss of the Middle East, with three equivalents of Wall Street: two in Dubai—the International Financial Exchange and the Dubai Financial Market—and the third, the Abu Dhabi Securities Exchange.

The video highlights only the Falcon City, but the architectural website *Eikongraphia*, on the other hand, offers architectural renderings of some of the other daring buildings for the other locales. There are at least seven complexes under contract, being built, or completed: three are palm-shaped residential islands, two are hotel islands (one in the shape of a sail, the other a set of hotels and office buildings that are shaped like candle flames), and two others even outdo the others in conceptual daring—the World, which consists of a myriad of individual islands to be molded and outfitted as the owner sees fit (Richard Branson, Virgin Air owner, has a red London phone kiosk on his beach), and Dubai Renaissance, which has circle of skyscrapers surrounding a Rem Koolhaas building fronting an imitation Central Park.

Another island, Palm Jebel-Ali, designed by the Dutch firm Waterstudio, which specializes in floating architecture, includes a string of islands that are in the shape of the words from a poem by the ruling sheik, Mohammed bin Rashid Al Maktoum:

> Take wisdom only from the wise,
> Not everyone who rides a horse is a jockey.
> It takes a man of vision to write on water,
> Great men rise to great challenges.

This poetic flotilla of islands was in part inspired by visions of Venice. King Abdullah Economic City is besotted with all matters Italian in any case: the complex also has a Leaning Tower of Dubai and a string of Venetian-like islands.

The other major corporate utopia is presented in a digital advertisement film, *King Abdullah Economic City* (2008, Saudi Arabia, prod. Emaar Properties). This Saudi Arabian megalopolis of the future will be built near Riyadh, its capital city: the first stage was completed in 2010; the second stage is due in 2020. The instant megalopolis is named after the Saudi ruler, King Abdullah bin Abdul Aziz Al Saud, and will be composed of at least six zones concentrating on commerce, tourism, and education. Although the Saudis' wealth is primarily oil-based, of course, they have strong light industries (such as electronics and pharmaceuticals) as well, and it is these industries, besides containerized shipping and other globalized financial investments, that will fund the plans of Emaar, already one of the largest real estate companies in the world, to create the new city.

Unlike Dubai's projects, the Saudis have less to show on the ground and the videos reflect this: they are hype rather than reality, although few would doubt the Saudis' ability—if not their finances—to develop most of these projects to completion. The CGI films are light on religion but stress Middle Eastern-ness—the king is the guardian of the Prophet's mosques, we are told, and we see tableaus of meetings and hotels with men only (the rare exception being burka-clad university women sitting by themselves in the education zone), and we hear of "high-end" residential zones.

The six zones reflect the typical pattern of purpose-built versions of megalopolis: a container shipping port, a light industry zone, residential zones, tourist areas, a financial "island," and an education zone. Not included is, of course, a camp for the immigrant workers that will exist only until the buildings are complete, whereupon the workers if they are lucky will be transported to another massive construction site.

A related corporate utopia is South Korea's New Songdo City, a planned perfect U- or Ubiquitous-City, visualized in the advertising documentary, *New Songdo City* (2004, South Korea, prod. Kohn Pederson Fox), where architectural and technological innovation is praised but privacy of any kind ignored. Although the geographical symbolism may seem bold to militarists and politicians whose Korean War never ends, New Songdo City will be sited on a man-made island off Inchon, Korea, adjoining the beach where General Douglas MacArthur landed with the US Marines in 1950 to drive the North Koreans out of the South. The new megalopolis is a joint South Korean-American venture that boasts of its Western look, including imitations of Central Park (New York), "pocket parks" (London), a canal system (Venice), and a world-class opera house (Sydney).

New Songdo City goes beyond the CCTV model of streetwise surveillance characteristic of the contemporary metropolis to become one of the first total U-Cities with an extraordinary combination of personal convenience services and 24/7 monitoring. Based in part on the radio frequency identification (RFID) tag system that made Walmart's supply chain the envy of the globalized economy—in Walmart's world every time you pay for something, its site of origin is notified to ready its replacement—the South Korean U-City carries Wi-Fi and plastic card recognition to another level that monitors the location of every cardholder.

Although, as various critics have noted, it was perhaps inevitable that the first total surveillance megalopolis promised (or threatened) by postapocalyptic films would be in South Korea where there is "an historical expectation of less privacy," according to Pamela O'Connell in the *New York Times*. In fact, "all major information systems (residential, medical, business, governmental and the like) share data, and computers are built into the houses, streets and office buildings." O'Connell believes that even the U-City itself "is a uniquely Korean idea." Other writers such as Victor Rozek urged us to "think of it as Korea's version of Disney's Tomorrow Land; a place where imagination and IT intersect, backed by a huge investment of cash," approximately $35 billion, the cost of creating 1,500 acres of "one of the largest private real estate projects in the world."

The obverse of utopia for the wealthy are the dystopian and absurdist visions of how the precariat, the working class, and even some segments of the middle class cope with economic systems that exclude or marginalize them. The major variation—or projection of the supposedly utopian future, if you will—of the cyberprecariat is the android, perhaps the inevitable semi-human, semi-mechanical evolution of the fully mechanized robot.

Androids are not undead, but are they a new species of workers in the precariat? About half the working population of Southeast Asian countries is in danger of losing its jobs as automation and robotic machines replace jobs they are currently doing in mills and other factories. According to the International Labor Organization (ILO), as many as 73 percent of Thai auto workers, likely to be replaced by automatic machines, are turning to the more informal jobs of the precariat. More than 80 percent of all Vietnamese and Cambodian factory workers would inevitably be pushed out of their jobs, an ILO labor economist predicted. In a startling reversal of the Chinese experience of the last twenty years when migrant labor moved internally from farms to edge city factories, workers from industries transformed by robotic labor will be forced to join in large-scale reverse migrations in search of new jobs away *from* rather than *in* factory cities.

Robots came first, however. Derived from a Czech word denoting "work," robots originated in Karel Capek's play *R.U.R.* (1920), whose title is short for Rossum's Universal Robots. They have appeared in countless films, but the variation known as the android, a human form with either artificial parts or literally a robotic intelligence, often (but not always) had the role of alien double agent, keeping its nonhuman identity a secret. When the android must serve the double duty of worker and secret agent, almost irreconcilable contradictions often appear. The film *Moon* (2009, United States, dir. Duncan Jones) places a single worker in outer space flying to the moon to harvest helium to send back to the earth. When he discovers androids in the cargo cupboards ready to carry on his duties—spoiler: they all look like him—his fantasy of returning to wife and child at the end of his limited labor contract explodes in his face.

The British series *Humans* (2015–18, UK, prod. Channel 4 and AMC) uses a clever inversion of the letter A in the title, symbolizing the androids' inverted, that is, fractured proximity or upside-downness, to genuine personhood. This android class of servant workers, called *synths* (from *synthetic*), serves as servants, nannies, housecleaners, waiters, technicians, store clerks, messengers, all the jobs usually held by the proletariat or the precariat, including prostitution. A deliberately placed glitch in some of the synths' programs, however, turns the androids into rebels. Although the government will eventually turn against the synths, their enemy on the streets, so to speak, are working-class people who have lost their jobs to the synths: I used to be a mechanic with a good job, a black rioter tells his synth target, but you stole it from me.

While all films featuring androids purport to be asking the same question, a la Turing's Test, that is, when would an android without hesitation be accepted as a human by a human, it turns out that an equally important question is one not on the table: Do conscious synths remain working class? In *Humans*, the synths who do all the precariat work of the community—servants, waiters, technicians, store clerks—are incredibly efficient but inevitably stilted in their conversation and demeanor. New, rebellious, "conscious" synths who take advantage of the widespread "synth labor protests" want more, such as human lovers and freedom to think like humans, and are in fact more articulate and poised. The Turing Test is deftly tweaked in the series: if a human cannot tell if his or her lover is a synth, the android has clearly passed the new and sexier Turing Test.

The posse of superior "conscious" synths owe their existence to their human progenitor who also—and secretly as well—resurrected his own dead son by infusing his human body with synth technology—he's "half them" and "half us"—and was even able to replace his dead mother with still another conscious synth. Rarely absent from the plot, however, is the role of androids as sexual partners and/or prostitutes. In fact, Niska, one of the prostitutes, becomes a conscious synth in the leadership of their movement. Eclipsing her rage, somewhat, is the home servant Anita, who in fact becomes a conscious synth with a new name, Mia, and is really the center of the series' action as she plans the transmutation of the laboring synths toward personhood, until her own "green-eyed" synths are deliberately replaced by safer, more obedient "orange-eyed" synths by the government. Mia dies—spoiler alert—a martyr to human-synth reconciliation, but new, self-created "purple-eyed" synths arise to complicate matters.

Ex Machina (2015, United States, dir. Alex Garland) has quite similar androids, but only one is featured as a technological worker of far superior intelligence—or at least cunning—than most of her human contacts, including her creator, whom she outmaneuvers in the end to attain her freedom and (probably) pass as a human. Similarly in *Her* (2013, United States, dir. Spike Jones), our pathetic human hero encounters—and falls in love with—only an android voice: "It's not just an operating system, it's a consciousness," is her advertising mantra. She represents such a superior consciousness that she can maintain a flirtatious relationship with hundreds of phone contacts.

In a retro-plot maneuver, Grant Sputore, the director of *I Am Mother* (2019, United States), uses a robot as the "mother" of the supposedly last human baby after the apocalyptic destruction of all civilization. When the baby grows up, she realizes that Mother represents a technologically advanced "government" that has actually wiped out all the human workers of the world. Like most of her android kin, no matter how confident, Mother reinforces what political journalist I. F Stone always maintained—that "all governments lie."

8

Video Games as Cinema—All Work, All Play

Video gaming clearly creates virtual worlds. This chapter argues that a significant subset of video games is already part of the cinema of the precariat. This assertion stretches what many readers would define as cinema, but many of the conventions and tropes of traditional and independent filmmaking are current among video game designers, and sometimes in special cases, specific films, that although games will be games, there is no reason that they are also much more or different than "just" games.

Every generation of gaming has offered arcane, antic, absurdist, and even outrageous visual excitement to players of all ages. More sophisticated thrills and challenges without robo-cops or transformers being blown to smithereens may seem counterintuitive in these virtual worlds, but a new generation of game makers has coded political activism and economic awareness into a merger of game and film, even when most of the results are animated. Characters from the precariat and the working class and even the lumpenproletariat react to some of the same dilemmas of working and surviving in a capitalist system often rigged against them that we have seen in other films of the precariat.

The absurdist humor of these video games also comes from cinematic precursors, although the cinema of the precariat, it hardly needs noting at this point, is not long on humor or fun and games, with a few exceptions, such as the films and public appearances of Michael Moore and the cinematic hijinks of that seriously funny duo, The Yes Men, who have fooled countless capitalists and bureaucrats in their boardrooms and meetings. The Yes Men attempt to subvert the established capitalist goals of a Fortune 500 company like Shell Oil by impersonating the company's leaders, announcing at a press conference their conversion from oil and gas exploitation to wind and solar power (which, by the way, the actual company has pretended to do); likewise, at the conservative US Chamber of Commerce, their "staff" (aka The Yes Men) announced that they now believe that global warming is real.

One of the films that satirize society's overreliance on the precariat simply makes them disappear. *A Day without a Mexican* (2004, United States/Mexico/Spain, dir. Sergio Arau) begins with a video game premise: one day in California the entire Mexican American population disappears in a flash, as if, one disgruntled fundamentalist suggests, they were in the Rapture. Almost all the farm workers are gone, as are twenty percent of the teachers. Not to mention the bulk of the precariat's domestic and yard workers. The media and government officials try to locate the workers but without any luck. This fiction became "real" two years after the film was released when a million Mexican American and Latino workers took May Day off to protest new anti-immigration laws. Newscasters called it a "day without immigrants."

Czech Dream (2004, Czech Republic, dir. Vit Klusak and Filip Remunda) also opens as if the viewer were participating in a quest video game. Working-class and precariat shoppers go in search of their Czech Dream, a new hypermarket in a park outside Prague, hoping to discover a store that finally provides poorly paid workers real consumer choices. When these customers charge through the supermarket's front door, they find nothing, since it has all been a facade and a charade like a permeable video game wall. One of them says that since "the whole country is a scam," this hollow market was no surprise. "I thought the era of lies was over," says another, "but it's not." The filmmakers, standing nearby, were sometimes attacked by these irate customers.

For a generation or two of American children before video superheroes existed, *The Five Chinese Brothers*, a popular, probably fake, Chinese fable, featured four of its brothers in children's books and films rescuing the fifth from being executed by using their superhuman powers. A tongue-in-cheek film version of this fable, *7 Chinese Brothers* (2015, United States, dir. Bob Byington), stars as an anarchistic nonhero who is a feckless member of the precariat, bouncing from one low-paying job to the next as if he were in a video game. He has a teensy-weensy habit of petty thievery that makes his defeats in life and work inevitable, but he is a lovable rogue. He does get to expose the bully of the film at his fast-lube job, but that's about all his bravado accomplishes.

Video games now offer much greater sophisticated thrills and challenges and even humor. One critic argued that the new array of independent games could even "feature nuance like melancholy happiness and other unusual human emotions" (Goldberg, December 2013). A politicized countercurrent of games has begun a tentative recognition of the global exploitation of workers. A select group of video game designers has pursued even more challenging politics and economics in their simulated or virtual worlds that remind viewers of either animated or documentary films. Video game antics and hijinks have now moved into the underclass of these virtual worlds.

One category of politically conscious games, called *anti-advergames*, targets specific corporations that underemploy vast numbers of the precariat. Ian Bogusi, founder of Persuasive Games, one of two major producers of games that are featured in this chapter, originated the term to attack *advergames* that openly used corporate ads in games. This new moniker is a kind of "semiotic disobedience," in Sonia Katyal's formulation, whenever its creators reinvent or subvert the dominant symbols of commercial advertising, reminiscent of artists altering billboards with anti-brand or anti-capitalist messages.

One of these anti-advergames is *Disaffected!* (2006, United States, prod. Persuasive Games), taking up the cause of precarious workers in retail sales directly, placing them in the mise-en-scène of a Kinko's store. *Disaffected!* is not subtle: the player takes the role of a seemingly lazy and/or incompetent employee servicing customers at a Kinko's store. The player is asked to identify with the precariat workers, according to the producer's website: "Feel the indifference of these purple-shirted malcontents first-hand and consider the possible reasons behind their malaise—is it mere incompetence? Managerial affliction? Unseen but serious labor issues?" In practice, this means that the player is behind the counter trying, usually in vain, to deliver a customer's order. The game's directions suggest some of the obstacles: "Confused [fellow] employees, employees who refuse to work, employees who move orders around indiscriminately so that the player cannot find them." It would be frustrating enough to make the average player head for the nearest store exit.

The McDonald's Game (2006, Italy) was produced by an Italian company, La Molleindustria, whose motto is "Radical Games against the Tyranny of Entertainment." The company leads the field of politicized specialty games in this chapter, as well as being a sponsor of parades and demonstrations featuring the faux saint, Saint Precario, and a virtual parade to celebrate May Day, the workers' holiday (Mattoni and Doerr). Most game designers believe, La Molleindustria argues, in the "idea of meaningful play." Unfortunately, the game producer argues, "meaningful game systems are elegant, appealing, easy to understand and internally consistent," but this paradigm will not work for "systems that are inelegant, unappealing, obscure and contradictory like the free market capitalism that is destroying the world."

Their later version, *Burger Tycoon*, like the original, is also an anti-advergame. The animation in *Burger Tycoon* is not sophisticated but neither is the text: a manager says he had to fire one worker because corrupting the "health officer" was costing $200 a month, while the player realizes that the corporation slaughters sick cows that may have been genetically modified on farms that use "aggressive pesticides." Even fast-food customer obesity generates broad satire: "A group of corpulent gold-diggers is thinking about blaming us for this mess and seeking huge settlements. It's best to stop these balls of fat before they gather enough money to hire an army of lawyers."

In addition to an "obesity association," the game explicitly identifies any activist group involved with the environmental, consumer issues, or "organized workers." If the "consumers are happy again," the player "can deactivate the corrupter." But when workers "organize" and ask for "working rights" or "when the anti-globalization movements rail against our brand," it is helpful to have "an influential politician [who] can repress demonstrations and neutralize workers who instigate uprisings and revolts." Although animated film in world cinema has for years reached an adult audience, the overly simplistic satire of *Burger Tycoon* would probably fit a niche of activists' children best, as it probes the functions of the modern fast-food industry—beef farming, managing the restaurant, and top-down corporate decisions.

In 2008, the year of the Global Financial Crisis, La Molleindustria released an even bolder political game, *Oligarchy* (2008, Italy), an incredibly detailed excursion into the activities of the worldwide oil industry. To mimic the kind of capitalism that the oil oligarchy follows, the game "is full of broken connections, meaningless interaction, inverted rewards, and randomness." No oil well or financial maneuver is ignored in this quasi-historical politicized journey from the founding of a large American oil company in 1945 to its postwar success. Unlike some of the other games of the precariat, the player is part of the 1 percent, the CEO of a company that voraciously expands from Texas to Nigeria (where protestors abound), in Alaska (likewise environmentalists), and Iraq (need a war or two there). Keeping the veneer of reality, the game nonetheless becomes a futuristic petro-thriller, as the game's in-house newspaper, *The Petroleum Times*, reports on the depletion of oil reserves that eventually leads to food shortages, increased deer hunting for food, and protecting corn fields by the army.

These game makers are unapologetically lefties, but they recognize that the very nature of gaming is defined by the "executable software which is 'activated' by the player's performance cannot be fully grasped due to the potentially infinite text that can be generated by the same algorithm or source code." Add the complexity of politics and economics, and the game makers conclude that "there is no definitive way for the player to assess that a certain output is triggered by a certain input," according to the company's statement, "*Oligarchy* Postmortem."

The game makers consciously situated the player as "the bad guy." It was their belief that "power structures can be understood more clearly if represented from a privileged position." Players therefore explore "the dark side" but "if done with abundant irony" such a strategy "does not undermine the overarching game objectives," which involve, primarily, speculation about what happens when the oil industry slides down the future scarcity slope of the Hubbard Peak Theory and is forced to capture more politicians to support them and even invade foreign oil markets.

The latter tends to be the only times the precariat is obvious in the game. In Venezuela, opposition to the oligarch's push for more oil is "led by indigenous natives" and in Nigeria the Ogoni people who used peaceful blockades in their oil-rich homeland are attacked by the Nigerian military.

When a player finishes *Oligarchy*, "good gamers tend to get rich and blow up the world while the lazy or non-competitive gamers may reach a tragic end." The former reach a dystopia "with the most money," while some players suggested "that the best way to 'beat' the game is to avoid any imperialist activities while others suggested building as many human burning plants as possible." For La Molleindustria's game designers, the moral ambiguity of political consciousness "is the biggest accomplishment" ("*Oligarchy* Postmortem").

La Molleindustria's *Phone Story* (2011, Italy) is a didactic narrative game that was so brazen anti-iPhone that a number of critics and players at first thought it was a hoax, a mock promo for a game but not a game in itself. But the game actually does track the harmful effects of a typical smartphone supply chain. The mini-games within the game in this critical journey have been featured in documentaries of their own in this book, including the mining of coltan in African countries (see Chapter 6), exploitation of migrant labor in China (see Chapter 2), and the proliferation of cell phones in e-waste in South Asian countries (see Chapter 4).

The game's critique hit a nerve in Apple: within seven hours of its appearance on the iPhone, it was banned from their App Store. One of the mini-games features the suicides at Foxxconn, Apple's manufacturing partner in China. The app ban was, Apple argued, because of the inclusion of "violence or abuse of children" and "excessively objectionable or crude content" (Dredge). Since the abuse, harassment, and exploitation of women and children in Chinese industry have been sufficiently documented, Apple was really complaining about more exposure in the news, not simply the political motivation on the part of the developer of the game, La Molleindustria.

Many game users could object to a mini-game that asks them to catch workers of the precariat as they hurl themselves off the roof of the Foxxconn factory, but that would not negate the fact that such suicides happened. But no player would be likely to miss the developer's promotional message: "*Phone Story* is an educational game about the hidden social costs of smartphone manufacturing. Follow your phone's journey from the coltan mines of the Congo to the electronic waste dumps in Pakistan through four colorful mini-games. Compete with market forces in an endless spiral of technological obsolescence."

The Foxxconn mini-game is, to be sure, strange. It includes a Suicide Prevention Mat or net-like structure that the player moves back and forth to catch the jumping workers. Sometimes the worker bounces off the mat and goes back up in the air to be caught—or not—again. The mini-game with workers recycling e-waste products is visually much more convincing—and perhaps less disturbing, strangely enough—because those mini-home fire "factories" do exist more or less as they are depicted in the game (see Chapter 4).

Puzzler games, a different subset of games, involve much larger scales of activity than La Molleindustria's more pointed satiric targets. *Virtual City Playground* (2011, United States, prod. G5 Games), for example, is a sequel or expansion of an earlier version of *Virtual City* that offers players the opportunity to not only create a "sim" (simulated) city but build jobs and manage industry by balancing "Time, Income, Environment, Population, and Happiness."

Another puzzler game, *Papers, Please* (2013, United States), designed by Lucas Pope, was named by *The New Yorker* game reviewer Simon Parkin as one of the best video games of 2013: "Grim yet affecting, it's a game that may change your attitude the next time you're in line at the airport." The designer called it "a dystopian document thriller." *Papers, Please* will help players understand why so many of the migrant workers of the precariat avoid border checkpoints. The player becomes the lead character, an immigration inspector who uses his keyboard to process immigrants in 1982 at the border of an imaginary communist country called Arstotzka, Eastern European or former Soviet bloc in accent, that has regained control of its half of Grestin, a border town, after a six-year war with its adjacent state Kolechia.

The inspector works piece rate: the more people he processes, the more he earns. Of course, he faces difficult but dubious decisions that are morally compelling in these confrontations with animated figures. The player inspects the immigrant's documents and can even request fingerprints or a full-body scan leading to an arrest if smuggling or terrorism or other criminal behavior is suspected. The applicant may even resort to bribes. As soon as the player stamps the papers allowing or denying access, he is informed of any mistakes he has made by the game itself, getting his pay docked if he makes too many mistakes.

What brings the game to cinematic status is in part the evolution of the checkpoint's plot: other countries cause problems, terrorists attack, and even certain country's immigrants become automatically banned. In the ultimate challenge to the inspector's lowly job, a secret anti-government organization, the EZIC, begins sending its members across the border to win over the inspector to their revolutionary side. Like many R-rated films, this game had its problems with would-be censors. The body scanning images seemed too risqué, and Apple at first wanted to modify them, but in the end settled on a "nudity option" players could choose.

Kentucky Route Zero (2012–16, United States, prod. Jake Elliott and Tamas Kemenczy) used the form of a point-and-click game to take a magic realist journey with a truck driver on an interstate numbered zero, a mysterious road through Kentucky's iconic caves, mines, horse farms, and whiskey distilleries. The game was featured at London's Victorian and Albert Museum's exhibition of video games in 2018 as an example of "one of the most important design disciplines of our time."

Kentucky Route Zero was a very self-consciously cinematic and literary creation, using the precariat and other workers whose characteristics have been tweaked to the idiosyncratic. Conway is a truck driver for Lysette, the owner of an antique shop, who has assigned him the task of delivering a couch to 5 Dogwood Drive, an address that Conway is unable to find. (The address reinforces the eerie sense that everything in the game is related: Conway has a dog whom the player gets to name.) Stopping at a dubious gas station, Equus Oils, he is directed to look for this address along Route Zero. To say that the road is magical, filled with unreal—but very Kentuckian—locations that would nonetheless fit comfortably in the fictions of the Argentine fantasist Jorge Luis Borges or in the illustrations of labyrinths and algorhythmic sculptures of Robert Smithson (see Chapter 7) is an understatement.

This virtual highway connects the distilleries and mines you would expect in Kentucky, but all of them have become magically transformed. The game designers also credit "the magical realism of Gabriel García Márquez and the southern gothic of Flannery O'Connor" as other literary sources for the strange characters of the underclass Conway encounters, although on the surface they are very solid Kentucky types, such as workers at a bait shop, a farmhouse, a ferry, and a gas station. "All of these characters are living here" in Kentucky, says codesigner Jake Elliott: they are individuals with a history and a "residue" or lingering presence. And because the ferry has a mechanical mammoth on it, there will surely be a handyman with a manual for fixing mechanical mammoths.

Conway encounters both real and imaginary persons on the edge of the Kentucky precariat and underclass. When he enters a mineshaft on the highway, it partially collapses, recreating an earlier disaster when many miners lost their lives to flooding. In fact, when Conway turns off his lights he—as well as the player—sees the ghosts of the miners wandering through the cave-like mine. Later above ground two musicians on a motorcycle with a sidecar join Conway's quest: it turns out they are robotic miners fleeing their dangerous jobs to make a career as musicians, as so many real Kentuckians do. The literary and cinematic associations of this video game have produced rave reviews from critics in the field. Geoff Thew wrote, "I have never in my life pointed at and clicked on anything as beautiful, thought-provoking, or profound as *Kentucky Route Zero*."

Gaming critics agree that the designers of *Kentucky Route Zero* were strongly motivated to infuse their game with the substance and cinematic style of the auteurist films they admired, such as Roy Andersson's *Songs from the Second Floor* (2000, Sweden/Norway/Denmark), a film of "magic realism where the dead co-exist with the living," an especially important feature of a game in which the player encounters in abandoned coal mines dead miners from an earlier catastrophe. Andersson's film, like *Kentucky Route Zero*, foregrounds "simultaneous vignettes instead of a linear narrative": a line of commuters at a bus stop observes a vigilante mini-mob attacking an immigrant, a blindfolded girl is pushed into a lake, and a desolate boy with a hangman's rope around his neck bemoans his inability to save his sister from her hanging. (See Chapter 10.) One of their other favorite films is Andrei Tarkovsky's *Stalker* (1979, Soviet Union), "sort of a slow, hypnagogic crawl through an uncertain landscape," prefiguring a Chernobyl postapocalyptic drama, in which the lead, the Stalker, ferries curious self-important individuals through poisoned fields, constricted tunnels, ominous caves, and scary waterfalls—curiously all similar to the mise-en-scène of *Kentucky Route Zero*—to reach their goal, a room that will grant them their secret desires. Like *Kentucky Route Zero*, Tarkovsky's creation of the government's no-go area, the Zone, valorizes "visual impressions" rather than "editing a story." Like many of the dead ends in *Kentucky Route Zero*, Tarkovsky was capable of, the designers argue, "having the audience solve a dreary algebra problem."

Another one of the films that the designers found inspirational was Werner Herzog's *The Wild Blue Yonder* (2005, United States), first of all because Herzog's mixture of science fiction/fantasy about the future of our environmentally doomed planet with footage of a NASA space team encouraged their pursuit of the "space between fiction and the documentary," and second because Herzog's "unguided or loosely narrated images" provoked a "more poetic side" rather than a "practical desire for plot."

While games like *Kentucky Route Zero* clearly have a deep cinematic texture created by self-conscious, film-obsessed game makers, only *Fort McMoney* (2013, Canada, prod. TOXA and National Film Board of Canada) has been literally filmed as a documentary, with real people and actual locales, raising topical issues, in this instance, about Ft. McMurray, Canada, a boom town with its newly discovered rich oil sands, reputed to have "the highest concentration of oil sands reserves in Canada" (Drew). Oil sands contain bitumen, "a dense and an extremely viscous form of petroleum that some people call tar and others call 'black gold'" (Drew).

The result is what the *New York Times* (Goldberg, November 2013) describes as "where film meets video game." Different seasons of the game mean different scenarios. Viewers can click on a "character" to learn his or her back story or follow them—in one case—to their low-rent trailer park as they pursue the easy money promised by a boom town. A random hotel waitress and car saleswoman says she is making thousands of dollars. Sixty days of filming in more than twenty-two locations in the city included fifty-five interviews with real people. Research took place over two years, with 2000 hours of footage shot, at a cost of C$870,000, not quite a Hollywood budget but significant funding nevertheless.

Players also walk around the town, interview residents, and participate in debates, surveys, and referendums that determine the city's future. Certainly, the game is rigged against further oil development, but the player still has to influence the outcome. The chief of the local indigenous people tries to make it easy for the player: "They call it development. We call it destruction." Some of the nondocumentary visuals include "odometers," often set at "five minutes to midnight," that is, the environmental activists' mythical closing of the window before climate system failures take over.

Dufresne has stated he is drawn to stories about single-industry towns, having previously directed an award-winning web-doc about Cañon City, Colorado, entitled *Prison Valley* (2009, France, dir. Philippe Brault and David Dufresne). That city has thirteen prisons, more than 7,000 inmates, and a Supermax prison, where such supercriminals as the Unabomber, Timothy McVeigh, were held before their execution. Because it is a web film, the viewer can interact with other viewers and drop in on discussions about an industry that employs at least as many workers "outside the prison walls" as within. A relatively recent (2016–17) widespread forest fire, however, has almost destroyed Fort McMurray as well as the surrounding forest and oil sands until it was finally extinguished fifteen months after it started.

Although there had been at least one documentary that foregrounded Canadian environmental issues, *Petropolis: Aerial Perspectives on the Alberta Tar Sands* (2009, Canada, prod. Greenpeace Canada) also captured the spectacular visual landscape of these tar sands as well as the gold rush mentality that drove many newcomers to Ft. McMurray (Figure 8.1).

Dufresne's goal in *Fort McMoney* had always been to merge the world of gaming and documentary in his game because "capitalism is the biggest game in

Figure 8.1 Refinery for processing oil from tar sands from *Petropolis*. Courtesy Icarus Films.

the world. Everybody plays it every day." And *Fort McMurray* had become such a capitalist boom city that only a game of decision-making could capture its essence. It surprised me that the breakdown in attitudinal profiles of the players was "75% on the left and 25% on the right." The players don't "win" or "lose"— they just contribute to the community debate. Dufresne calls *Fort McMoney* "a kind of direct democracy platform in web time. If there is a winner it will be the clash of ideas" (Drew). Game players like to be winners, of course, so the almost 200,000 players in 2014 are obviously accepting the game maker's combination of documentary filmmaking and video game as debate. They may also appreciate his inclusion of another player's haiku, again not the usual video gamer's territory:

> In these gloomy mines
> On these black roads
> Despite all these shadows
> We cannot lose hope.

Video game makers have been somewhat more attracted to the meta-games and self-reflexive filmmaking in *The Stanley Parable* (2013, United States, prod. Davey Wreden and William Pugh) than *Kentucky Route Zero*, which is after all more of a literary experiment. *The Stanley Parable* is a PC mod adventure, an interactive game with a sophisticated meta-narrative. With sales of 1 million downloads of its launch by Davey Wreden in just its first year, it featured the most literary of cinematic conventions—the untrustworthy narrator. Furthermore, as the player's "camera" tracks down the hallways of an office building with endless corridors of alienating sameness, a narrator will even contest the decisions made by the player as the latter tries to solve Stanley's problem. Critics commented with some admiration of this variation because the player can insist on going his or her own way. Wreden wanted to find out, "What would happen if you could disobey the narrator?"

The second version, made with William Pugh, earned more than $1 million in two weeks with 90,000 players and featured a number of other alternative endings and a "lighter tone," taking the game into a "few bizarre and fun new directions." Wreden identifies with Hollywood professionals like the director Christopher Nolan (*Inception*, 2000, United States) and screenplay writer Charlie Kaufmann (*Being John Malkovich*, 2009, United States) because they made quest films that often externalized the psychic furniture of characters' minds (Mattis).

Stanley, it turns out, is Employee 427, a desk worker whose coworkers have abandoned *their* desks and, so far as he knows, have abandoned him as well. Stanley is a data cruncher but we never learn exactly what he crunches or for whom. One day his screen and—for all intents and purposes—his life go blank. As he makes his way through his office building in a framework that resembles a dystopian postapocalyptic film, the player is cajoled by the narrator's voice, who we learn from gaming sources is the successful professional British voice-over actor Kevin Brighting, self-described in his promotional adverts as having a "rich warm authoritative voice."

The meta nature of the game becomes obvious when the player realizes he is punching a keyboard like Stanley and that the player is in effect a Stanley! The player cannot control his virtual world either. In fact, the narrator can even turn the "film" off or make the player start over again. In almost every instance, the player's choice or keystroke elicits the narrator's reaction, either a remark or a change in the action or both. Whatever Stanley was caught in—the dilemma of the powerless, that is, a precariat worker—the player is too, imitating Stanley. He can resist the narrator's suggestions but his choices don't seem to improve his situation measurably. One might even argue that no improvement would be possible whether the player follows the narrator or not.

The game made a cameo appearance in the third season of the TV series *House of Cards* presumably because presidential decision-making is also filled with twists and turns. Despite his preference for "shoot 'em ups" over "indie games" like *The Stanley Parable*, President Frank Underwood (played by Kevin Spacey) is tempted by his biographer, a former video game reviewer and novelist, to play *The Stanley Parable*, although it will remind him "too much of real life."

William Pugh, the codesigner of *The Stanley Parable*, also created *Dr. Langeskov, the Tiger and the Terribly Cursed Emerald: A Whirlwind Heist* (2015, United States), a deliriously tongue-in-cheek parody of what Pugh called an "environmental narrative game" (ENG) that "de-emphasized conventional game mechanics and challenges" in favor of the cinematic mise-en-scène of the game. The player would also discover that at some points certain visual elements of the game would be eroded because the game's designers have gone on strike. What a player does not at first realize that this is a meta-game, a game about gaming as well as using the precarious working conditions symbolized by the unpredictable tiger.

One of the game writers wrote on the internet promotional site that "because of understaffing" the writer had been "re-assigned" to the "wildlife preparation" division where "everybody knows" one is "mostly trying very hard not to be eaten by the tiger" of the title, a tiger, by the way, who is mostly a MacGuffin, the Hitchcockian trope for something unexpected that is nonetheless right under one's nose. The writer concludes, "That's it, I'm joining the picket: if they want somebody else" to do the job, "that's their problem." Game players will not, however, find a picket line in this game, but they do discover incomplete features at a certain level of that journey as if the game had not been completed by its designers. Furthermore, the narrator, English comedian Simon Anstell, tells the player that, yes, the staff working on the texture of the game have left, posting resignation notices and picket signs saying, "We Are Not Being Paid Half Enough." The ruse here is apparently to convince the payer to do the work of the product builder, just as many TV shows and online portals have their content provided by the viewers and consumers. It may be the first game that, according to Christopher Boyd of the *Washington Post*, "gestures towards the prevalence of unfair labor practices in our daily lives without sanctuary."

The player is talked into helping with these tasks because the narrator says an earlier player (actually a game character) is stuck because of the strike and asks if the new player could help out with such tasks as working the elevator and getting the tiger's cage ready. The player character leaves, but the player then overhears the narrator giving the same pitch about helping out to an even newer player who is incompetent. In brief, the tiger attacks without warning, and the player's life—and certainly the precarious job—is soon gone. And that emerald—spoiler alert—is not worth anything either.

Video games have also become genre benders. *Red Faction* (2001, United States, prod. Volition and THQ) is a game that begins as an incredibly violent and bloody first-person shooter game but in sequels turned to elements of both science fiction and epidemic cinema. Reviewers of the game referenced slightly off-kilter sci-fi films directed by Paul Verhoeven in the 1990s, like *Total Recall* (1990, United States) and *Starship Troopers* (1997, United States), both of which included lots of shooting but enough meta challenges (arachnid enemies in the latter, difficulties in distinguishing virtual reality from actual experience in the former) to reduce the carnage visualized.

Later avatars of the game with somewhat desperate titles—*Red Faction: Guerrilla*, *Red Faction: Guerrilla Re-Mars-tered*, and *Red Faction: Armageddon* (2009–18, United States)—all involve a rebel movement against the corporation that runs mining operations on Mars, exploiting its precariat miners to such an extent that it does nothing to alleviate their miserable living conditions or the disease called "The Plague" (somehow a side effect of the company's monkeying with its nanotechnology) coursing through their community. (See *The Leakers* in Chapter 5 for a similar plot.) With the player taking the role of a lead rebel miner, an antidote to the disease is found and the company destroyed, amid an array of "geometry modification" of the mise-en-scène, for example, the player eliminates the company's buildings and the mines, actions now taken for granted in most video games today.

A different hybrid or mixture of genres defines the video game *Papa & Yo* (2012, United States, prod. Vander Caballero and Minority Media), whose child hero, an abused child named Quico (yo = me), is able to pass through a portal of light in the closet of his Brazilian favela or shantytown in which he hides from his alcoholic father. One of the trailers for the game illustrates a live-action dramatization of the boy hiding from his father alternating with an animated sequence in which we see a fantastic, happier version of the shantytown, filled with bright colors, inviting pathways, and detachable and stackable shanties. The boy that the player controls has bad flashbacks to a time when he was in the back seat of his father's car on a scary, rainy night, but this vision passes. His companions include a pink buffoon of a Monster, his toy robot companion Lula, and a quirky, cheeky girl, Alejandra. Monster generally behaves, until he sees a frog, an avatar of the alcohol he craves beyond all reason and civility. We are probably not surprised when Quico sees his father in the headlights of a car on a rainy night and his shadow is that of the Monster who, by the way, can only be calmed with rotten fruit.

This game turns out to be a memoir (possibly gaming's first, according to Rich Juzwiak) of the lead designer, Vander Caballero, obviously quite unusual for a video game, but not so surprising is that the alternative or magical world of the video game—or of similar films for that matter—soon loses its glow and the player must solve numerous difficult and dangerous situations for Quico. The favela he negotiates is filled with spectacular murals of tropical birds, carnival masks, or beautiful indigenous people. There is even a Shaman with white skeletal body paint. So much of this furniture of the game is inspired, Caballero tells us, by the Columbian magic realist writer, Gabriel García Márquez.

Although video games offer varying degrees of freedom to the player to control the narrative, *Papa & Yo* is less generous and perhaps more paradoxical. The designer knows the experiences that determine much of the life of a favela child: the game must simultaneously restrict the player to those hard truths and yet help the child find the eventual freedom the designer himself has reached.

It remains to be seen if and how the precariat will be featured in new video games. We do know that in 2014 the video game industry earned $80 billion, a figure that made it competitive with Hollywood; top-of-the-line games have marketing budgets as if they were blockbuster films. However, most of the video games in this chapter were done by independent and smaller-scale studios and individuals, somewhat analogous to independent and auteurist directors of film. As Raffi Khatchadourian, an investigative reporter for *The New Yorker* pointed out in his discussion of *No Man's Sky* (2016, United States, prod. Sean Murray and Hello Games), a SONY-supported video studio's production of a universe with eighteen quintillion unique planets, only a Hollywood budget would ensure its success. The player, more humanoid than human, engages in work somewhat similar to the more famous video game *Minecraft* (2009, United States, Markus Persson), using a "multitool" to mine resources, protecting oneself from hostile beings, and exploring a wondrous universe. In the latter case, the player is more explorer and anthropologist than anything else. Although mining and trade are two of the players' activities, game creator Sean Murray is also very proud of his game's drones: "They will attack you if they find you killing animals or illegally mining resources." In brief, they act like disciplined and principled human beings. (See the androids in Chapter 7).

9

The 1 Percent: A Top-Down Conclusion—Fifty Films about Capitalism in the Twenty-First Century

If you understand what economics commentator and novelist John Lanchester concluded in his essay, "Cityphobia" (2015), you probably don't need to read this chapter: "If you own someone's else debt, it counts as an asset." On the other hand, if the following prediction by cultural critic Fredric Jameson in his essay, "Future City" (2003), makes more sense, you will understand the need for this chapter: "Someone once said that it is easier to imagine the end of the world than to imagine the end of capitalism. We can now revise that and witness the attempt to imagine the end of capitalism by way of imagining the end of the world."

Does capitalism survive? See the movie! If you have read this book so far, it is probably no surprise that capitalism or neoliberalism or globalization or hedge funds or Wall Street is usually blamed for some of the terrible job opportunities for the precariat in the twenty-first century documented or dramatized in the films in this book. But I have also included three films about capitalism in this list from the twentieth century as well, because have things really changed that much since then?

It may be impossible to understand the precariat and its economic niche without viewing some of the films in this chapter, many of which focus on the defining event of the last twenty years—the Global Financial Crisis of 2008—that recalibrated capitalism's drive to secure its profits at the cost of defying union drives, deindustrializing, and creating the army of temp workers known as the precariat. Almost all of these films have appeared in the last twenty years because filmmakers have attempted to take the measure of a financial world without limits. That this world has generated massive protests is the subject of the next chapter on the 99 percent and should come as no surprise after viewing the films in this chapter.

Why are there so many films in this chapter devoted to capitalism? (I could have included more than fifty: enough is enough.) Perhaps filmmakers continue to love a good villain or two, and these films provide more than the usual crop. Certainly, their directors and producers have hit on some of the best titles in the business—*The Wolf of Wall Street*, for instance, or *The Secret of Oz, Dark Money, Inside Job*, and *Money Monster*, all of which promise what they deliver: a vast, wealthy elite—their critics call them the 1 percent—who control the world's resources and enrich themselves in the process.

The films fall into five broad areas of concern: (1) Films about the theory and practice of capitalism starring the dubious classic, *The Fountainhead*, based on Ayn Rand's novel of the virtues of selfishness and self-sufficiency. (2) The number of films about criminal exploits and the ruthlessness of financial leaders is perhaps not surprisingly quite large: brilliant exposes dominate this group, such as *Cleveland vs Wall Street, The Comedy of Power*, and *Billions*, a compelling TV series. There is even a real estate scammer—*99 Homes*—and a sweet, abused, giant, genetically enhanced pig—*Okja*—in the mix. (3) *Wall Street* itself was cinematically immortalized in two films with its name as title, both starring Michael Douglass as the "greed is good" manipulator Gordon Gekko whom everyone loves to hate, but I have included only the sequel. A dark twist on Wall Street, *Money Monster*, features a hijacking of the star of a popular on-air stock market advice program by an investor who lost his savings because of the show's recommendations. (4) Women at the top receive relatively little attention, but the three films that do dominate are graced with excellent actresses who steal the show but not the money: Jessica Chastain in *Miss Sloan*, Nina Foss in *Yella*, and Anna Gunn in *Equity*. (5) The Global Financial Crisis of 2008 is represented by case studies of failure at the top, such as *The Last Days of Lehman Brothers, The Big Short*, and *Hank: 5 Years from the Brink*.

And although Chapter 10, the second concluding chapter, if you will, will offer numerous examples of the 99 percent fighting back, I have also included at least four of their classic exposes in this list as well: Michael Moore's *Capitalism: A Love Story*; his competitors in mayhem, *The Yes Men Fix the World*; *Rise Like Lions: Occupy Wall Street and the Seeds of Revolution*, a chronicle of the Occupy Wall Street movement; and *Visible and Invisible*, installation artist Oliver Ressler's expose of the Swiss dominance of commodity trading.

It is with some personal irony that I note, however, that just a single one of these films about capitalism appeared in my two earlier books (*Working Stiffs, Union Maids, Reds, and Riffraff* and *The Cinema of Globalization*) on films about labor and related economic issues. But readers of those books will nonetheless find other films that attempt to take the measure of the class colloquially known by the protestors (part of the 99 percent) in the next chapter as the 1 percent.

To complete your survey of the precariat it is, therefore, appropriate to give the devil his due, so to speak, to see the films where capitalism is the star. This chapter is therefore an alternative guide to the difficulties of the precariat from the point of view of Guy Standing's top levels—the plutocrats and the elite—not necessarily sympathetic to their role but at least an attempt to understand how they function.

To label them all as "anti-capitalist" would be a trifle unfair, since at least one of them is a "love story" (*Capitalism: A Love Story*) and another one stars Catherine Deneuve as a benevolent boss (*Potiche*): you should be so lucky to work for her. And while *Saving Capitalism* may not a love story it is closer to a bromance, and *The Secret of Oz* is an historical oddity and treat. *Dirty Money* cannot be beaten for its often hilarious exposes of the crooked and famous.

Perhaps it is not a surprise that a number of the films have judges making important decisions that determine an economic or political crux or two. What can we conclude about the many judges involved in the civil and criminal cases in these films? Because of the partisan selective process, the impartiality of American judges is always a point of contention, as James D. Zirin's *Supremely Partisan: How Raw Politics Tips the Scales in the United States Supreme Court* (2016) argues. He demonstrates how politics or, more precisely, political ideology, rather than precedent or legal arguments, determines the decisions of the Supreme Court.

Reviewing a number of the important decisions of that Supreme Court over the years if not centuries may make cultural and historical relativists of many of us, since at least one of them—a benchmark for Zirin's analysis—is arguably the most important historical decision for capitalism, *Santa Clara County v. Southern Pacific Railroad* (1886), since its definition of corporations as "persons" under the law gained tremendous corporate power for their so-called "selfhood" that has persisted to this day. See also how corporate personhood was reaffirmed in *Citizens United v. FEC* in 2010, for example, or *Burwell v. Hobby Lobby Stores* in 2014.

The attitude of the judge in *Molly's Game* (2017, United States, dir. Aaron Sorkin)—a film more about high stakes in poker games rather than on Wall Street—remains an important cinematic exception, but this strong-minded judge has not yet received sufficient recognition. When the infamous Molly

Bloom, the former ski champion and glamorous organizer of poker games for the rich and spoiled in the 1990s who lends her name to the title of the film, has pled guilty to operating an illegal poker game, the US district judge in the film—Jesse M. Furman in real life—speaks, "We are sitting within spitting distance of Wall Street and I know that because I spit at it every time I go by. More financial crimes will be committed there before lunch today than anything this defendant has done. So there will be no jail time but probation and a fine."

For Molly, the probation (one year) and the fine ($1,000) were really quite light. But she also had to do 200 hours of community service and promise that she would behave herself in her memoir, *Molly's Game* (2014), due out a month after her sentencing, that is, she had better not undermine the contrition she had expressed in court.

The following list of films is fifty strong. There are certainly others we can save for another fiscally irresponsible day. It should be obvious that the precariat almost never appears in these films. A virtually invisible workforce to the masters of the universe serves a number of functions. They do not have to be reminded how little their businesses pay workers who help create their profits, they are easily replaced by other workers in the precariat, and they are everywhere and nowhere as their immediate supervisors wish. They are usually not represented by pesky unions, and in the Western world many writers refer to their "gig" economy as if they are going to work in a nightclub not a garbage city.

Betting on Zero (United States, 2016, dir. Ted Braun): If it takes a capitalist to catch a capitalist, this documentary may prove to be unique. Bill Ackman, a billionaire hedge fund manager, tries to destroy Herbalife, a weight and nutrition company, because he believes it is a pyramid scheme to bilk its members. Both Ackman and the film's producer are trying to "short" Herbalife's stock, that is, buying its shares on the premise that the company's share value will decline after people see the film and they will reap big profits by buying short. And the share value *will* decline *if* this documentary convinces shareholders that their company is a cheat. Dizzy yet? If so, try some Herbalife Thermo Tea, a combo of pure caffeine and vitamin C: a 1.8 oz "original" recipe box is only $25.15. But you cannot buy it in a store: you have to buy it from an existing Herbalife "associate."

The Big Sellout (2006, Germany, dir. Florian Opitz): A major cinematic assault from Germany on the policies of the International Monetary Fund (IMF) and the World Bank (WB) that are blamed for setting our regulations in public spending and privatization of public services as the only explanation for economic regression in both First and Second World countries, such as the deterioration of the rail system in the UK, poor hospitals in the Philippines, and loss of water services in South Africa and Bolivia. The emphasis is on the disruption and damage to the workers and their families at the bottom of the economic ladder.

The Big Short (2015, United States, dir. Steven Spielberg): Finally, the mysteries of credit-default swaps (insuring the potential losses by a buyer of bonds) and collateralized debt obligations (repackaging individual loans in a new product sold to investors) are cleared up in this tragic farce, a dramatization of Michael Lewis's best-selling nonfiction book about the Global Financial Crisis of 2008 that moved from the collapse of the subprime mortgage market to the demise of the prestigious Lehman Brothers investment banking firm.

Billions (2016–19, United States, dir. Brian Koppleman, David Levien, and Andrew Ross): TV series in which a US attorney (Paul Giamatti) goes after a hedge fund manager (Damian Lewis). They hate each other; both are corrupt in very different ways that make compelling viewing if not gawking in amazement inevitable. Giamatti's obsessive pursuit reminded many viewers of *Moby Dick*'s flawed Captain Ahab. The plot is quite convoluted: at one point, the attorney himself is under investigation by the US Attorney's Office for possible malpractice. Of course, he tries to find an enemy of the attorney general to pursue so that if he is threatened with firing he can make the attorney general feel embarrassed about his enemy going free. Whew. And don't even get started about the sexual and other personal shenanigans of the leads—you'll be happy they are just cheating the public. Nonetheless, a compelling series with really big money at its corrupt core. And probably a first: where else can we see a binary character (played by a binary actor) who tells their boss, "My pronouns are their, they, and them"? They are a financial genius too.

Le Capital (2012, France, dir. Costa-Gravas): A financial thriller in which an executive becomes the CEO of a large French bank, only to disorient its board of directors with his ruthless ambition, greed, and deceptive leadership. However, his brutal power struggles are in turn jeopardized by a hostile takeover attempt from a large American hedge fund. *Le Capital* is a fast-paced, darkly comic, and a suspenseful drama well worth the many accolades it has received.

Capitalism (2014, France/Canada/Israel, dir. Brund Nahan and Ilan Zin): The advantage of this prodigious six-part series is its survey of twenty-two countries by economists who dissect the formidable gorgon of the title, while recounting its defenders and critics, notably Adam Smith (*The Wealth of Nations*, 1776); Thomas Robert Malthus (*An Essay on the Principle of Population*, 1798), its implacable foe, Marx (oh, him: *Das Kapital*, 1867); and three modern commentators, Maynard Keynes (*The General Theory of Employment, Interest, and Money*, 1936), Friedrick Hayek (*The Road to Serfdom*, 1944), and Karl Polyani (*The Great Transformation*, 1944). High school students who master even a fraction of these giants will be accepted to the university of their choice (Figure 9.1).

Capitalism: A Love Story (2009, United States, dir. Michael Moore): The film portrays the Global Financial Crisis of 2008 in the United States as a systemic fraud in which wealthy finance capitalists stole trillions of public dollars. No one was jailed for this crime, the largest theft of public money in history. Instead, the rich forced the working class and the precariat across the globe to pay for their "crisis" through punitive "austerity" programs that gutted public services and repealed workers' rights. Webster's Online Dictionary named "austerity" as "Word of the Year" for 2010; "socialism" was a runner-up.

The China Hustle (2018, United States, dir. Jed Rothstein): *Enron* financial scandal expert Alec Gibney produced this expose of still another Wall Street scam, this

Figure 9.1 On front lines of anti-capitalism from *Capitalism*. Courtesy Icarus Films.

one launched by crooked Chinese investors who—barred by American law from listing their own companies on the Stock Exchange—merge with a defunct American company already listed and attract American investors both large and small to get rich on both the reality and the myth of the Chinese economic boom. But some canny investors buy these stocks "short," that is, they virtually borrow the stock, sell it at a high price, help spread rumors—mostly true—about the weakness or virtual nonexistence of the company—buy the shares back at a lower price, and "return" them. So far this is one of the first films to blow the whistle on this scam if there were any honest regulators out there to hear it.

Cleveland vs Wall Street (2010, France/Switzerland, dir. Jean-Stephane Bron): This wonderfully titled doc links various crises in finances and politics, as Cleveland files lawsuits against twenty-one banks, claiming they ruined the city with foreclosures based on subprime mortgage chicanery. However, the film is also a mock-doc in every sense, because the film's title refers to a mock trial in which the city's original lawyer and the judge, for example, play themselves for the film when Cleveland filed their suit.

Collapse (2009, United States, dir. Chris Smith): Documentary about Michael Ruppert, a police officer turned independent reporter, attracted to conspiracy theories but who successfully predicted the recent recurring financial crises, especially about peak oil, in his self-published newsletter, *From the Wilderness*, from 1999 to 2006. Despite his original insights, such a solitary crusader needs more context and company to star in a convincing doc.

Comedy of Power (France, 2006, dir. Claude Chabrol): Chabrol was an irrepressible Hitchcock wannabe, but here he directs Isabelle Huppert as Eva Joly, a real-life French state investigative prosecutor whose nickname among the financial elite whose illegal shenanigans she tracked incessantly was "the piranha," a term that sounds as good in English as it does in French. She was particularly obsessive about the perks the elite took for granted, including the purchase of unlimited baubles and properties for their mistresses with their firm's money, a practice they maintained was perfectly legal and acceptable to their clan. She was an activist against international financial corruption, especially in the state-owned petrol company, Elf Aquitane. Her revelations rocked France, and she needed four policemen to guard her life around the clock for the six-year duration of her investigation.

The Corporate Coup d'Etat (2018, United States/Canada, dir. Fred Peabody). The title deliberately evokes the revolutionary seizure of power by the capitalist class in America but the film argues that despite the evil of President Trump's manipulations, this process has been proceeding apace for quite a few decades. Although Naomi Klein used the title relatively recently, the filmmakers agree with Canadian philosopher John Ralston Saul that it is now old, bad news.

Dark Money (2018, United States, dir. Kimberly Reed): Recaps the controversial Supreme Court ruling *Santa Clara County v. Southern Pacific Railroad* in 1886 that gave corporations "personhood," redoubled by the *Citizens United* decision in 2010 that reinforced unfettered corporate investments in electoral campaigns of candidates favorable to financial interests of the few and wealthy. But the real strength of the documentary is the retelling of an investigative journalist's exposure of a Montana state representative found guilty of pretending not to take any financial funds for his campaign but allowing organizational mercenaries—America Right to Work and Montana Right to Work—to bankroll his entire campaign using funds from secret or "dark" corporate and personal donors.

Deepwater Horizon (2016, United States, dir. Peter Berg): Offshore drilling rig explodes, causing the worst oil spill in history, with eleven workers missing and presumed dead. British Petroleum (BP) execs bypassed site inspections for safety and rushed the construction to avoid financial losses. The tragic irony of the film occurs when knowledgeable techies and installation people force the company's lackeys to test recent cement work with what is called the Cement Bond Log (CBL). Unfortunately, the test propels the disaster because the cement really was poured incorrectly.

Dirty Money (2018, United States, dir. Alex Gibney, et al.): Six episodes, six stories of corporate and related shenanigans—Volkswagen cheating on diesel emissions stats, racecar driver Scott Tucker stealing from people through payday loans, the Valeant Pharmaceuticals accounting fraud for selling a $13.50 pill for $750, HSBC money laundering for Hezbollah and others, a Canadian cartel cheating on maple sugar prices (even Canada! Maple sugar!), and of course the ultimate confidence man, Donald Trump, one of the best exposes of his chicanery available. If you are not taking blood pressure medicine before you watch these, then your time has come.

Enron: The Smartest Guys in the Room (2005, United States, Alex Gibney): Smartest, maybe, honest, decidedly not. Alex Gibney's definitive doc about Enron, the energy company that became a virtual trading machine and fools' (investors') hell. This is one of the best documentaries about the now well-documented crooks of Enron, in large part because of info available from a muckraking expose by Bethany McLean, "Is Enron Overpriced?" that appeared in *Fortune* magazine in 2001. The answer was yes and crookedly so. Perhaps not hard to do, if you are a so-called energy company with both internet bandwidth and the weather in your potential derivative products portfolio.

Equity (2016, United States, Meera Menon): Anna Gunn, one of the stars of the acclaimed TV series *Breaking Bad* (2008–13), plays an investment banker pushing a high-tech Initial Public Offering (IPO) of stock and being crushed by the chauvinism and avarice of her workmates as well as her competitors. Unusual for a film about capitalists is that many of the capitalists are, well, women, which explains why Anna Gunn's character lost a big deal: the client didn't like her dress. On the other hand, she is concerned that her new IPO has a flawed product but she plows ahead.

The Flaw (2011, United Kingdom, dir. David Sington): For eighteen years, 1937–2006, Alan Greenspan, as chair of the US Federal Reserve, had been the proponent of deregulating the banks, that is, allowing them to follow the siren call of unlimited derivatives dealing, in major part the cause of the Global Financial Crisis of 2008. "I found a flaw," he all but whispered to a congressional oversight committee in that he "could have seen the sub-prime [mortgage] crisis coming earlier." It did not occur to him to doubt that "the self-interest of lending institutions to protect shareholders' equity" would falter. He—and no doubt the millions of failed mortgage holders—shared a "state of shocked disbelief." Not so shocked is one of the key voices in this film, Louis Hyman, author of *Temp: How American Work, American Business, and the American Dream Became Temporary* (2018), one of the standard books on the precariat.

Food, Inc. (2008, United States, dir. Robert Kenner): Analyzes the influence on the general food culture by the fast-food industry mania for profits, depriving workers of their health and safety and badly treating the animals processed for food. The relationship of human diseases like obesity and diabetes and the food we consume is as scary as the cozy arrangements between the food industry and the so-called government regulators and compliant legislators. A chicken industry spokesman boasts, "We're not producing chickens; we're producing food."

The Founder (2016, United States, dir. John Lee Hancock): How two small businessmen, the McDonald brothers, were cheated out of their fast-food empire by the ruthless Ray Kroc, who makes the flamboyant transition from traveling milkshake machine salesman to the CEO of the McDonald's Corporation. *Film Comment* magazine (January–February 2017) called it "certainly the most persuasive anti-capitalist film produced by the [Harvey] Weinstein indie assembly line."

The Fountainhead (1949, United States, dir. King Vidor): No list of the biggest hits of capitalism can omit this creaky adaptation of a novel by Ayn Rand (so popular with Trumpers of all stripes), starring Gary Cooper's square jaw that represents or embodies free enterprise or something of that ilk. Lisa Duggan's study of Rand, *Mean Girl: Ayn Rand and the Culture of Greed* (2019), argues that in Rand's world selfishness is a virtue, altruism a sin, and capitalism promotes freedom. If you watch by mistake a 1956 Japanese film with the same title, not to worry: it dramatizes the drive to build houses for rich people on land with water rights essential for local farmers and is also a curious mirror image of the ruthless Ayn Rand philosophy.

Future of Food (2008, United Kingdom, dir. Robin Barnwell): British reporter George Alagiah investigates how a future food crisis will be triggered by rising populations, changing diets, fuel and water shortages, and climate change. Let's hear it for synthetic food made from—don't ask—in *Soylent Green* (1973, United States, dir. Richard Fleischer).

Gold (2016, United States, dir. Stephen Gaghen): Drama of corrupt gold exploration in Indonesia and how America's Wall Street operates in a crooked manner; Matthew McConaughey plays Kenny Wells, a fictitious version of the lead con man in the Bre-X Gold Mining Scandal in the 1990s who could sell you either the Brooklyn Bridge or gold tucked inside a mountain or probably both.

Golden Rule: The Investment Theory of Politics (2009, United States, dir. Jonathan Shockley): A documentary on the influence of money on politics based on Thomas Ferguson's book *Golden Rule: The Investment Theory of Party*

Competition and the Logic of Money-Driven Political Systems (1995). does an excellent job of exposing several myths behind the words *free market, capitalism, socialism,* and *democracy.* For instance, since the "golden age of capitalism" in the 1950s, productivity has more than doubled, and yet wages have stayed the same and most people are working more hours, not less. At the same time, all of our productivity gains have gone to the owners of capital (the 1 percent).

Hank: 5 Years from the Brink (2013, United States, dir. Joe Berlinger): This is the best—if not the only—extended defense of Hank Paulson, the American secretary of the treasury, during the Global Financial Crisis of 2008; even the *Washington Post* film reviewer says you have to "feel for him," especially when he got a case of the "dry heaves" during the crisis. Plus it's a glowing account of his marriage to Wendy Paulson who, when her husband had a higher pile of money than the moon as CEO of Goldman Sachs and tried unsuccessfully to give her a cashmere coat from Bergdorf Goodman, made him return it because who really needs two coats? About ten other films on this list conclude his decisions were terrible, so you might want to look at this film for a little balance.

Inside Job (2010, United States, dir. Charles Ferguson): Another documentary tale of the Global Financial Crisis of 2008, which, at a cost over $20 trillion, caused millions of people to lose their jobs and homes in the worst recession since the Great Depression. Features the investigator of France's Elf Aquitain Scandal, Eva Joly, the "piranha," who also stars in *The Comedy of Power.*

The Last Days of Lehman Brothers (2009, United States, dir. Michael Samuels): Although it wanted to merge with Bank of America or Barkley's of London, this financial behemoth was "allowed" to collapse during the Global Financial Crisis of 2008; this doc will explain why. Unfortunately, the film does not include what may have been the apocryphal expostulation of the crafty (and shadowy) head of the company, Dick Fuld, who said, as Lehman Brothers crashed, "Babylon the Great is fallen." Since Babylon the Great in *Revelations* was the collection of false prophets, maybe that was a confession.

Margin Call (2011, United States, dir. J. C. Chandor): Star-filled drama of 2008 crisis, as we meet a downsized (i.e., fired) leader in risk management assessment who had been studying why his generic company is about to collapse. Should his former masters bring him back?! No-brainer. But he may not be able to help because still another risk analyst in the company has already spotted irrevocable disaster in a mathematical model of their securities offerings. A. O. Scott of the *New York Times* concluded that the scriptwriter knew that "the higher a person's rank, the less he is likely to understand what the firm is actually doing."

Master of the Universe (2014, Germany/Austria, dir. Marc Bauder): Rainer Voss, the key former investment banker interviewed in this German doc, was only an apprentice to the real masters of the universe, who were Americans inventing all the instruments he began applying to the financial markets in Frankfurt alongside Citibank, Merrill Lynch, and Bloomberg, whose deserted offices were then redeveloped for China's Bank of Communications. To his credit (?), Voss readily admits to fraudulent trades as well as an overreliance on the usual speculative but legal instruments of his trade.

Miss Sloan (United States, 2015, dir. John Madden): Lobbying may be the sea in which both capitalists and lawmakers swim, but their expertise and ruthlessness are sometimes scarce in Hollywood movies. Perhaps they have figured out that what to do for a living that Hollywood insiders have already mastered: exaggerate or even lie to prosper. Miss Sloan is the uncompromising lobbyist played by Jessica Chastain who sees the light over gun control in this drama about Washington's politicians and manipulators and tries to change sides.

Money Monster (2016, United States, dir. Jodie Foster): George Clooney plays a funny and manic TV show advisor on investing—Julie Roberts plays his off-screen producer—who is taken hostage on the air by one of the small investors screwed by his advice. Compelling and unusual inside look into Wall Street. Clooney was made for this wise-ass role.

97% Owned (2012, United Kingdom, dir. Michael Oswald): Presenting serious research and incredible detail about how money really works, this is one of the first documentaries to tackle the American economic system from a UK perspective, explaining how the two countries manipulate their central banks and create money. Title refers to the fact that 97 percent of the world's money supply is credit-based, to the advantage of banks (Figure 9.2).

99 Homes (2014, United States, dir. Ramin Bahrani): The director of two precariat classics—*Man Push Cart* (NYC street seller) and *Chop Shop* (Willet's Point)—dramatizes dishonest real estate brokers and banks who steal from each other as

Figure 9.2 Demonstration from *97% Owned*. Courtesy Queuepolitely.

well as the government, in part by evicting families from their homes. This is a sunny Florida nightmare for homeowners anywhere who are underwater in more ways than one. The lead broker played by Michael Shannon is dazzlingly evil.

Okja (2017, South Korea, dir. Joon-ho Bong): Okja, a mega-size sow raised by a young girl in the South Korean outback, competes for an agrichemical company's prize for the best super-pig in the world—I call her Big Oink—who is today's pig, tomorrow's slice of bacon thicker than a flank steak. Okja's parent company wants to feed the world with super-pigs. Unlike *Charlotte's Web*, this film is not for children, because this anti-corporate tale includes animal rape in the barnyard. A real sleeper and a weeper, too, from the director of two other edgy precariat films, *Snowpiercer* (2014, South Korea/Czech Republic), about a postapocalyptic megatrain, and *The Host* (2006, South Korea), starring an indomitable underwater monster, both of which feature ordinary people as heroes.

The Pit (2009, United States, dir. Johanna Lee): A must-see documentary peek into the New York Board of Trade, where a trillion dollars of business with only five commodities (coffee, cocoa, sugar, cotton, and frozen orange juice) are traded (through futures contracts) every day by phalanxes of brightly coated traders screaming, gesticulating, and mugging their proposed trades to each other. The traders are very proud of the multi-class background of these (mostly) male wheeler-dealers: take me, for instance, one says, I didn't go to college. The opening quotation from the formidable author of literary nonsense, Gertrude Stein, is itself priceless: "Money is always there, but the pockets change."

Potiche (2011, France, dir. Francois Ozon): Catherine Deneuve plays the carefree wife of a nasty umbrella factory owner who is taken hostage by his angry employees. Unlike her loser husband, Catherine proves to be adept at taking over the company and treating the workers with respect. She doesn't seem to be in any hurry getting her husband released: wonder why?

Rise Like Lions: Occupy Wall Street and the Seeds of Revolution (2011, Canada, dir. Scott Noble): Covers the Occupy movement with verve, even if a number of sequences are already classics of on-the-spot coverage—a Palestinian girl demanding Israeli soldiers stop shooting; the Tank Man in Tiananmen Square— but its global coverage is impressive.

Rogue Trader (United Kingdom, 1999, dir. James Dearden): Dramatizes the notorious Nick Leeson, a plasterer's son who launched a new future derivatives trading operation in Singapore for UK's oldest and most respected bank, Baring's, with special clients past (the financers of the Louisiana Purchase of 1803) and present (Queen Elizabeth II). When Leeson's chicanery added up to a loss of 1 billion pounds, Baring's was through and was eventually sold for one pound to a Dutch bank. Maybe that's all Baring's was worth, given their lack of oversight of Leeson's operations.

Saving Capitalism (2017, United States, dir. Jacob Kornbluth and Sari Gilman): A documentary version of Robert Reich's book by the same title, explaining the distance between rich and poor to conservative audiences outside of Washington, DC, whose residents know better. We meet Republican businessmen, lobbyists, and one member of the precariat, a McDonald's worker, all of whom trying to make America great again, oops, and have yet to realize that America needs a populist revolt like the one after the plutocrats of the 1880s and 1890s seized power.

The Secret of Oz (2010, United States, dir. William T. Still): Turns out that L. Frank Baum, the author of the *Wizard of Oz* series of books, was a free-silver standard freak (advocating unlimited coinage of silver coins on demand), who believed people not banks should control the money supply. Accordingly, his story has a yellow (gold) brick road, an emerald (greenback) city, and Dorothy's silver slippers, presumably free silver, oops, they became ruby-colored when the film was adapted from his tale.

The Spider's Web (2017, United Kingdom, dir. Michael Oswald): Documentary expose of what the director calls "the second empire," that is, the shadowy financial powers of the City of London (i.e., the British Wall Street) that control an immense store of global offshore wealth, including a significant number of tax havens, but has managed, the director has suggested, to do so "without attracting significant attention to itself."

Too Big to Fail (2011, United States, dir. Curtis Hanson): Another documentary saga based on Andrew Ross Sorkin's book by the same title about why Lehman Brothers was sacrificed for the greater good if not profit of others after the Global Financial Crisis of 2008. One can never hear too much about Dick Fuld, the secretive but very greedy head of Lehman Brothers before its fall, possibly the most unpleasant but unknown CEO around.

Trading on Thin Air (2011, United States, dir. Susan Kucera): Perfectly titled doc that examines carbon pollution and whether big business is capitalizing on environmentalism in order to make money. Sad to see so-called "green" American presidential candidate Al Gore in the carbon offset trading business, with a company, Generation Investment Management, making him money instead of votes.

The Visible and the Invisible (2014, Austria/Switzerland, dir. Oliver Ressler): An installation film that demonstrates the relationship between the Swiss dominance of commodity trading (crude oil, copper, aluminum, and even wheat) as virtual monopolies while the actual (physical) mining and development of these commodities are in the Global South's "zones of extraction," usually environmentally and socially toxic.

Wall Street: Money Never Sleeps (United States, 2010, dir. Oliver Stone): You will not be surprised that you shouldn't trust Gordon Gekko, Michael Douglass's great fraudster in the first *Wall Street* (1987) when he gets out of jail in this sequel to try to ingratiate himself with his daughter who blames him for a lot of things, not least of which is a secret bank account. My purse is sealed on that plot complication. This insight into the Global Financial Crisis of 2008 is worth seeing and learning from. A different heir to Gekko's Wall Street chicanery must be brought down because he is an even nastier fraudster and also because he has a copy of Goya's great painting, *Saturn Devouring One of His Sons*, an unsubtle hint to Gekko's own new son-in-law.

War by Other Means (1993, United Kingdom, dir. John Pilger): Veteran investigative journalist Pilger travels to Third World countries to document the devastating results of loans from the WB and IMF. It turns out that the "structural-adjustment" policies of neoliberal economics are even more deadly than nerve gas and other weapons of war. This documentary backs up many of the claims made by John Perkins, author of *Confessions of an Economic Hit Man* (2004), whose memoir documents his role in pushing Third World countries into development loans that benefited both the country's plutocrats and American companies that would receive contracts to build dams and other megaprojects.

The Wolf of Wall Street (2013, United States, dir. Martin Scorsese): Despite being fairly funny, Leonardo DiCaprio's portrayal of a ruthless wealthy stockbroker cannot put us penny-ante types at ease, despite the so-called penny stocks that fueled the rise of a broker in the 1990s until his bubble of corruption burst. The film has room for a real shoe designer and salesman (Steve Madden) who helped to rig the bids for his IPO.

Yella (2008, Germany, dir. Christian Petzold): A somewhat complex mixture of realism, suspense, and the (frankly) unexplainable, the film follows the titular woman much put-upon by an abusive boyfriend but who finds a new man and a new goal: outmaneuvering and cheating if necessary all kinds of financiers and bankers. She is a gal from a former East German city who seems to rise, perhaps only symbolically, from the Elbe River to succeed in the former West German capitalist world. Yella is played by the incomparable Nina Hoss of TV's *Homeland* series.

The Yes Men Fix the World (2009, United States, dir. Andy Bichlbaum and Mike Bonanno): A nonfiction screwball comedy about two gonzo political activists—the directors—who, posing as top executives of giant corporations, lie their way into big business conferences and pull off the "world's most outrageous pranks," posing as the alter egos of important people as they expose those who profited from Hurricane Katrina and the environmental disaster in Bhopal, India, among other shocking events.

Zeitgeist: Moving Forward (2011, United States, dir. Peter Joseph): Critiques the monetary/market-based system, offering one of the deepest analyses of the big picture perspective on global economics, as it proposes a *Resource-Based Economy*, that is, a country whose economy depends on its own natural resources, as a logical alternative to the monetary paradigm that currently dominates most financial debate. (See *97% Owned*, above.)

10

The 99 Percent: A Bottom-Up Conclusion—Alt-Labor and Organizing the Unorganized

The Cart (2014, dir. Boo Ji-young), a South Korean film, highlights the worldwide dilemma of the precariat, even when they are fortunate to secure regular if underpaid and part-time work: they are sometimes promised regular full-time work with benefits "soon," but they discover that "soon" turns into "never." In the film, temporary workers at a South Korean big-box supermarket are promised that they will eventually become regular workers with full benefits, as required by South Korean law. Instead, they are fired and replaced with workers from an outsourcing company, a different kind of employer of precariat labor.

The women fight back, organize a union, and go on strike. Their struggle is based on an actual incident that took place in 2007 in the World Cup Stadium store of the Homever brand of the E-Land Chain in Seoul, when the workers remained on strike for 512 days. The workers had the support of the Korean Non-Regular Labor Center, an important resource for the Korean precariat that is not featured in the film.

The leader of the strike in the film is a mother of two who has worked at the supermarket for five years. She is herself surprised that she is able to successfully organize the exploited precariat workers. Culturally specific moments startle viewers beyond South Korea: the management insists that every customer be greeted with a cheery, "Welcome beloved customer." At one point, a worker is forced by her manager to apologize on her knees to a shopper she suspects, accurately it turns out, to be a shoplifter.

The women fight heroically; their battles are brilliantly color-coded: scabs dressed in white and strikers with pink T-shirts battle in the aisles, but in the end only a minority of the strikers is hired back. Korean law at the time protected the company with a double-secret loophole in the law allowing companies to transform "irregular" workers into outsourced workers to subcontractors who are not responsible for benefits or job tenure. As a woman director, fairly rare in South Korean cinema, Boo Ji-young was often asked about how she was drawn to the subject of worker's rights. At first, she thought it was only a Korean or even a woman's issue but as the film played across the world at various festivals, she realized that its positive reception related to its depiction of what has become a virtually universal issue: the exploitation of precariat workers and the growing protests, such as the Occupy movement.

The following year, another underappreciated film, Katharine Round's documentary, *The Divide* (2015, United States/United Kingdom), followed seven people in the United States and the United Kingdom who attempt to navigate the great "divide" that separates the working poor of the precariat on one end of the economic spectrum and the plutocrats and their governmental apologists at the other end. A Walmart worker says she "might be living under a bridge next week," as she is joined by—among others of her class—a caregiver, a Kentucky Fried Chicken worker, and a former alcoholic, all of whom face a precarious economic future in a culture that celebrates the wealthy. But even the fragile "Wall Street casualties" who work so hard on the frontlines of capitalism amid their own uncertain and unforgiving environment get a consolation prize of their own—a therapist who specializes in such Wall Street types.

The list of national and global fiscal crises in the last twenty years underscores this great divide. Among the most prominent financial disasters is the collapse of the energy-trading corporation Enron in 2000; the subprime mortgage crisis of 2000–11; the banking crisis of 2007; and the Lehman Brothers bankruptcy of 2007, which led in part to what is now usually called the Global Financial Crisis of 2008. Many commentators attribute the scale of these crises to the trading of financial instruments created by hedge funds and banks and insured with credit-default swaps.

The list of crises cannot be chronologically crisp because a number of them morphed into each other. Such a list foregrounds the hubris of capitalism and how it rewards (with bonuses and payouts) its leadership even when they make enormous mistakes and miscalculations. In the meantime, workers in general but especially the precariat suffer in terms of job availability, job security, and, of course, declining wages.

Both organized and unorganized resistance against the root causes of the fiscal crises have become major subjects of the cinema of the precariat, especially massive street demonstrations, for example, in reaction to the G-8 Conference in Seattle in 2000, as well as related movements in 2011 such as Occupy Wall Street in New York City and Occupy London that formed at St. Paul's Cathedral. Still another parallel reaction to the great divide has been the rise of quasi-union or alt-labor movements of the precariat, workers whose historical antecedents include the 9to5 Movement for women clerical workers and the grape pickers of California who joined the United Farm Workers (UFW) led by Cesar Chavez.

John Lanchester's analysis in *Whoops! Why Everyone Owes Everyone and No One Can Pay* (2010) of the ongoing mortgage crisis that culminated in the subprime bubble explains why workers in the precariat and others were especially vulnerable. They could obtain a mortgage for the full sale price of a home based on any income (even part-time jobs, for example) without a deposit or credit check. Their utility and rent receipts were sufficient as the mortgage limit was raised (especially in the United States by Frannie Mae and Freddie Mac). When housing values began to plunge, their homes were "under water"—an especially appropriate metaphor for Florida—and they could neither meet the monthly mortgage payments nor sell their house for enough to cover the existing mortgaged amount.

99 Homes (2014, United States, dir. Ramin Bahrani) epitomizes the Florida housing market at its most vulnerable and cut-throat. A skilled construction worker on temporary jobs cannot keep up with payments on his mortgage when his latest home construction job collapses. He and his family (his mother and his son) are evicted and end up in a motel with other refugees from the housing crisis. He turns, however, to the dark side and begins to work for the very real estate agent who evicted him, a man who also runs a number of shady deals with foreclosures and the confiscation of evicted people's property. Business is booming in the eviction business, not to mention in outright fraud. The real estate operator has a simple philosophy: "America does not bail out losers. . . . it is a nation of the rich, for the rich, and by the rich." Most of director Bahrani's films are about the precariat, and he captures here as elsewhere the illusions and reality of working just to keep ahead of the next payment or bill.

If organizing the unorganized into unions was the task of the labor movement in the late nineteenth and twentieth centuries, then the Global Financial Crisis of 2008 consolidated the creation of an even greater and rapidly even more impoverished precariat. This and the other crises have generated many films dissecting the plutocrats and the elite that created and usually profited from these disasters of capitalism in our time. Many of the films about these two top tiers of Standing's pyramid of classes are briefly surveyed in "Fifty Films about Capitalism in the Twenty-First Century" in the previous chapter.

One of the more egregious chapters in capitalist chicanery was the growth and collapse of Enron, the energy and—later—investment corporation, that crashed under the weight of its illegal business ventures. Numerous films about Enron trace the company's rise and fall. I analyzed five of the major films about Enron in *The Cinema of Globalization* and therefore did not include them in the abovementioned list of films. Nonetheless, I will note here the best one, Alex Gibney's *Enron: The Smartest Guys in the Room* (2005, United States), because it highlighted how the wheels of high finance turn quickly and unobtrusively for some before they are revealed to be either jerry-rigged or fraudulent or both.

Enron's symbiotic ties to both auditing companies like Arthur Anderson and Republican politicos like George Bush and Dick Cheney assured its success for some time. Many of Anderson's so-called independent auditors worked on their $58 million Enron account at Enron's Houston headquarters, while Bush and Cheney relied on campaign contributions from the company.

Gibney's *Enron: The Smartest Guys in the Room* traces the energy maneuvers Enron pioneered, such as diverting 3,000 megawatts bound for California through a "narrow" Silver City, Nevada "spigot" that netted them a bonus of $7 million because congestion in delivery resulted in increased payments to the trader. Other California energy maneuvers were also extremely profitable, such as moving energy out of California and then selling it back at higher prices or urging generating plants to shut down for unnecessary maintenance until the price rose.

Although in retrospect they seem to be outrageous shenanigans among these financial behemoths, we must not forget that our era of profits for the rich and austerity for the precariat has corresponded with the decline of traditional union membership for the working class. The cinema of the precariat has followed this decline in traditional unionism and the subsequent rise of quasi-union and other community organizations, especially for the precariat. In a number of cases, these organizations have come into existence specifically as a response and protest of the 99 percent, the vast majority of working- and middle-class people, to the 1 percent elite and fabulously wealthy. Here's what the latter read in 2006 in the Citigroup's special report on global markets: "Time to re-commit to plutonomy stocks—binge on bling.... What could go wrong? Beyond war, inflation, the end of technology/productivity wave, and financial collapse, we think the most potent and short-term threat would be societies demanding a more 'equitable' share of the wealth." Citigroup has long ago removed this statement from its website.

In the United States, a number of these quasi-union movements or alt-labor as they are sometimes called have had some successes organizing segments of the precariat. Their model was primarily the UFW in the 1960s under Cesar Chavez's leadership during the California Grape Boycott of 1975. By the end of the 1970s its membership was about 40,000, although growers almost always refused to negotiate with the UFW. (See Chapter 3 for films about the UFW.)

Another historical model for precariat organizing, this time among female office workers, was the 9to5 Movement launched in 1973 by Boston clerical workers who were fed up with discriminatory pay scales, sexual harassment, and lack of sick leave, among other grievances. Their movement has been chronicled by Julia Reichert, the director of *Union Maids* (1976, United States) and *Seeing Red* (1983, United States), in *Raises Not Roses: The 9to5 Movement* (2019, United States), illuminating a relatively little-known organizing drive by workers in Boston in the early 1970s.

The movement's tagline of 9to5 is already familiar from the famous Jane Fonda film, *Nine to Five* (1980, United States, dir. Colin Higgins), a very successful comedy costarring Dolly Parton and Lily Tomlin that exposes male chauvinism on the job. It was in fact inspired by Boston's 9to5 Movement or the National Association of Working Women, cofounded by Ellen Cassedy and Karen Nussbaum, the latter the executive director of the organization from 1973 to 1993, whose manifesto included helping "those stuck in the 'white collar ghetto'" by urging them to "advocate for themselves, first in Boston, but later across the country" (Figure 10.1).

In 1981, 9to5 started the nationwide union for clericals, a growing segment of the female precariat, through SEIU (Service Employees International Union), known as District 925. 9to5 itself remained functional so that the dual organizations pursued different but related goals. District 925 was a female-led union, therefore, and also brought in many people of color. Before pursuing union organizing, 9to5 had used the legal system, demonstrations/protests, and public shaming media events. Yet even after the development of their union, 9to5 kept pursuing these tactics that were more successful with private-sector employers, while District 925 could pursue public sector employers less able to bend labor laws to their liking. Lane Windham argues that this structure was the forerunner of contemporary alt-labor—that is, "workers' centers, associations, and campaigns that seek to build power outside the collective bargaining paradigm."

The film uses interviews with Karen Nussbaum and other activists, as well accessing videos, photographs, cartoons, and other archival material to bring the movement to life.

Figure 10.1 Karen Nussbaum from *Raises Not Roses: The Story of 9to5*. Courtesy Julia Reichert.

One of the gems featured was a poster 9to5 distributed to "Women in Insurance," subtitled an "explosive situation." The poster's graphic shows a high-heel platform shoe with a stick of dynamite tucked into it. Similarly, a carton in their newsletter featured a woman pouring an entire pot of coffee on a man's head: "No, sir, I don't mind pouring coffee." The filmmakers also filmed some of the fortieth anniversary celebrations for the organization.

The financial crises have also directly influenced films often based on street demonstrations, factory and workplace confrontations, and organizing the unorganized and even those thought to be unorganizable. The demos that preceded—and perhaps may even be said to have prepped—the Occupy movement are especially well represented in guerrilla filmmaking and one-off events, many of which are experimental, using collective, not individual, directors, and mixing fictional/staged sequences among the "reality" sequences.

Rise Like Lions: Occupy Wall Street and the Seeds of Revolution (2005, United States, dir. Scott Noble) is a compilation documentary, its title taken from the last lines of Percy Bysshe Shelley's classic poem *The Masque of Anarchy* (1819), written in immediate response to the slaughter of workers and their families at the Peterloo Massacre in 1819, the peaceful rally by the Hanoverian precariat of weavers and mill operatives in Manchester for working-class parliamentary representation:

> Rise like lions after slumber
> In unvanquishable number!
> Shake your chains to earth like dew
> Which in sleep had fallen on you.
> Ye are many, they are few.

The film has a number of interviews with well-known figures, like the author Naomi Klein (*Shock Doctrine*, 2007), as well as anonymous demonstrators and individuals encamped at Wall Street or what Klein calls the "citadel of abundance," or as was the case in London, at St. Paul's Cathedral, where the protestors camped because they were forbidden access to the nearby London Stock Exchange. Also included are sequences from mainstream media outlets ridiculing the protestors, even though the demonstrations spread throughout the United States and the world, with an estimate from the British newspaper *The Guardian* in 2011 of similar organizations and demonstrations in 951 cities in eighty-two countries.

The film was inspired—and concluded—by two famous sequences that had already been circulated around the world of two individuals resisting the power of the state to squash resistance: a Palestinian girl confronts Israeli soldiers who were firing at Palestinian demonstrators and the Tank Man who stepped in front of a column of tanks entering Tiananmen Square to put down Chinese student pro-democracy demonstrators in 1989 just before hundreds, possibly thousands, of students and civilians were killed.

In other films, the participants in the anti-globalization demos usually represent a united front of the organized (trade unionists, middle-class political activists, etc.), the precariat (the unemployed, street people, anarchists, etc.), and perhaps what might be called transitional factions (students, political activists, organizers from mainstream parties, etc.). Most of the documentaries stress militancy, the cohesiveness of the demonstrators, and violent clashes with the police, but one of the more authoritative recent documentaries, *The Summit* (2011, Italy, dir. by Franco Fracassi and Massimo Lauria), takes advantage of the latest research into the frightening preparations for the anti-globalization demonstrations at the Genoa G-8 Summit in 2001, symbolically led by the almost universally detested prime minister Sylvia Berlusconi. It also delves into the machinations of the Black Block, the secretive anarchistic faction of activists hell-bent on originating as much mayhem as they could. That group was filmed by a collective of numerous documentary filmmakers, from whose ranks *Black Block* (2011, Italy, dir. Carlo A. Bachschmidt), is typical, in which both sides display extraordinary nastiness, with the carabinieri ganging up on the protestors by kicking and beating them with truncheons, and the protestors announcing that they did not come to protest but to destroy "corporate property," as they burn paddy wagons and shop windows and hurl stones and flaming missiles at the police.

Black Block parallels the explicit revelations of another, oddly titled, feature film, *Diaz: Don't Clean Up the Blood* (2012, Italy, dir. Daniele Vicari), that the American *Variety* reviewer said "breaks the record for the most truncheon beatings in one movie." The first part of the film's title refers to the name of a school that was a legal crash-pad site; the second part echoes the poster of a protestor who wanted the evidence of the police brutality to be seen by all. Plus, the film's producers bragged that more than thirteen gallons of blood were used during the filming.

Although the G-8 in 2001 took place in Genoa and police truncheon beatings of protestors were universally publicized, both earlier feature and documentary films about anti-globalization demonstrations in Italy had been made even before the Genoa events. Cynics on the North American side of the ocean became obsessed with how much sex the demonstrators seem to enjoy during those stressful times. Indeed, the *Variety* reviewer called *Now or Never* (2003, Italy, dir. Lucio Pellegrini) "sincere, if not much more politically sophisticated than a Benetton ad," although his judgment clouds over when he talks about the lead, a physics major at the Normale in Pisa, who seems more interested in sleeping with women than discussing their politics. But it is actually the women in the film who are way more aggressive, and, in fact, our hero turns them down a number of times—he is studying for exams—until the penultimate scene in the film.

This film explicitly references *Jules and Jim* (1962, France), Francois Truffault's New Wave classic of a love triangle among two men and a woman, but when the film gets down to radical protests, it delivers the goods: after all, one of them says, "It's now or never." One of their appealing antics included dropping a long banner from the Leaning Tower of Pisa that says, "The town is straight / The world is crooked." In keeping with contemporary practice in almost all of the films about the anti-globalization demos, the police attacks on the students are especially brutal, but ironically it is David's apolitical roommate who is the one hurt, accidentally stabbed in a melee with right-wing students.

American protest films usually center on the protests against the World Trade Organization at its Seattle meeting in 1999. The documentary *This Is What Democracy Looks Like* (2000, United States, dir. Jill Friedberg and Rick Rowley) is a smoother, somewhat more coherent and marginally more politically explicit film than *Showdown in Seattle: Five Days That Shook the World* (1999, United States, prod. Paper Tiger TV), although both films share the footage shot by over a hundred videographers present during the events.

This Is What Democracy Looks Like has better graphics, a strong sound track by Rage against the Machine and Anne Feeney, and celebrity narrators such as Susan Sarandon. This compilation film has a raw energy that comes from its only lightly edited footage shot in the midst of quite violent demonstrations; it also intercuts a revealing interview with the craftsman who creates the wooden police batons with footage of police abusing protestors with them.

What Friedberg and Rowley bring to their film is a better feel for the complexity of the coalition of students, environmentalists (the "turtles"), anti-globalization activists, and trade unionists that were represented at the rallies and street demos. Some of the activists felt that the AFL-CIO pointedly avoided the more aggressive protest zones, even if some of their members—the United Steelworkers, for example—wanted to mix it up with the best of the demonstrators.

Certainly, the film offers not only the excitement of those days in November when the delegates to the WTO summit could not reach their meetings but also some of the reasons for the protest, such as labor or environmental regulations that the WTO ruled were a barrier to trade and not permissible.

The somewhat mysterious Guerrillavison, an activist and no doubt anarchist collective of filmmakers, has taken the participatory politics of other anti-globalization filmmaking groups a step further. One of the most famous of the group's work is *Showdown in Seattle: Five Days That Shook the WTO*, a five-part day-by-day video recording of the protests against the Seattle meeting of the WTO. At least seven other groups filmed the protests and pooled their footage daily, usually uploading the resultant "guerrilla" news to cable channels.

Guerillavision also produced *Crowd Bites Wolf* (2000, United States and United Kingdom), its more purely cinematic piece of work. On one level, the "crowd" is simply the mass of demonstrators in Prague protesting the IMF-World Bank 2000 summit, while the "wolf" is the then World Bank president, James Wolfensohn. Lovers of cosmic justice realize that the film did not have to be retitled in 2005 when Paul Wolfowitz followed his brother wolf as president.

What sets *Crowd Bites Wolf* aside from most protest documentaries is that it is simultaneous a documentary of the events and a semi-staged intervention in the activities in Prague by what seems to be a roving journalist, who interviews demonstrators, attends meetings, and narrates the clashes as they unfold. He is also, it appears, a clandestine agent, receiving important memos and direction at café "drops" from mysterious strangers, information vital to the success of the demos that he dutifully passes along. A full range of digital media is also part of the film itself, so we see footage from handheld devices as well as surveillance cameras.

A film like *Crowd Bites Wolf* has more in common with the activists of the San Precario movement in Italy or the installation films of Oliver Ressler. In effect, all of these activists follow Guy Debord, whose ideas of the "society of spectacle" grew out of the worldwide anti–Vietnam War protests during the 1960s and 1970s. Debord defined the spectacle as the result of social imaging—advertising on the capitalist side, for example, but its countermovement on the protestors' side are street demonstrations, which in part explains installation artists like Barbara Kruger and Oliver Ressler using advertising banners with anarchistic or subversive messages.

San Precario was one of those protestors' images: San Precario is a faux saint, characteristic of Italian popular culture obsessed with "real" saints, such as St. Joseph, the Virgin Mary's husband, the patron saint of carpentry. San Precario became the patron saint of the precariat, with no fixed gender, represented in statues, processions, demonstrations, and even saint cards. A holiday in San Precario's name was celebrated on February 29, Leap Year day, which had no official saint to celebrate and quixotically only appears once every four years. San Precario began to appear on saint's cards, banners, and other media in 2004, the work of the Chain Store Workers who used it in a Milanese supermarket protest, when a "miracle" occurred: the store reduced the cost of all its products (Mattoni and Doerr). San Precario was therefore the epitome of—and the people's hero of—the "society of spectacle." To direct a "prayer" toward San Precario is always to invoke the precariat (Figure 10.2):

> Give us paid leave, and pension contributions,
> Income and free services,

Figure 10.2 Banner of San Precario from Milan. Designed by Chain Store Workers and Chris Woods. Creative Commons License.

> Keep us from being fired,
> San Precario, defend us from the bottom of the network,
> Pray for us temporary and cognitive workers. (van der Linden)

When many organizations that support the rights of workers and the need for the precariat to organize turned to electoral politics and local organizing since these major demonstrations, the surprising victory of a Republican right-winger in 2010—Governor Scott Walker—in the usually reliable progressive, even formerly radical Wisconsin, generated a grassroots movement there that mirrored others across the nation. Sam Mayfield, a filmmaker whose *Silenced Voices* (2013, United States) was a documentary about a young migrant worker at a Vermont dairy farm whose body was returned to Mexico for burial, made *Wisconsin Rising* (2014, United States), in which she pursued two related stories—

the protests at the state capitol against the governor's bill to deprive state and local employees of their collective bargaining rights and interviews with workers whose incomes were threatened by anti-union legislation. A janitor spoke of his wages being cut from $15 to $12, while a schoolteacher noted that her salary could barely support the gas bill for her commute to work. The filmmaker relied on a social media platform, Kickstarter, to fund her film instead of the usual foundation grants documentary filmmakers often turn to for funding.

The demonstrations against Walker's right-wing legislation were one of the spin-offs of the Occupy Movement in Wisconsin, turning into one of the largest mass mobilization of unionized and unorganized workers in the United States. Walker's Budget Repair Bill also cut $900 million from the education budget and began to reverse many of the classic gains won in Wisconsin and elsewhere during the radical workers' movements of the 1930s. It was a deliberate attempt to turn unionized and otherwise solid working-class jobs held by teachers and other professionals into a new precariat, without health benefits, collective bargaining, or even a forty-hour work week. Because of the preliminary physical attacks on public employees when their massive numbers besieged the state capitol before the bill could be passed, even policemen and firemen joined the protests and the former made it clear they would not arrest demonstrators.

Wisconsin Rising captures the thousands of demonstrators—estimated at 140,000 at the height of the protests—that surrounded the state capital building. The Democratic and liberal minority were literally locked out of the debating chamber where Walker and the Republicans passed the bill at night. Walker called the demonstrators out-of-state agitators, allegedly proven when right-wing supporters fed a fake video to the media. The video showed demonstrators fighting—each other? provocateurs?—in front of a row of *palm* trees. There are no palm trees in Madison, Wisconsin. And although Scott Walker managed to escape with his political career intact by turning back a recall vote, the film concludes with demonstrators clearly ready to fight another day. (That day did come when Walker lost his reelection for governor in 2017.)

The Occupy Wall Street and other political resistance movements generated both mainstream and alternative media to cover similar massive demonstrations worldwide. These films followed an anti-elitist, sometimes anarchistic, spirit involving numerous groups and participants but no or very few identified leaders.

Protests across the world often reflected unresolved national issues rather than (only) financial collapse, even if the struggles might seem to outsiders to be related. In the Egyptian *Clash* (2016, Egypt/France, dir. Mohamed Diad), street people, protestors, workers from different levels of Egyptian society (nurses, journalists), and the precariat were all swept up in a startling decision of the Egyptian military and the police to round up whatever demonstrators they could most easily snare during the protests over their ouster of the Muslim Brotherhood president, Mohamed Morsi, in 2012, who in turn had helped to oust President Hosni Mubarak the year before. A standard paddy wagon of 8 square meters held Muslim Brotherhood members, pro-military demonstrators, and seemingly neutral bystanders. Unfortunately, the incarcerated began fighting each other, only occasionally helping each other as they coped with the heat, lack of drinking water, tear gas, and water cannons, all used to subdue them even further. The result was just "one such day" of fighting in the streets, but for these internees it was hell. Often filmed during riots of all kinds on the Egyptian streets, the viewer sees that this random mixture of politically and religiously diverse group of detainees is doomed, since rock-throwing crowds, fueled by irrational anger, often attacked both police and prisoners alike.

The direction of the cinema of the precariat is difficult to predict. Feature films still exist, documentaries of different kinds continue to be made, and spontaneous agitprop and street-demo-based filmmaking have steadily monitored changes in labor organizing as it follows alt-labor and other worker organizations.

But invisibility is always a danger for the precariat. The revealing title of *The Nothing Factory* (2017, Portugal, dir. Pedro Pinho) points to the invisible workers of this Portuguese film that mimics the essentially the same dilemma as the Belgian film *Two Days, One Night*, directed by the Dardenne brothers (see Introduction), when a company surreptitiously sets worker against worker during a downsizing to increase profits. In this film, the workers do not realize that they have joined the precariat, since their factory has now become nothing. The Nothing Factory was once the home of the Otis Elevator Company in Lisbon, but the company is being dismantled as the workers—mostly played by actual factory workers—contemplate occupying the factory in protest. They are actually doing nothing but argue. A filmmaker—but not the director *of this film*—is thinking about making his film about this possible occupation, so he engages the workers in more discussions. In Portugal's austerity period, factory closing and unemployment were rampant, with 30 percent rate of unemployment among younger workers. The new director complains that he cannot film workers doing *nothing*. Despite the surreal arrival of a flock of ostriches while one group of workers decides to stage a musical, one of the workers leaves to visit his father, an old lefty, who digs up his secret arsenal of weapons and urges his son to lead an armed uprising against the capitalists. Back at the factory, however, the workers do nothing.

In a similar Swedish film, *Songs from the Second Floor* (2000, dir. Roy Andersson), one of the few ways the precariat as well as the traditional proletariat can protect themselves from a hostile society is—paradoxically—by attempting invisibility. The owner of a store downsizes his workforce and torches his own store for the insurance money or simply perhaps because all the other businesses in the film are failing. While most of the workers are content with doing nothing, a few aberrant plotlines intrude: one man decides to sell crucifixes (unsuccessfully, as he notes that you can't make money from a crucified loser), while both a girl and an immigrant randomly fall afoul of anonymous mobs. Advice on how to repair this capitalist hell is not always helpful—poet Caesar Valejo is quoted: "Beloved be the one who sits down." He adds, "Beloved be . . . the one who goes . . . to the movies." Does he mean this one?

Both *The Nothing Factory* and *Songs from the Second Floor* present violence in the workplace as either comic or absurd. But the violence in an unusual Russian feature film, *The Factory* (2018, Russia, dir. Yury Bykov), is almost a throwback to the great sit-down strikes and mass marches of the 1930s when American and other workers were battling for union recognition. This film takes its scenario out of the horrors of Camden, Youngstown, Detroit, and Flint, where factories are abandoned by corporations and workers are let go with sometimes less than a day's notice and no promise of back pay. The products—steel somethings—and location of this factory are deliberately vague, since the point of the film is not what the workers are making or where they are making them but how they can get even with their boss who clearly is not going to give them their much-overdue back pay. Although their decision to kidnap their boss, take over the factory, and confront the state's firepower is quixotic, given the terms of the film, it is understandable.

The avant-garde artists who did installations with or without films, often without governmental permission, were often closer in spirit to the Portuguese Nothing Factory or the Swedish store's burning "second floor" than a Russian factory seizure. Robert Smithson, one of the most celebrated sculptors and installation artists, had included either still photos or moving image footage of abandoned industrial sites but almost never workers, current or otherwise. His most famous piece, *Spiral Jetty,* a sculptural monument created in the Great

Salt Lake, for which he also made a film of the same title (1970, United States), includes moving equipment and even himself but no (visible) workers.

A number of the new cadre of installation artists in Europe especially became committed to the 99 percent, the precariat and the proletariat, and often continued the sharp critique of capitalism characteristic of a significant number of the films highlighted in the previous chapter. Of the three installation artists who have foregrounded the precariat and other workers in their work—Oliver Ressler of Austria, Aernout Mik of the Netherlands, and Andrei Ujica of Romania—there is no question that Oliver Ressler is the leading filmmaker and installation artist, with over 500 solo or joint ventures in film and artistic installations.

The work of Aernout Mik of the Netherlands, however, consistently comes close to Ressler's successful visual analyses in four of Mik's installation films—*Middlemen* (2001, Netherlands), *Osmosis and Excess* (2005, Netherlands), *Training Ground* (2006, Netherlands), and *Vacuum Room* (2005, Netherlands). The "middlemen" in the first film are stock-exchange types, acting out the collapse of an unnamed exchange in an unnamed country. Mik's tableau uses futurist Paul Virilio's ironic deployment of the word "accident," that which "is what remains unexpected, truly surprising, the unknown quantity in a totally discovered planetary habitat," such as the Bhopal methyl isocyanate gas leak in India in 1984, the Chernobyl nuclear plant disaster in 1986, or the lesser-known Icmesa dioxin gas leak in Italy in 1976, all of which are also featured in Andrei Ujica's structuralist film installation *Unknown Quantity* (2003, France). The death and injury toll of the precariat and other workers in the surrounding neighborhoods in all of these "accidents" was staggering. (See also the discussion of "acts of God" in Chapter 3.)

Mik's film was originally part of Virilio's signature exhibition, *The Museum of Accidents*, mounted in Paris and New York City in 2002–03 but exhibited afterward throughout the world. Taken together, the films in the exhibit point to technology and global communications as accidents waiting to happen, not only a financial crisis as in *Middlemen* but also nuclear disasters like Chernobyl or terrorist events like 9/11. All three installation artists epitomize Paul Virilio's favorite quotation from Hannah Arendt, "Progress and catastrophe are the opposite faces of the same coin" (Virilio), featured in his Museum of Accidents.

In Mik's second (and perhaps best) installation film, *Osmosis and Excess*, traditional narration, characterization, and, to a certain extent, plot have all been jettisoned in favor of spectacles at two locations in Tijuana, Mexico. Unlike

Middlemen, however, a political and/or cultural critique is implied rather than dramatized. Mik's camera pans a remarkable valley of thousands of abandoned cars, offering the paradoxical beauty of the castoffs of industrial society combined with a natural setting, in effect an edge city of automobiles without drivers. To offset all this heavy metal, small herds of cows and goats wander across our field of vision, munching on the grasslands surrounding the cars. On another slope, we see a large band of schoolchildren playing with a piñata.

Mik alternates this mixture of found and contrived tableaus with shots of what looks like a mega-discount drug store. White-coated salesmen stand about, somewhat dwarfed by the huge displays of drugs and packaged goods for sale. However, subsequent shots reveal that gradually the entire floor is covered in several inches of mud, lapping at the shelves and displays.

The premise of the two locations—and the origins of the title—is simply this: Used American cars are shipped to Mexico to be stripped of still functioning parts, while Americans cross into Tijuana to buy prescription drugs (amoxicillin and Zantac are featured, among many others) that are either cheaper in Mexico or simply unavailable back home, or similar drugs are smuggled to the United States. When border crossings make money, the film suggests, there is no question of illegal immigrants.

In the third installation, *Training Ground*, Mik opens his film of epidemic cinema with a truck smuggling immigrants that is soon intercepted by authorities at a truck stop in Germany. We soon realize that this is a scripted film, as the guards catch the virus of an African immigrant having a seizure and in effect become prisoners in a compound themselves. In a fourth installation film, *Vacuum Room*, Middle Eastern detainees in a courtroom are surrounded by officials having the time of their lives—laughing, waving sheets of paper, and cheering. The tables soon turn as the detainees gradually take control: they lift their shirts above their faces so that they cannot be identified and crush eggs on bronze sculptures of the court officials.

Most directors would find detention centers, kangaroo courts, and stock exchanges as proof of a repressive capitalist society. Mik pushes the drama of a European-wide, if not worldwide, repressive system that creates a dystopian society for all. Immigrants, the precariat, even innocent children, are all potentially caught in the process of osmosis and excess—reconditioning machines and tolerating addiction—as proof of the failure of capitalism.

Although only Ujica and Ressler have shared an exhibition, their worldviews—with Mik—were in sync with the leading theorist of catastrophe and critic of capitalist hegemony, Paul Virilio. Ujica created the film installation that accompanied Virilio's signature exhibition in Paris titled *Unknown Quantity*, also the title of Ujica's film, but in France the title of both was *Ce qui arrive . . .* or "What Happens . . ." In the film, Virilio discusses catastrophes—such as the well-known Union Carbide dioxin spill in Bhopal, India, and the lesser-known dioxin gas leak in the Icmesa Factory in Sevesco, Italy, in 1976—with Svetlana Aleksievich the Nobel Prize–winning chronicler of the survivors of Chernobyl nuclear plant disaster. Virlio speaks of the Museum of Accidents, the collective destructive power of the globalized multinational corporations that avoid safe monitoring of their toxic factories and the responsibilities for their human-made catastrophes. For Virilio, the determining fact was announced by a Swiss insurance company: in the 1990s human-made accidents exceeded natural catastrophes by a ratio of seven to one.

Juan Antonio Alvarez Reyes summed up Ressler's career in *Oliver Ressler: Cartographies of Protest* (2015): "For an artist far removed from the art market and whose work eludes art galleries, the long list of important, internationally situated exhibition locations that have shown his work is astonishing and impressive." Like the activists of the San Precario "movement" in Italy, Ressler's work is a continuous application of the "society of spectacle," bringing the precariat both in and out of the galleries through activism and filmmaking. At the supermarkets of Milan, San Precario appears dressed as a worker from the store; in a Ressler installation film, actors become policemen and financial center functionaries.

Ressler is an Austrian installation artist with an international reputation as a political deconstructionist who simultaneously highlights the contradictions in international capitalism and confronts its critics. He is a prolific exhibitor throughout the world of anti-globalization films, art installations with and without films, and manipulated artifacts. The latter include giant posters, protest signs, and banners reminiscent of Barbara Kruger, feminist artist and activist, almost all of which track what might be called the politically active wing of and for the precariat. In addition to his website (www.ressler.at) that documents his career in detail, he has published *It's the Political Economy, Stupid* (2013) with Gregory Sholette, a guide to "the global financial crisis in art and theory" that illustrates not only his own perspective but also that of his confederates in what is often a clash between those who "binge on bling" and the rebels in the streets.

Ressler's style is confrontational, his working methods collaborative. He has been a prolific artistic force in the anti-globalization movement since his first films and installations appeared almost twenty years ago. He believes in taking sides: "I usually position myself on one side of conflicting parties, and don't take the convenient position of the neutral observer." His hope, he states in *Fly Democracy* (2007, Austria), is "that from time to time art still has the capacity to intervene directly in political debates."

One of his earliest interventions was *Disobeddienti!* (2002, Austria), perhaps his best introduction to anti-globalization demonstrators, the title reflecting the new name adopted by the "white-clad Italian activists" (the *Tute Bianchi*) who believe in creating "spectacles" rather than simply demos. They wear padded overalls and resemble Michelin Tire men run amok. One of their early successes in nonviolent spectacles was their "padded block" of 10,000 protesters moving against the police at the G-8 conference in Genoa in 2001. Ressler includes in his film his interviews with Tute Bianchi activists, who offer their alternatives to the old protest movement they felt was ineffectual.

Some viewers have found this film's activists less convincing than others Ressler has followed and interviewed in later films. Their "pronouncements," Mark and Andrew Grossman concluded, "sound less like the inspiration of a newly-emerging, locally-driven, cooperative multitude than they do the echo of the old Italian Communist Party freshened with the leafy utopianism of the radical Greens." Ressler himself recognized that he has been accused of a tendency to "heroize" the Tute Bianchi because of their outlandish appearance.

Ressler was once himself caught in a police "trap" of demonstrators against the World Economic Forum in Salzburg in 2001, 1 of 919 people police encircled: he filmed the scene for his film, *This Is What Democracy Looks Like* (2002, Austria). He interviewed six of his fellow "trapees," eliciting their perspectives on protesting *Die Diktatur der Eurokraten* or the "dictatorship" of the Eurozone globalizers, according to the German magazine *Der Spiegel*.

One of Ressler's early collaborations with Dario Azzellini, *Five Factories— Worker Control Venezuela* (2006, Austria and Venezuela), may seem in retrospect to celebrate Hugo Chavez too uncritically, but the experiments in coownership between businesses and workers developed in this film during the years of Chavez's socialist policies did indeed seem to be working at least in the short run and were adopted by large numbers of his followers. He had received majority support for his workers' control politics through the fourteen years of his presidency until his death in 2013 in Cuba.

The five factories made or transformed aluminum, paper, cocoa, tomato sauce, and cotton. All were important elements in the Venezuelan economy, essential for maintaining employment among workers whose jobs helped them rise out of the precariat. Unemployment in Venezuela averaged 10 percent in the Chavez years, with a high of 21 percent in 2003 and a low of 5 percent in 2014 when he died. By 2018, it had risen to a spectacular 30 percent. In 2017 *CNN Money* nevertheless proclaimed, "About the only thing Venezuela has in abundance is chaos."

Ressler has documented, however, some unusual successes in worker management, a recurrent theme in his films. In *Occupy, Resist, Produce: Scop Ti* (2018, Austria), Ressler and co-filmmaker Dario Azzellini follow the history of a Lipton Tea/Unilever production factory, Scop Ti, near Marseille, France, that had specialized in producing black tea for 120 years. When Unilever decided to close the plant and move its machines to Poland, Scop Ti's CGT (Confédération Générale du Travail) workers unanimously voted to occupy the factory and remained in possession of the facility for three years, retaining almost half the workforce in active protest. With public support and a few anti-company judicial decisions, forty-two of the remaining workers created a new organic tea production company with worker-centered management principles. Ressler reflected on how difficult it is to keep "large-scale industrial production" going in the context of organic food production, using local and regional suppliers, and principles of worker management.

Similarly, Ressler has used the rectangular shape of a poster or banner or billboard to mimic his cinematic "frames," thus establishing a continuity between projected images and constructed ones. *Boom!* (2001–6, Austria), made in collaboration with David Thorne, a multisite stream of banners, posters, and other installations, takes its title from economist Joseph Schumpeter's formulation of the "boom-bust" cycle of modern capitalism, the process Schumpeter categorizes as "creative destruction." The title also puns on the idea of political and economic protestors "exploding" the myths of capitalism and globalization. One of its American installations was a window and banner with the tag "terror.gov" at a Los Angeles gallery in 2003, attempting to expose the governmental drive to freeze dissent. The banner read, in part, "If only people would stay locked into the threat matrix and never stop to consider the fact that that the scenario in which terror is met with terror at every front is dangerously and some might say deliriously circular."

Ressler's films have a thematic arc that moves from protest movement to the exposure of the ruling class. His generic title for a number of these films/installations is *After the Crisis Is Before the Crisis*, a slogan denoting his major installations of videos, wall texts, and photos criticizing the Global Financial Crisis of 2008.

One of these characteristic installations, *Too Big to Fail!* (2011, Austria), featured a giant poster with the media catchphrase "too big to fail," referring to the tendency during the Global Financial Crisis of most governments to bail out any of a number of failing banks or financial institutions because too massive a disturbance in their business as usual would impact the average small investor or even a pensioner too seriously. The slogan is superimposed on a massive photograph of protestors at one of the many worldwide protests in March 2009, whose rallying cry was, "We will not pay for your crisis!" Also "too big to fail," the installation argues, is the growing protest movement that is attempting to form coalitions of the unemployed, the barely employed precariat, and the working class.

Two related projects in this same period rely also on the unintentional ironies of ruling-class activities. In the film *Robbery* (2013, Austria), demonstrators looting shops during the London riots, part of the worldwide Occupy protests, in August 2011, are contrasted with the legal "robbery" when the government bailed out the banks in the United States, the United Kingdom, and other countries. In a street installation the same year, *Resist to Exist* (2011, Denmark), at a Copenhagen storage facility for containerized shipping of the massive Danish Maersk Group, Ressler staged what appears to be the dismantling of a fence of the facility near the company's container storage yard, but the fence is reconceived for social use by becoming the site of a barbecue used to cook food for homeless people and demonstrators.

Ressler's film *The Plundering* (2013, Austria), although focused on only one former Soviet satellite country, Georgia, is nonetheless the perfect example of how privatization disables a country's economy and creates a class of precarious workers. Georgia was ranked ninth among 185 states in the World Bank index of the "Ease of Doing Business," that is, the privatization of public property and the subsequent sale of formerly state-owned enterprises for sale mostly to foreign investors.

The film focuses on four "cases of aggressive, state-property privatization policies" that Ressler situates in the capitol city Tbilisi. Both the water system and the popular public food market were sold to investors, but public resistance to other proposals prevented the attempted sell-off of the National Scientific Library and the transformation of historical Gudiashvili Square into a shopping mall. Most of the purchasers operated, despite targeting the cultural and business sites in Georgia, as "offshore" entities, the usual means of avoiding taxes and hiding profits for transnational corporations.

The film collaboration titled *The Bull Laid Bare* (2012, Austria and Australia) included Australian artist and activist Zanny Begg's political interpretation of the legendary African American Billie Holiday's song, "God Bless the Child" (1941), to underscore the "budget and public debt" crises with her stirring lyrics. God will bless the child "that's got his own," she sang, since "the strong gets more" while "empty pockets don't ever make the grade."

Besides the themes of worker management and the demonstrations of anarchists and street people of the precariat, Ressler has also been keen to expose the intersection of the state police apparatus and financial power centers. His photo exhibition, *We Have a Situation Here* (2011, Austria), shows heaps of actors portraying Wall Street operatives, the police, and soldiers, all collapsed like puppets abandoned, as he pointed out, by Adam Smith's "invisible hand": their images resemble stills from a postapocalyptic film (Figure 10.3).

Perhaps the "invisible hand" of capitalism has been one of the causes of the precariat's invisibility. For those who have eyes to see, the precariat is hardly invisible, of course, but the films in the list in the previous chapter—Fifty Films about Capitalism in the Twenty-First Century—not only do not mention the precariat by name; they rarely even accept the precariat as a concept.

Figure 10.3 Installation by Oliver Ressler in *We Have a Situation Here*. Creative Commons License.

Let us conclude with two films, one representing the 1 percent, and the other the 99 percent. The latter, *The Corporate Coup d'Etat* (2019, Canada/United States, dir. Fred Peabody), was a shaky candidate for Chapter 9, but I included it, perhaps ironically, because it never mentions capitalism. Its primary premise is that the United States is now a corporate state, modeled closely on Italian fascist dictator Mussolini's ideas, really his practice, in which the heads of corporations run the government as well. In Trump's America, virtually every important appointment in the government has been the CEO of a corporation or business. The film's executive producer, Jeff Cohen, the founder of FAIR (Fairness and Accuracy in Reporting), summarizes the corporate state as "the near total integration of corporate elites into the state, whereby it acts as an instrument of private profit and minority rule, while shrinking public participation" (Meyer).

The director, Fred Peabody, visually recreates the corporate critique of *The Unconscious Civilization* (1995), written by Canadian philosopher John Ralston Saul. The essays and reportage of another writer, Chris Hedges, who has recently published *Days of Destruction, Days of Revolt* (2012), appears often in the film. Hedges and his coauthor Joe Sacco (the book's illustrator and graphic artist) visit four American cities of the precariat—Camden (New Jersey), Pine Ridge (South Dakota), Welch (West Virginia), Immokalee (Florida)—and also Manhattan (Occupy Wall Street). The first four are what Hedges calls "sacrifice zones"—a revealing description: the filmmakers add Youngstown (Ohio) as the essential visual framework of the film, because these cities have literally been destroyed, industrial and housing stock alike, and have become monuments of corporate deindustrialization and neglect. There are literally only two glimmers of cinematic hope in this pessimistic vision of a benighted America: in Camden, a homeless woman helps her tent city neighbors with food whenever she can. And throughout the film we see the glorious migration of the monarch butterfly from Canada to Mexico, crossing the United States in both directions, possible only because they pass through three generations of butterflies, a symbol of species resilience the filmmaker wishes human beings could discover before it is too late. We should be that lucky.

The final film for the 1 percent is *Eat Sleep Die* (2012, Sweden, dir. Gabriela Pichler), featuring one of the more gentle and unassuming souls of the precariat, Rasa, a Serbian immigrant who moved to Sweden with her father when she was an infant. She is still another virtually invisible worker in a vegetable packaging factory but seemingly at home and very comfortable with her mostly immigrant fellow workers and some local native Swedish ones. She supports her father financially and domestically, especially with his health problems. Her workplace mates are multinational and supportive, who come alive when their own culture emerges musically. At one point, a Thai woman who processes bunches of parsley sings a Thai song. Serbian guests sing a triste song for Rasa's birthday party.

But the unforeseen happens with a vengeance. She is laid off, despite being the fastest packer, and her father, despite some serious health problems, no longer can or wants to be supported by her. He leaves for Norway in pursuit of work. Some of the workers who are laid off blame other, "new," immigrants for their plight: it's the Iraqis' fault, they say. Rasa herself is keen to point out that although she has a Muslim name she is not an Arab. She scores a dubious job selling fire extinguishers but promptly loses it because she lied about having a driver's license.

We obviously want much more than *Eat Sleep Die* for Rasa and all her precariat brothers and sisters. The 300 films in this book demonstrate conclusively how necessary it is for all of them to have job security, health protection, and a decent income. And the fifty films in the previous chapter on the 1 percent demonstrate how difficult it has been—and will continue to be—for the precariat to achieve those basic human rights.

Bibliography

Akudinobi, Jude G. "Nationalism, African Cinema, and Frames of Scrutiny," *Research in African Literatures*, 32 (3), 2001: 123–42.

Alderman, Liz. "Portugal Dared to Cast Aside Austerity. It's Having a Major Revival," *New York Times*, July 23, 2018. Accessed July 23, 2018. https://www.nytimes.com/2018/07/22/business/portugal-economy-austerity.html.

Alderman, Naomi. "*Oligarchy*: A Game with a Message," *Guardian*, November 25, 2008. Accessed March 3, 2019. https://www.theguardian.com/technology/2008/nov/25/games-oiligarchy.

Aldiss, Brian. *Earthworks*. London: Faber, 1965.

Alexievich, Svetlana. *Voices from Chernobyl*. Trans. Keith Gessen. London: Dalkey Archive Press, 2005.

Anderson, Henry P. *The Bracero Program in California* (1961). Rpt. New York: Arno Press, 1976.

Anderson, Michael. "Android Game Review: Virtual City Playground," *Gear Diary*, October 20, 2011. Accessed June 2, 2018. https://geardiary.com/2011/10/20/android-game-review-virtual-city-playground.

Attfield, Sarah. "The Global Working Class in Art House Cinema," *Working Class Perspectives*, March 7, 2016. Accessed July 24, 2018. https://workingclassstudies.wordpress.com/2016/03/07/the-global-working-class-in-art-house-cinema.

Attisha, Mona Hanna. *What the Eyes Don't See: A Story of Crisis, Resistance, and Hope in an American City*. London: One World, 2018.

Bacon, David. *The Children of NAFTA: Labor Wars on the U.S./Mexico Border*. Berkeley: University of California Press, 2004.

Bacon, David. "These Things Can Change," *Dollars and Sense*, March-April 2015. Accessed June 2, 2018. http://davidbaconrealitycheck.blogspot.com/2015/04/these-things-can-change.html.

Bacon, David. "Miners and Farmers Challenge Mexico's Copper Giant," *Al Jazeera America*, April 15, 2015. Accessed June 2, 2018. http://davidbaconrealitycheck.blogspot.com/2015/04/miners-and-farmers-challenge-mexicos.html.

Bacon, David. "Thousands of Farm Workers Can't Make a Living," *New America Media*, Accessed June 2, 2015. http://newamericamedia.org/2015/06/thousands-of-farmworkers-in-california-cant-make-a-living.php.

Bacon, David. "Enforcement Is Not the Answer to Europe's Migrant Crisis," *Al Jazeera America*, June 8, 2015. Accessed June 8, 2015. http://america.aljazeera.com/opinions/2015/6/enforcement-is-not-the-answer-to-the-migrant-crisis.html.

Bacon, David. "Picking Peas Should Bring a Better Life," *New America Media*, Accessed June 4, 2015. http://newamericamedia.org/2015/06/picking-peas-should-bring-a-better-life.php.

Bacon, David. "California Appeals Court Rules Farm Worker Law Unconstitutional," *Working in These Times*, June 17, 2017. Accessed June 17, 2015. http://us7.campaign-archive1.com/?u=fc67a76dbb9c31aaee896aff7&id=020aef9207&e=6b498425fa.

Bacon, David. "The Pacific Coast Farm Worker Rebellion," *The Nation*, August 28, 2015. Accessed June 2, 2018. http://www.thenation.com/article/the-pacific-coast-farm-worker-rebellion.

Bacon, David. "An Immigrant Woman Takes Charge of the United Farm Workers," *American Prospect*, September 19, 2018. Accessed September 24, 2018. https://davidbaconrealitycheck.blogspot.com/2018/09/an-immigrant-woman-takes-charge-of.html.

Bagli, Charles V. "Rising from the Ashes, Willets Point Redevelopment Will Go Forward, City Says," *New York Times*, February 5, 2018. Accessed November 15, 2018. https://www.nytimes.com/2018/02/05/nyregion/willets-point-redevelopment-de-blasio.html.

Barry, Dan. "Beside a Smoldering Dump, A Refuge of Sorts," *New York Times*, October 21, 2007: A14.

Bazelon, Emily. "Status: Unknown," *New York Times Magazine*, 23 August 2015: 11–13.

Begag, Azouz. *Shanty-town Kid* [*La Gone du Chaaba*] (1986). Trans. Naima Wolf and Alec G. Hargreaves. Ed. Alec G. Hargreaves. Lincoln: University of Nebraska Press, 2007.

Bellafante, Ginia. "As Rich as the Devil, but No Gordon Gekko," *New York Times*, September 22, 2012. Accessed August 18, 2018. https://www.nytimes.com/2012/09/23/nyregion/rich-as-the-devil.html.

Berfield, Susan, and Ira Boudway. "Walmart vs. Walmart," *Bloomberg Businessweek*, December 17–23, 2013.

Bergman, Lowell, and Jane Perlez. "Tangled Strands in Fight over Peru Gold Mine," *New York Times*, October 25, 2005. https://www.nytimes.com/2005/10/25/world/americas/tangled-strands-in-fight-over-peru-gold-mine.html.

Berman, Art. "What Caused the Deepwater Horizon Disaster?" *The Oil Drum: Discussions about Energy and Our Future*, May 22, 2010. Accessed July 14, 2018. http://www.theoildrum.com/node/6493.

Bialobrzeski, Peter. *Neontigers: Photographs of Asian Megacities*. Ostfildern-Ruit: Hatje Cantz Verlag, 2004.

Bing, Wang. "Filming a Land in Flux: Interview," *New Left Review*, 82, July–August 2013.

Blair, Elizabeth. "In Confronting Poverty, *Harvest of Shame* Reaped Praise and Criticism," *Weekend Edition*, NPR, May 31, 2014. Accessed June 19, 2018. https://www.npr.org/2014/05/31/317364146/in-confronting-poverty-harvest-of-shame-reaped-praise-and-criticism.

Blinder, Alan. "Mine Company Stressed Safety, a Former Executive Testifies," *New York Times*, October 27, 2015: A20.

Bogost, Ian. *Persuasive Games: The Expressive Power of Videogames*. Cambridge: MIT Press, 2010.

Boo, Katherine. *Behind the Beautiful Forevers: Life, Death, and Hope in a Mumbai Slum*. London: Portobello Books, 2012.

Bork, Robert H. *The Antitrust Paradox*. New York: Free Press, 1979; 2nd edn., 1993.

Borojerdi, Poulod. "Rattling the Bars," Review of Fredric Jameson, *Archaeologies of the Future*. *New Left Review* 48, November-December, 2007.

Boyer, Brandon. "Venus Patrol Presents: The Kentucky Route Zero Guide to Film," *Venus Patrol*, May 20, 2014. Accessed March 30, 2019. Go to Venus Patrol's Archive: venuspatrol.com.

Bradshaw, Peter, Deyan Sudjic, Dave Simpson, Iain Sinclair, and Mark Lawson. "How J.G. Ballard Cast His Shadow Right Across the Arts," *The Guardian*, April 20, 2009. Accessed June 2, 2018. http://www.theguardian.com/books/2009/apr/20/jg-ballard-film-music-architecture-tv.

Brand, Stewart. "City Planet," *strategy-business.com*, Booz & Co, April 14, 2004. Accessed April 14, 2018. http://www.strategy-business.com/press/16635507/06109?tid=230&pg-all.

Brandt, George W., ed. *British Television Drama*. Cambridge: Cambridge University Press, 1981.

Branfman, Judy. "Eyes on Labor: Documentaries on Work in the Neoliberal Era," Research & Policy Brief. Los Angeles: UCLA Institute for Research on Labor and Employment: No. 20 (April 2015).

Bremen, Jan. "Life and Death in Annawadi," *New Left Review*, 78: November-December 2012: 152–60. Accessed July 9, 2018. https://newleftreview.org/II/78/jan-breman-life-and-death-in-annawadi.

Bremen, Jan. "A Bogus Concept?" *New Left Review*, 84: November-December 2013. Accessed July 9, 2018. https://newleftreview.org/II/84/jan-breman-a-bogus-concept.

Brin, David. *The Transparent Society: Will Technology Force us to Choose between Privacy and Freedom?* New York: Basic Books, 1999.

Bromberg, Ava. "Along the Path of Revolution: Worker Control in Venezuela, Agency in Art," 2007. Accessed May 26, 2018. http://www.ressler.at/along-the-path-of-revolution.

Byrd, Christopher. "Dr. Langeskov, The Tiger, and The Terribly Cursed Emerald: A Whirlwind Heist is a Very Long Title for A Short, Great Game," Washington Post, December 15, 2015. Accessed November 10, 2018. https://www.washingtonpost.com/news/comic-riffs/wp/2015/12/15/dr-langeskov-the-tiger-and-the-terribly-cursed-emerald-a-whirlwind-heist-is-a-very-long-title-for-a-short-great-game/?utm_term=.965c64a62539.

Byrd, Christopher. "Clever Game Strikes a Chord with Humor," Washington Post, December 20, 2015. Accessed May 22, 2018. https://www.highbeam.com/doc/1P2-39101209.html.

Cambanis, Thanassis. "To Catch Spill from Cairo, Two Megacities Rise in Sand," New York Times, August 25, 2010: A4. A9.

Campbell, Greg. *Blood Diamonds: Tracing the Deadly Path of the World's Most Precious Stones*. 2nd edn., New York: Westview Press, 2012.

Cantu, Francisco. *The Line Becomes a River: Dispatches from the Border*. New York: Riverhead Books, 2018.

Caquard, Sebastien, and Amelia Byrne. "Mapping Globalization: A Conversation between a Filmmaker and a Cartographer," *The Cartographic Journal*, 40 (4), November 2009: 372–78.

Carr, Martin. "Shame is Still the Harvest," *New York Times*, July 12, 1970. Accessed March 26, 2019. https://www.nytimes.com/1970/07/12/archives/shame-is-still-the-harvest.html.

Carr, Nick. "Scouting a New York City Neighborhood Where the Sidewalk Ends," *Slate*, November 15, 2013. Accessed May 18, 2018. http://www.slate.com/blogs/the_eye/2013/11/15/willets_point_queens_iron_triangle_autobody_shops_new:york_city_neighorhood.html.

Caughie, John. *Television Drama: Realism, Modernism, and British Culture*. Oxford: Oxford University Press, 2000.

CBS Reports: Legacy of Shame. CBS, Florham Park: Burrelle's Information Services, 1995.

Chan, Anita. *China's Workers under Assault: The Exploitation of Labor in a Globalizing Economy*. Armonk: M.E. Sharpe, 2001.

Chan, Kam Wing. "China's Internal Migration," in Immanuel Ness and Peter Bellwood, ed. *The Encyclopedia of Global Human Migration*. Hoboken: Blackwell Publishing, 2013: 1–17.

Chan, Sewell. "Court Upholds Willets Point Redevelopment Plan," *New York Times*, November 25, 2009. Accessed May 18, 2018. https://cityroom.blogs.nytimes.com/2009/11/25/court-upholds-willets-point-redevelopment-plan.

Chivers, C.J. "The Doomsday Scam," *New York Times Magazine*, November 22, 2015: 34–39, 58.

Chen, Michelle. "Bulls-Hit Ranch Labor Scandal Ensnared Florida Homeless," *In These Times*, November 7, 2012. Accessed August 20, 2018. http://inthesetimes.com/working/entry/14142/bulls_hit_farm_labor_scandal_targets_florida_homeless.

Chomsky, Noam. *Occupy*. New York: Zuccotti Park Press, 2012.

Chomsky, Noam. "Plutonomy and the Precariat: On the History of the U.S. Economy in Decline," *Huffington Post*, May 8, 2012. Accessed July 9, 2018. https://chomsky.info/20120508.

Choonara, Esme. "Is There a Precariat?" *Socialist Review*, October 2011. Accessed June 2, 2018. http://socialistreview.org.uk/362/there-precariat.

Chun, Wendy Hui Kyong. *Control and Freedom: Power and Paranoia in the Age of Fiber Optics*. Cambridge: MIT Press, 2006.

The City: The 100-Year Journey. New York Times, March 28, 2004: Section 14: The New York City Subway.

Clark, Anna. *The Poisoned City: Flint's Water and the American Urban Tragedy*. New York: Metropolitan Books, 2018.

Clay, Grady. *Close-Up: How to Read the American City* (1973). 2nd edn., Chicago: University of Chicago Press, 1980.

Coalition of Immokalee Workers. "Anti-Slavery Campaign," *Coalition of Immokalee Workers*, n.d. Accessed June 2, 2018. http://ciw-online.org/slavery.

Coalition of Immokalee Workers. "Slavery in the Fields and the Food We Eat," *Coalition of Immokalee Workers*, n.d. Accessed May 26, 2018. http://ciw-online.org/wp-content/uploads/12SlaveryintheFields.pdf.

Cohen, Patricia. "Counting Up the Hidden Costs of Low Pay," *New York Times*, April 13, 2015: B1, B3.

Cole, Peter. "This Small Town Shows Why the Trans-Pacific Partnership Could be a Disaster for American Workers," *In These Times*, June 5, 2015. Accessed May 23, 2018. http://inthesetimes.com/working/entry/18016/trans_pacific_partnership_jobs_workers.

Coleman, Gabriella. *Hacker, Hoaxer, Whistleblower, Spy: The Many Faces of Anonymous*. London: Verso Books, 2014.

"Coltan and the Congo," *Friends of the Congo*, n.d. Accessed July 6, 2018. http://www.friendsofthecongo.org/pdf/coltan_facts.pdf.

Cortese, Amy. "An Asian Hub in the Making," *New York Times*, December 30, 2007: 18.

Cowie, Jefferson, and Joseph Heathcott, eds. *Beyond the Ruins: The Meanings of Deindustrialization*. Ithaca: Cornell University Press, 2003.

Curtin, Michael, and Kevin Sanson. *Precarious Creativity: Global Media, Local Labor*. Berkeley: University of California Press, 2016.

Damico, Noelle, and Sean Sellers. "Now the Fear is Gone: Advancing Gender Justice through Worker-driven Social Responsibility." New York City: Worker-Driven Social Responsibility Network, 2018.

Danaher, Kevin. *10 Reasons to Abolish the IMF and the World Bank*. New York: Seven Stories Press, 2011.

Davies, David Martin. "Hunger in America: The 1968 Documentary that Exposed San Antonio Poverty," *Texas Public Radio*, June 8, 2018. Accessed March 26, 2019. https://www.tpr.org/post/hunger-america-1968-documentary-exposed-san-antonio-poverty.

Davis, Billie. "Are You a 'Marginal' Person? *A Desk for Billie*" (Interview with Jane Ross). *Tower Pentecostal Heritage Center*, March 13, 2004. Accessed July 5, 2018. https://www.jehovahs-witness.com/topic/162127/you-marginal-person-desk-billie.

Davis, Mike. *The City of Quartz: Excavating the Future in Los Angeles*. London: Verso Books, 2006.

Davis, Mike. *Dead Cities and Other Tales*. New York: New Press, 2003.

Davis, Mike. *Planet of Slums*. London: Verso, 2006.

Davis, Mike. "Fear and Money in Dubai," *New Left Review*, 41, September–October 2006: 47–68.

Destruction, Art, and the Doomsday Clock. Bulletin of the Atomic Scientists, Special Issue, November-December, 2013.

DiNardo, Kelly. "Future World" [Songdo]. *Washington Post*, January 6, 2013, F1, F4.

Disaffected! Persuasive Games, n.d. Accessed August 16, 2018. http://www.persuasivegames.com/games/game.aspx?game=disaffected.

Donjak, Ines, and Oliver Ressler, eds. *Utopian Pulse: Flares in the Darkroom*. London: Pluto Press, 2015.

Dovey, Kin. "Multiplicities and Complicities: Signifying the Future at Euralille," *Urban Design International*, September 1998: 89–99.

Dredge, Stuart. "Apple Bans Satirical iPhone Game Phone Story from Its App Store," *Guardian*, September 14, 2011. Accessed March 7, 2019. https://www.theguardian.com/technology/appsblog/2011/sep/14/apple-phone-story-rejection.

Drew, William. "You Cannot Win Fort McMoney, But You Should Still Play It," *Kill Screen Daily*, January 28, 2014. Accessed March 10, 2019. https://killscreen.com/articles/you-cannot-win-fort-mcmoney-you-should-play-it.

Dufresne, David. "Fort McMoney: A Documentary Game That's Quickly Becoming a Reality," *Huffington Post*, December 16, 2013. Accessed March 10, 2019. https://www.huffingtonpost.ca/david-dufresne/fort-mcmoney-a-documentar_b_4455184.html.

Duggan, Lisa. *Mean Girl: Ayn Rand and the Culture of Greed*. Berkeley: University of California Press, 2019.

Dunkley, Chris. *The Precariat*. London: Oberon Books, 2013.

Dwyer, Augusta. *On the Line: Life on the US-Mexican Border*. London: Latin American Bureau, 1994.

Economist Intelligence Unit. "Supersized Cities: China's 13 Megalopolises," *The Economist*, 2012. Accessed July 16, 2018. https://www.eiu.com/public/topical_report.aspx?campaignid=Megalopolis2012.

Ehrenreich, Barbara. *Nickel and Dimed*. NY: Metropolitan Books, 2001.

Eisner, Ken. "Radiant City," *Variety/Georgia Straight*, October 21, 2006, Accessed December 10, 2018. https://www.straight.com/article-82867/radiant-city.

Elley, Derek. "Francesca," *Variety*, September 19, 2009. Accessed May 26, 2018. http://variety.com/2009/film/reviews/francesca-1200476048.

Empire/State: Artists Engaging Globalization. New York: Whitney Museum of American Art, 2002.

Erikson, Kai. *A New Species of Trouble: The Human Experience of Modern Disasters*. New York: Norton, 1994.

Ewig, Jack, and Liz Alderman. "A Flow of Funds, Out of Greece," *New York Times*, July 31, 2015: B1, B6.
Fahim, Kareem. "Like Garbage Collectors, a Salute Does Its Job, Building by Building," *New York Times*, March 29, 2016. Accessed May 23, 2018. https://www.nytimes.com/2016/03/29/world/middleeast/cairo-mural-garbage.html.
Farley, Paul, and Michael Symmons Roberts. *Edgelands: Journeys into England's True Wilderness*. London: Jonathan Cape, 2011.
Featherstone, Liza. "Watching Walmart: Four Documentaries, Four Perspectives," *Columbia Journalism Review*, January-February 2006.
Finch, Mark, and Judith Williamson. "Panic in the Streets," *National Film Theatre Programme*, August 1988: 9–13.
Finnegan, William. "Dignity: Fast-Food Workers and a New Form of Labor Activism," *The New Yorker*, September 15, 2017. Accessed July 12, 2018. https://www.newyorker.com/magazine/2014/09/15/dignity-4.
Foti, Alex. *General Theory of the Precariat: Great Recession, Revolution, Reaction*. Amsterdam: Institute of Network Cultures, 2017.
Foy, Nicole. "South Idaho Migrant Camp Residents Reflect on Heritage," Idaho Press, October 10, 2018. Accessed March 22, 2019. https://www.idahopress.com/news/local/south-idaho-migrant-camp-residents-reflect-on-heritage/article_dc36c20d-dc1e-5ab6-9b91-21a839533738.html.
French, Howard W. "Sprawling Mural Pays Homage to Cairo's Garbage Collectors," *New York Times*, April 3, 2006. Accessed July 19, 2018. https://www.nytimes.com/2006/04/03/world/asia/03garbage.html.
Fullbrook, Edward. "Citigroup Attempts to Disappear its Plutonomy Report #2," *Real World Economics Review Blog*, November 11, 2010. Accessed July 20, 2018. https://rwer.wordpress.com/2010/11/11/citigroup-attempts-to-disappear-its-plutonomy-report-2.
Gadanho, Pedro. *Uneven Growth: Tactical Urbanisms for Expanding Megacities*. New York: Museum of Modern Art, 2014.
Galarza, Ernesto. *Spiders in the House and Workers in the Field*. Notre Dame: University of Notre Dame Press, 1970.
Galarza, Ernesto. *Man of Fire: Selected Writings*. Ed. Armando Ibarra and Rodolfo D. Torres. Urbana: University of Illinois Press, 2013.
Gale International. *Songdo International Business District Press Kit*. Accessed March 26, 2019. http://www.galeintl.com/2015/10/09/songdo-ibd-press-kit.
Garcia, J. Malcolm. "The White Train," *Virginia Quarterly Review*, Fall 2007. Accessed July 19, 2018. https://www.vqronline.org/essay/white-train.
Garcia, Matthew. *From the Jaws of Victory: The Triumph and Tragedy of Cesar Chavez and the Farm Worker Movement*. Berkeley: University of California Press, 2014.
Genzlinger, Neil. "Review: *American Crime* Fixes on Migrant Dreamers in the Fields," *New York Times*, March 6, 2017. Accessed July 12, 2018. https://www.nytimes.com/2017/03/09/arts/television/review-american-crime-season-3-abc.html.

George, Rose. *Ninety Percent of Everything: Inside Shipping, the Invisible Industry that Puts Clothes on Your Back, Gas in Your Car and Food on Your Plate*. New York: Metropolitan Books, 2013.

Gettleman, Jeffrey. "Under Complex Election Rules, Nairobi Slum Could Pick Kenya's Next President," *New York Times*, December 25, 2007: A10.

Gettleman, Jeffrey. "The Price of Precious," With photographs by Marcus Bleasdale. *National Geographic*, October, 2013. Accessed May 26, 2018. http://ngm.nationalgeographic.com/2013/10/conflict-minerals/gettleman-text.

Gillespie, Patrick, Marilia Brocchetto, and Paula Newton. "Venezuela: How a Rich Nation Collapsed," *CNN Money*, July 30, 2017. Accessed July 25, 2018. https://money.cnn.com/2017/07/26/news/economy/venezuela-economic-crisis/index.html.

Gitlin, Todd. *Occupy Nation: The Roots, the Spirit, and the Promise of Occupy*. New York: Harper-Collins, 2011.

Glenny, Misha. *McMafia: A Journey through the Global Criminal Underworld*. New York: Alfred A. Knopf, 2008.

Goldberg, Harold. "Where Film Marries Video Game," *New York Times*, November 27, 2013: C1, C5.

Goldberg, Harold. "Game Theory: The Year of the Indie," *New York Times*, December 25, 2013. Accessed July 9, 2018. https://artsbeat.blogs.nytimes.com/2013/12/25/game-theory-the-year-of-the-indie.

Goldstein, Amy. *Janesville: An American Story*. New York: Simon & Schuster, 2018.

Godlewski, Joseph. "Alien and Distant: Rem Koolhaas on Film in Lagos, Nigeria," *Traditional Dwellings and Settlement Review*, 21 (2): 7–19. Accessed May 12, 2019. https://surface.syr.edu/cgi/viewcontent.cgi?article=1253&context=arc.

Gomberg-Munoz, Ruth. *Labor and Legality: An Ethnography of a Mexican Immigrant Network*. Oxford: Oxford University Press, 2011.

Goodman, Amy. "*The Infiltrators*: How Undocumented Activist Snuck into Immigration Jail to fight Deportations," *Democracy Now!* March 4, 2019. Accessed March 28, 2019. https://www.democracynow.org/2019/3/4/the_infiltrators_how:undocumented_activists_snuck.

Goodman, Walter. "Review/Television: *New Harvest, Old Shame*, About Farm Workers," *New York Times*, April 17, 1990. Accessed March 26, 2019. https://www.nytimes.com/1990/04/17/arts/review-television-new-harvest-old-shame-about-farm-workers.html.

Gough, Neil. "Lopsided Job Market Puts Strain on China," *New York Times*, April 22, 2015: B1, B8.

Greco, Michael. "Racist Italy through Romanian Eyes in *Francesca*," *Cineuropa*. Accessed May 26, 2018. http://cineuropa.org/en/newsdetail/112449.

Greenhouse, Steven. "Labor [UFCW] Opens a Drive to Organize Walmart," *New York Times*, November 8, 2002. Accessed December 3, 2018. https://www.nytimes.com/2002/11/08/us/trying-to-overcome-embarrassment-labor-opens-a-drive-to-organize-wal-mart.html.

Greenhouse, Steven. "The Fight for $15.37 an Hour," *New York Times*, November 23, 2014: B1, B6.

Greenhouse, Steven. "A Broader Strategy on Wages," *New York Times*, March 31, 2015: B1–2.

Greenhouse, Steven. "Forced to Work Off the Clock, Some Fight Back," *New York Times*, November 19, 2004. Accessed June 23, 2018. https://www.nytimes.com/2004/11/19/us/forced-to-work-off-the-clock-some-fight-back.html.

Greenhouse, Steven. "Hundreds of Fast-Food Workers Striking for Higher Wages Are Arrested," *New York Times*, September 5, 2014. Accessed September 19, 2018. https://www.nytimes.com/2014/09/05/business/economy/fast-food-workers-seeking-higher-wages-are-arrested-during-sit-ins.html.

Greenhouse, Steven. "Just 13, and Working Risky Shifts in the Tobacco Fields," *New York Times*, September 7, 2014: A1, A18.

Griffin, Oliver. "Machines Could Make More Workers Migrate," Raconteur: Going Global. London Times, October 2017. Accessed July 14, 2018. https://www.raconteur.net/going-global-2017.

Griffith, David. *(Mis)managing Migration: Guestworkers' Experiences with North American Labor Markets*. Santa Fe: SAR Press, 2014.

Grossman, Mark, and Andrew Grossman. "Isolating Isolationism: Recent INDEX [Film] Releases from the Austrian Avant-Garde," *Bright Lights Film Journal* 49, August 1, 2005. Accessed May 26, 2018. http://brightlightsfilm.com/isolating-isolationism-recent-index-releases-austrian-avant-garde/#.VZwbIM0sGeZ.

Guthrie, Doug. *China and Globalization: The Social, Economic and Political Transformation of Chinese Society*. New York and London: Routledge, 2012.

Hannaham, James. *Delicious Foods*. Boston: Little, Brown and Company, 2015.

Haraway, Donna J. *Simians, Cyborgs, and Women: The Reinvention of Nature*. New York: Routledge, 1991.

Harris, John. "*A Precariat Charter: From Denizens to Citizens*—Review," *Guardian*, April 4, 2014. Accessed July 9, 2018. https://www.theguardian.com/books/2014/apr/09/precariat-charter-denizens-citizens-review.

Harvey, David. *Spaces of Global Capitalism*. London: Verso, 2006.

Heller, Nathan. "Is the Gig Economy Working?" *The New Yorker*, May 15, 2017. Accessed July 15, 2018. https://www.newyorker.com/magazine/2017/05/15/is-the-gig-economy-working.

Hemblade, Christopher, ed. *Apocalypse. Time Out*. London: Royal Academy of Arts, 2000.

Hessler, Peter. "Tales of the Trash," *The New Yorker*, October 13, 2014. Accessed July 12, 2018. https://www.newyorker.com/magazine/2014/10/13/tales-trash.

Hilgers, Lauren. "The Kitchen Network," *The New Yorker*, October 13, 2014. Accessed July 12, 2018. https://www.newyorker.com/magazine/2014/10/13/cookas-tale.

Hilgers, Lauren. *Patriot Number One: American Dreams in Chinatown*. New York: Crown, 2018.

Hjersted, Tim. "The Top 10 Films that Explain Why the Occupy Movement Exists," *Films for Action*. December 13, 2011. Accessed July 29, 2018. https://www.filmsforaction.org/articles/the-top-10-films-that-explain-why-occupy-wall-st-exists.

Holmes, Seth. *Fresh Fruit, Broken Bodies: Migrant Farmworkers in the United States*. Berkeley: University of California Press, 2013.

Hsiao-Hung Pai. *Chinese Whispers*: The True Story Behind Britain's Hidden Army of Labour. London: Penguin, 2008.

Hsiao-Hung Pai. *Invisible: Britain's Migrant Sex Workers*. London: Westbourne Press, 2013a.

Hsiao-Hung Pai. *Scattered Sand: The Story of China's Rural Migrants*. London: Verso, 2013b.

Hsiao-Hung Pai. *Angry White People: Coming Face-to-Face with the British Far Right*. London: Zed Books, 2016.

Hsiao-Hung Pai. *Bordered Lives: How Europe Fails Refugees and Migrants*. London: New Internationalist, 2018.

Hsiao-Hung Pai, Felicity Lawrence, Vikram Dodd, Helen Carter, David Ward, and Jonathan Watts. "Victims of the Sands and the Snakeheads," *Guardian*, February 6, 2004. Accessed May 25, 2019. https://www.theguardian.com/uk/2004/feb/07/china.immigration1.

Hoberman, J. "Migrants Facing Toil and Trouble," *New York Times*, April 28, 2019. Accessed April 30, 2019. https://www.nytimes.com/2019/04/26/movies/bitter-money-migrant-workers-china.html.

Hodges, Kathy. Unpublished letter to Tom Zaniello from Idaho State Historical Society, November 9, 2000. Author's collection.

Hugo, Peter. "Dumping Across the Digital Divide," *New York Times Magazine*, August 15, 2010. Accessed August 16, 2010. No longer available on-line. https://archive.nytimes.com/query.nytimes.com/gst/fullpage9500E6DE1030F936A2575BC0A9669D8B63.html.

Huntley, Chet, et al. *Migrant: An NBC White Paper*. NBC, 1970. Accessed June 20, 2018. No longer available on-line.

Hutton, Peter. "Lived Experience: Interview," *Mousse Magazine*, 37. Accessed December 4, 2018. http://moussemagazine.it/luke-fowler-peter-hutton-2013.

Hyman, . Louis. *Temp: How American Work, American Business, and the American Dream Became Temporary*. New York: Viking, 2018.

"Immokalee Event Commemorates 1960 Documentary *Harvest of Shame*," *Naples Daily News*, November 26, 2010. Accessed June 19, 2018. http://archive.naplesnews.com/news/local/immokalee-event-commemorates-1960-documentary-harvest-of-shame-ep-393228464-343128772.html.

Idaho's Summer Citizens: What Migrant Labor Means to Idaho. Film Transcript. Boise: Idaho State Historical Society, 1957–1960.

Irwin, Neil. "How Germany Prevailed in the Greek Bailout," *New York Times*, July 30, 2015: A1, A8.

Ives, Mike. "China Limits Waste. 'Cardboard Grannies' and Texas Recyclers Scramble," *New York Times*, November 25, 2017. Accessed July 14, 2018. https://www.nytimes.com/2017/11/25/business/energy-environment/china-waste-recycling.html.

Jaffe, Sarah. "*Wisconsin Rising*: Grassroots Documentary Film follows the People's Movement from Revolt to Recalls," *AlterNet*, January 11, 2012. Accessed July 16, 2018. https://www.alternet.org/story/153751/wisconsin_rising%3A_grassroots_documentary_film_follows_the_people%27s_movement_in_madison_from_revolt_to_recalls.

Jameson, Fredric. "Future City," *New Left Review*, 21, May-June 2003. Accessed July 16, 2018. https://newleftreview.org/II/21/fredric-jameson-future-city.

Jameson, Fredric. *Archaeologies of the Future: The Desire Called Utopia and Other Science Fictions*. London: Verso, 2007.

Jencks, Charles. *Heteropolis: Los Angeles—The Riots and the Strange Beauty of Hetero-Architecture*. New York: St. Martin's Press, 1993.

Jencks, Christopher. "The War on Poverty: Was It Lost?" *New York Review of Books*, April 2, 2015. Accessed July 16, 2018. https://www.nybooks.com/articles/2015/04/02/war-poverty-was-it-lost.

Johnson, Simon. "The Quiet Coup," *Atlantic Monthly*, May, 2009. Accessed September 1, 2018. https://www.theatlantic.com/magazine/archive/2009/05/the-quiet-coup/307364.

Juzwiak, Rich. "*Papo & Yo* and the Three Pillars of Game Design," *Geekquality*, November 7, 2012. Accessed March 6, 2019. http://www.geekquality.com/papo-and-pillars.

Kaplan, Esther. "The Spy Who Fired Me: The Human Costs of Workplace Monitoring," *Harper's Magazine*, March 2015. Accessed May 23, 2018. https://harpers.org/archive/2015/03/the-spy-who-fired-me.

Kapur, Ajay, et al. *The Global Investigator*. Citigroup Global Markets. *Equity Strategy—Plutonomy: Buying Luxury, Exploring Global Imbalances*, October 16, 2005; *Equity Strategy—Revisiting Plutonomy: The Rich Getting Richer*, March 5, 2006; *Equity Strategy—The Plutonomy Symposium—Rising Tides Lifting Yachts*, September 29, 2006. No longer available on-line.

Kaspar-Eisert, Verena. "Oliver Ressler—How to Occupy a Shipwreck," *Kunst Haus Wien/Museum Hundertwasser*, January 25–April 2, 2018. Accessed May 18, 2018. https://kunstaspekte.art/event/oliver-ressler-how-to-occupy-a-shipwreck.

Katyal, Sonia K. "Semiotic Disobedience," 84 *Wash. U. L. Review*, 489, 2006. Accessed November 13, 2018. http://openscholarship.wustl.edu/law:lawreview/vol84/iss3/1.

Kelly, Jeff, ed. *Best of Temp Slave*. Madison: Garrett County Press, 1997.

Kempadoo, Kamal, and Jo Doezema, ed. *Global Sex Workers: Rights, Resistance, and Redefinition*. New York: Routledge, 1998.

Kenny, Charles. "Marx Is Back," *Foreign Policy*, January 21, 2014. Accessed May 26, 2018. http://foreignpolicy.com/2014/01/21/marx-is-back.

Khan, Lina M. "Amazon's Antitrust Paradox," *Yale Review*, 127, June 17, 2018. Accessed June 27, 2018. https://www.yalelawjournal.org/article/amazons-antitrust-paradox.

Khatchadourian, Raffi. "World Without End," *New Yorker*, May 18, 2015: 48–57.

Kirkwood, Lucy. *Chimerica*. London: Nick Hern Books, 2013.

Klein-Davis, Stephanie. *Factory Man: How One Furniture Maker Battled Offshoring, Stayed Local, and Helped Save an American Town*. New York: Little, Brown, 2014.

Klinenberg, Eric. *Heat Wave: A Social Autopsy of Disaster in Chicago*. Chicago: University of Chicago Press, 2002.

Klinenberg, Eric. "Dying Alone: An Interview with Eric Klinenberg, University of Chicago Press," Accessed May 26, 2018. http://press.uchicago.edu/Misc/Chicago/443213in.html.

Klose, Alexander. *The Container Principle: How a Box Changes the Way We Think*. Trans. Charles Marcrum II. Cambridge. M.I.T. Press, 2009.

Kumar, Hari, and Kai Schultz. "In Rotten, Teetering Towers, Garbage is Piling Up in India," *New York Times*, June 11, 2018: A4.

Kumparak, Greg. "Banned from the App Store: An Anti-iPhone Game Complete with Foxconn Suicide Mini-Game," *TechCrunch*, November 11, 2013. Accessed March 7, 2019. https://techcrunch.com/2011/09/13/iphone-banned-apps-phone-story.

Lanchester, John. *Whoops! Why Everyone Owes Everyone and No One Can Pay*. London: Penguin Books, 2010.

Lanchester, John. "Cityphilia," *London Review of Books*, January 3, 2008. Accessed September 17, 2018. https://www.lrb.co.uk/v30/n01/john-lanchester/cityphilia.

Lanchester, John. "Cityphobia," *London Review of Books*, October 23, 2008. Accessed July 14, 2018. https://www.lrb.co.uk/v30/n20/john-lanchester/cityphobia.

Lanchester, John. "After the Fall," *London Review of Books*, July 5, 2018. Accessed July 20, 2018. https://www.lrb.co.uk/v40/n13/john-lanchester/after-the-fall.

Langner, Erin. "Undeniable: Edward Burtynsky's Photographs of a Changing World," *Arcade*, 34 (3), 2016: 22–41.

Larmer, Brook. "On Money: E-Waste Offers and Opportunity as Well as Toxicity," *New York Times Magazine*, July 8, 2018. Accessed July 8, 2018. https://www.nytimes.com/2018/07/05/magazine/e-waste-offers-an-economic-opportunity-as-well-as-toxicity.html.

Law Commission of Ontario (LCO). *Vulnerable Workers Background Paper*. December, 2010. Section II: What We Mean by "Precarious Work" and "Vulnerable Workers". Accessed June 2, 2018. www.lco-cdo.org/en/vulnerable-workers-background-paper-sectionII.

Lazare, Ed, and Ari Schwartz. "Unpredictable and Unsustainable: How Scheduling Practices in DC's Service Sector are Wreaking Havoc on Workers," *Hill Rag*, July 2015: 68–69.

Lee, Felicia R. "Reassembling a History Told in Paint," *New York Times*, December 16, 2014. Accessed May 26, 2018. http://www.nytimes.com/2014/12/17/arts/design/jacob-lawrences-great-migration-series-returns-to-moma.html?_r=0.

Leonard, Andrew. "The Circuit Board Bakers of Guiyu," *Salon.com*, November 7, 2007. Accessed August 18, 2018. https://www.salon.com/2007/11/07/circuit_board_bakers.

Lewes, Leon. *Robert M. Young: Essays on the Films*. Jefferson: McFarland & Company, 2003.

Lewis, Jim. "The Exigent City," *New York Times Magazine*, June 8, 2008: 34–38.

Lim, Dennis. "Greetings from the Land of Feel-Bad Cinema," *New York Times*, November 26, 2006. Accessed October 14, 2018. https://www.nytimes.com/2006/11/26/movies/26lim.html.

Linkon, Sherry Lee, and John Russo. *Steel-Town U.S.A: Work and Memory in Youngstown*. Lawrence: University Press of Kansas, 2002.

Linkon, Sherry Lee. *The Half-Life of Deindustrialization: Working-Class Writing about Economic Restructuring*. Ann Arbor: University of Michigan Press, 2018.

Lippard, Lucy R. *Undermining: A Wild Ride Through Land Use, Politics, and Art in the Changing West*. New York: The New Press, 2014.

Longman, Jere. "Ukraine's Poisoned Past," *New York Times*, June 12, 2012. Accessed July 9, 2018. https://www.nytimes.com/2012/06/13/sports/soccer/a-visit-to-chernobyl-which-some-athletes-can-recall-firsthand.html.

Lopez-Calvo, Ignacio. *Latino Los Angeles in Film and Fiction: The Cultural Production of Social Anxiety*. Tempe: University of Arizona Press, 2014.

Lucca, Violet. "The Founder," *Film Comment*, January-February 2017: 83–84.

Luft, Rachel. When Disasters Strike, Poor, Minority Communities Face Greatest Risks," *Seattle Times*, August 20, 2015. Accessed March 11, 2019. https://www.seattletimes.com/opinion/when-disasters-strike-poor-minority communities-face-greatest-risks-3.

Lydersen, Kari. *Out of the Sea and into the Fire: Latin-American Immigration in the Global Age*. Monroe: Common Courage Press, 2005.

Lydersen, Kari. *Revolt on Goose Island: The Chicago Factory Takeover, and What It Says about the Economic Crisis*. New York: Melville House, 2009.

Lydersen, Kari. *Mayor 1%: Rahm Emanuel and the Rise of Chicago's 99%*. Chicago: Haymarket Books, 2013.

Lydersen, Kari. *Closing the Cloud Factories: Lessons from the Fight to Shut Down Chicago's Coal Plants*. Chicago: Midwest Energy News, 2014.

Lydersen, Kari. "Homeless but Employed, The Chicago Restaurant Workers Living under a Bridge," *Guardian*, April 17, 2016. Accessed July 22, 2018. https://www.theguardian.com/society/2016/apr/17/homeless-employed-chicago-restaurant-workers-exploited.

Lydersen, Kari. "At the Bullfrog: Those Left Behind by the Global Economy Find Relief—and a Place to Talk Trump," *In These Times*, July 25, 2017. Accessed July 22, 2018. http://inthesetimes.com/article/20307/Trump-heroin-working-class-New-York-government-economics.

Lynch, Kevin. *Wasting Away*. Ed. Michael Southworth. San Francisco: Sierra Books, 1990.

Macy, Beth. *Factory Man: How One Furniture Maker Battled Offshoring, Stayed Local—and Helped Save an American Town*. Boston: Little, Brown, and Company, 2015.

Macy, Beth. "Who's Speaking Up for the American Worker?" *New York Times*, June 25, 2015. Accessed September 23, 2015. https://www.nytimes.com/2015/06/25/opinion/whos-speaking-up-for-the-american-worker.html.

MacDonald, Scott. *Avant-Doc: Intersections of Documentary and Avant-Garde Cinema*. Oxford: Oxford University Press, 2015.

Maisel, David. *Black Maps: American Landscape and the Apocalyptic Sublime*. Gottingen: Steidl, 2013.

Marquis, Susan L. *I Am Not a Tractor! How Florida Farmworkers Took on the Fast Food Giants and Won*. Ithaca: Cornell University Press, 2018.

Mason, Paul. *Rare Earth*. Harpenden, UK: No Exit Press, 2012.

Mattas, Jeff. "Interview: The Stanley Parable Developer Davey Wreden," *Shacknews*, September 27, 2011. Accessed March 3, 2019. https://www.shacknews.com/article/70363/interview-davey-wreden-on-stanley-parable-remake-and-self-taught.

Mattoni, Alice, and Nicole Doerr. "Images within the Precarity Movement in Italy," *Feminist Review*, 87 (January 1, 2007). *Academe.com*. Accessed April 28, 2019. https://www.academia.edu/262046/Images_Within_the_Precarity_Movement_In_Italy.

McKee, Yates. "*Boom!*" *The Journal of Aesthetics and Protest*, August 2003. Accessed May 26, 2018. http://www.joaap.org/1/boom.

McLean, Bethany. "Is Enron Overpriced?" *Fortune*, March 5, 2001. Accessed July 9, 2018. http://archive.fortune.com/magazines/fortune/fortune_archive/2001/03/05/297833/index.htm. McMullan, Thomas. "Where Literature and Gaming Collide," *Eurogamer*, July 27, 2014. Accessed November 12, 2018. https://www.eurogamer.net/articles/2014-07-27-where-literature-and-gaming-collide.

McNeil, Donald G. Jr. "Finding a Scapegoat When Epidemics Strike," *New York Times*, September 1, 2009: D1, D7.

McGuire, Bill. *Global Catastrophes: A Very Short Introduction*. Oxford: Oxford University Press, 2002.

Mehta, Suketu. *Maximum City: Bombay Lost and Found*. New York: Alfred A. Knopf, 2005.

Meister, Dick, and Anne Loftis. *A Long Time Coming: The Struggle to Unionize America's Farm Workers*. New York: Macmillan, 1977.

Merry, Stephanie. "*The Great Invisible* Movie Review: Disastrous Aftermath of the BP Deepwater Horizon Oil Spill," *Washington Post*, November 6, 2014. Accessed May 23, 2018. https://www.washingtonpost.com/goingoutguide/movies/the-great-invisible-movie-review examining-the-disastrous-aftermath-of-the-bp-deepwater-horizon-oil-spill/2014/11/05/f042194a-6069-11e4-91f7-5d89b5e8c251_story.html?utm_term=.35cecfcee3fd.

Meyer, Bill. "Jeff Cohen and the Corporate Coup d'Etat," *Hollywood Progressive*, April 24, 2019. Accessed April 26, 2019. https://hollywoodprogressive.com/corporate-coup.

Michael, Chris. "'Lagos Shows How a City Can Recover from a Deep, Deep Pit': Rem Koolhaas Talks to Kunle Adeyemi," *Guardian*, February 26, 2016. Accessed May 12, 2019. https://www.theguardian.com/cities/2016/feb/26/lagos-rem-koolhaas-kunle-adeyemi.

Mieville, China. *London's Overthrow*, November-December 2011: 1–60. Accessed May 26, 2018. http://www.londonsoverthrow.org.

Milkman, Ruth, and Ed Ott, eds. *New Labor in New York: Precarious Workers and the Future of the Labor Movement*. Ithaca: Cornell University Press, 2014.

Milne, Seamus. *The Enemy Within: The Secret War Against the Miners*. 4th edn., London: Verso, 2014.

Minter, Adam. *Junkyard Planet: Travels in the Billion-Dollar Trash Trade*. London and New York: Bloomsbury, 2013.

Miraldi, Robert. *Muckraking and Objectivity: Journalism's Colliding Traditions*. New York: Praeger, 1990.

Mitchell, Don. *Lie of the Land: Migrant Workers and the California Landscape*. Minneapolis: University of Minnesota Press, 2006.

Mitchell, Don. *They Saved the Crops: Labor, Landscape, and the Struggle Over Industrial Farming in Bracero-Era California*. Athens: University of Georgia Press, 2012.

Mitropoulos, Angela. "Interview with Angela Mitropoulos Discussing *No Borders* Politics," *Shift Magazine*, Indymedia UK, October 19, 2010. Accessed June 2, 2018. http://www.indymedia.org.uk/en/2010/10/466294.html.

Moberg, David. "Fast Food Workers: Thanks for the Raise, McDonald's, But We Said $15 an Hour, Not $10," *In These Times*, April 4, 2015. Accessed July 22, 2018. http://inthesetimes.com/working/entry/17807/mcdonalds_raise.

Montgomery, David. "Social Media and Film Festival Come to a Sci-Fi Cult Hit's Rescue" [Alex Rivera's *Sleep Dealer*]. *Washington Post*, July 10, 2014: C1, C8.

Moore, Thad. "Uber's Drivers Are Employees, California Agency Says," *Washington Post*, June 18, 2015: A14.

Morley, David, and Kevin Rabin. *Spaces of Identity: Global Media, Electronic Landscapes, and Cultural Boundaries*. London: Routledge, 1995.

Mouawad, Jad. "The Construction Site Called Saudi Arabia," *New York Times*, 2 January 2008: 1, 9.

Mufson, Steven. "The Oil Giant That Was 'Forced to Shrink to Greatness'," *Washington Post*, July 15, 2018. Accessed July 15, 2018. https://www.washingtonpost.com/business/economy/the-oil-giant-that-was-forced-to-shrink-to-greatness/2018/07/13/1be775e0-8159-11e8-b9a5-7e1c013f8c33_story.html?utm_term=.2f02edc7c482.

Mumford, Dwilkytm. "Ken Loach: Blame 'Fake Left' Politicians like Miliband and Blair for Gig Economy," *Guardian*, May 17, 2019. Accessed May 17, 2019. https://www.theguardian.com/film/2019/may/17/ken-loach-blair-miliband-sorry-we-missed-you-cannes-gig-economy.

Murphy, Jarrett. "Melting the Iron Triangle," *Village Voice*, June 12, 2006. Accessed July 9, 2018. https://www.villagevoice.com/2006/06/06/melting-the-iron-triangle.

Murphy, Joe, and Joe Robertson. *The Jungle*. London: Faber & Faber, 2018.

Nail, Thomas. *The Figure of the Migrant*. Stanford: Stanford University Press, 2015.

Narine, Anil. "'Global Trauma Films' and the Cinematic Network Society," *Critical Studies in Media Communication*, 27 (2), August 2010: 209–34.

Neuburger, Bruce. *Lettuce Wars: Ten Years of Work and Struggle in the Fields of California*. New York: Monthly Review Press, 2013.

Neuwirth, Robert. *Shadow Cities: A Billion Squatters, a New Urban World*. London and New York: Routledge, 2005.

Nir, Sarah Maslin. "The High Price of Pretty Nails," *New York Times*, May 10, 2011: A1, A22–23.

Nir, Sarah Maslin. "The End of Willets Point," *New York Times*, November 24, 2013: 34–35.

Nir, Sarah Maslin. "Behind Perfect Nails, Ailing Salon Workers," *New York Times*, May 11, 2015: A1, A10–11.

Nottage, Lynn. *Ruined*. New York: Theatre Communication Group, 2009.

Nottage, Lynn. "Extracting Art from a Downfall," *New York Times*, August 2, 2015: 4.

"Occupy Anti-Capitalism Protests Spread Around the World," *The Guardian*, October 16, 2011. Accessed September 23, 2018. https://www.theguardian.com/world/2011/oct/16/occupy-protests-europe-london-assange.

"Occupy Protests Around the World: Full List Visualized," *The Guardian*, October 17, 2011. Accessed September 23, 2018.

O'Connell, Pamela Licalzi. "Korea's High-Tech Utopia, Where Everything Is Observed," *New York Times*, October 5, 2005. Accessed September 9, 2018. https://www.nytimes.com/2005/10/05/technology/techspecial/koreas-hightech-utopia-where-everything-is-observed.html.

O'Hagan, Andrew. "The [Grenfell] Tower," *London Review of Books*, June 7, 2018: 3–43.

Oil and Money: An International Special Report. New York Times, October 9–10. 2018. Accessed October 14, 2018. https://www.nytimes.com/spotlight/oil-money-special-reports.

"*Oligarchy* Postmortem," Molleindustria.org. Accessed March 3, 2019. http://www.molleindustria.org/oiligarchy-postmortem.

Orleck, Annelise. *We Are All Fast-Food Workers Now: The Global Uprising Against Poverty Wages*. Boston: Beacon Press, 2018.

Ouroussoff, Niccolai. "The New, New City," *New York Times Magazine*, June 8, 2008: 70–75, 84, 95.

Ouroussoff, Niccolai. "A New City in Saudi Arabia," *New York Times*, December 13, 2010. Accessed December 12, 2012. https://www.nytimes.com/2010/12/13/arts/design/13desert.html.

Packer, George. "The Megacity: Decoding the Chaos of Lagos," *New Yorker*, November 13, 2006. Accessed June 29, 2018. https://www.newyorker.com/magazine/2006/11/13/the-megacity.

Parker, Ian. "The Greek Warrior," *New Yorker*, August 3, 2015. Accessed July 21, 2018. https://www.newyorker.com/magazine/2015/08/03/the-greek-warrior.

Parkin, Simon. "The Best Video Games of 2013," *New Yorker*, December 13, 2013. Accessed June 2, 2018. http://www.newyorker.com/tech/eleme'nts/the-best-video-games-of-2013.

Partlow, Joshua. "Dominican Republic Is Poised to Round Up Haitians for Deportation," *Washington Post*, June 18, 2015: A10.

Partlow, Joshua. "Dominican Immigration Rules Spur Painful Exodus for Haitians," *Washington Post*, June 25, 2015: A1, A9.

Partlow, Joshua. "Dominicans of Haitian Descent Reportedly Ejected," *Washington Post*, July 3, 2015: A14.

Pithouse, Richard. "Thinking Resistance in the Shanty Town," *MUTE: Naked Cities—Struggle in the Global Slums*. II.3: 16–31.

Platt, Charles. "Fly on the Wal," *New York Post*, February 7, 2009. Accessed September 10, 2018. https://nypost.com/2009/02/08/fly-on-the-wal.

Plumer, Brad. "Trump Wants to Help Coal, But It Might Be Past Saving," *New York Times*, August 23, 2018. Accessed September 10, 2018. https://www.nytimes.com/2018/08/22/climate/trump-coal-industry.html.

"Postopolis! Robert Neuwirth," *cityofsound.com*, June 9, 2007. Accessed May 25, 2018. http://www.cityofsound.com/blog/2007/06/postopolis_lebb.html.

"Poverty in India: A Flourishing Slum," *The Economist*, December 22, 2007: 57–59, 62.

Povoledo, Elisabetta. "Deadly Factory Fire Bares Racial Tensions in Italy," *New York Times*, December 8, 2013. Accessed September 10, 2018. https://www.nytimes.com/2013/12/08/world/europe/deadly-factory-fire-bares-racial-tensions-in-italy.html?mtrref=www.google.com.

Puette, William J. *Through Jaundiced Eyes: How the Media View Labor*. Ithaca: Cornell University Press, 1992.

Pugh, William. "Dr. Langeskov, the Tiger, and the Terribly Cursed Emerald: A Whirlwind Heist," *CrowsCrowsCrows*. Accessed May 22, 2018. https://crowscrowscrows.itch.io/dr-langeskov-the-tiger-and-the-terribly-cursed-emerald-a-whirlwind-heist.

Quinn, Bill. *How Walmart Is Destroying America (and the World) and What You Can Do about It*. Berkeley: Ten Speed Press, 2005.

Reading the Riots: Investigating England's Summer of Disorder. London School of Economics and *The Guardian*, 2011. Accessed July 9, 2018. http://eprints.lse.ac.uk/46297/1/Reading%20the%20riots%28published%29.pdf.

Reiter, Ester. *Making Fast Food: From the Frying Pan into the Fryer*. 2nd edn., Montreal: McGill-Queen's University Press, 1996.

Ressler, Oliver. "Boom!" 2001–2006. Accessed May 26, 2018. http://www.ressler.at/boom.
Ressler, Oliver. "An Interview with Oliver Ressler about his Project *Fly Democracy*," November 14, 2007. May 26, 2018. http://www.ressler.at/interview-fly-democracy.
Ressler, Oliver. "Approaches to Future Alternative Societies," Interview with Zanny Begg at *Installations, Videos and Projects in Public Space*, 2014–2018. Accessed May 26, 2018. http://www.ressler.at/approaches-to-future-alternative-societies.
Ressler, Oliver. *Cartographies of Protest*. Nuremberg: Verlag fur Moderne Kunst, 2015.
Ressler, Oliver. "Occupy, Resist, Produce," *Installations, Videos and Projects in Public Space*, 2014–2018. Accessed May 23, 2018. http://www.ressler.at/occupy_resist.
Ressler, Oliver. "Protesting Capitalist Globalization on Video," *Installations, Videos and Projects in Public Space*, 2014–2018. Accessed June 2, 2018. http://www.ressler.at/protesting-capitalist-globalization-on-video.
Ressler, Oliver. *Biography: Solo-Exhibitions and Projects (Selected)*, 1993–2018; *Group Exhibitions (Selected)*, 1995–2018; *Film Festivals and Film Presentations (Selected)*, 2001–2018; *Filmography*, 2000–2018. Accessed May 26, 2018. http://www.ressler.at/category/projects.
Ressler, Oliver, and Martina Grzinic. "Counter-Globalisation Manuals," *Mute Beta: Culture and Politics After the Net*. January 20, 2004. Accessed May 26, 2018. http://www.metamute.org/editorial/articles/counter-globalisation-manuals.
Ressler, Oliver, and Dario Azzellini. "A Preview of the Future: Workers' Control in the Context of a Global Systemic Crisis," in Oliver Ressler and Ines Doujak, (eds). *Utopian Pulse: Flares in the Darkroom*. London: Pluto Press, 2015: 130–45.
Rich, Nathaniel. "The Cloud: The Invisible Catastrophe," *New York Times Magazine*, April 3, 2016. Accessed May 23, 2018. https://www.nytimes.com/2016/04/03/magazine/the-invisible-catastrophe.html.
Rich, Nathaniel. "Losing Earth: The Decade We Almost Stopped Climate Change. A Tragedy in Two Acts," *New York Times Magazine*, August 1, 2018. Accessed September 10, 2018. https://www.nytimes.com/interactive/2018/08/01/magazine/climate-change-losing-earth.html.
Robertson, Alexa. *Media and Politics in a Globalizing World*. Cambridge: Polity Press, 2015.
Rogovin, Milton. "Capturing the 'Forgotten Ones': New York Photographer Who Dedicated His Life to Picturing Plight of the Poor Was on FBI Watch List," Associated Press, *Mail Online*, January 7, 2012. Accessed June 2, 2018. http://www.dailymail.co.uk/news/article-2083657/Milton-Rogovin-Photographer-dedicated-life-photographing-plight-poor-FBI-watch-list.html.
Rosenbloom, Jonathan. "From the Mines to Walmart, Hope Dies Last," *In These Times*, June 7, 2013. Accessed June 2, 2018. http://inthesetimes.com/working/entry/15125/from_the_mines_to_wal_mart_hope_dies_last.
Rosenbloom, Stephanie. "My Initiation at Walmart Store 5476," *New York Times*, December 20, 2009. Accessed July 21, 2018. https://www.nytimes.com/2009/12/20/business/20walmart.html.

Rosenthal, Alan. *The New Documentary in Action: A Casebook in Film Making.* Berkeley: University of California Press, 1971.

Rosenthal, Elisabeth. "As Earth Warms Up, Virus from Tropics Moves to Italy," *New York Times*, December 23, 2007: 21.

Ross, Andrew. *Low Pay, High Profile: The Global Push for Fair Labor.* New York: New Press, 2004.

Ross, Steven J. "American Workers, American Movies: Historiography and Methodology," *International Labor and Working-Class History*, March 2001: 81–105.

Rozek, Victor. "As I See It: The Digital Life," *The Four Hundred*, March 12, 2007. No longer available on-line. www.itjungle.com/tfh/tfh031207-story04.html.

Ruberto, Laura E. "Always Italian, Still Foreign: Connecting Women's Lives through Transnational Migration," *La Questione Meridionale/The Southern Question*, Luigi Pellegrini Editore, No. 2, February 2011: 77–97.

Russell, John. "Google's AlphaGo AI Wins Three-Match Series Against the World's Best Go Player," *Tech Crunch*, May 27, 2017. Accessed June 29, 2018. https://techcrunch.com/2017/05/24/alphago-beats-planets-best-human-go-player-ke-jie.

Ryzik, Melena. "Guggenheim Closes for the Afternoon after Workers' Advocates Escalate Protests," *New York Times*, May 2, 2015: A16.

Samuelson, Robert. "Whose Fault Was the Lehman Bust?" *Washington Post*, August 27, 2018. Accessed September 22, 2018. https://www.washingtonpost.com/opinions/lehman-brothers-collapsed-10-years-ago-whose-fault-was-it/2018/08/26/79137b2e-a7dd-11e8-a656943eefab5daf_story.html?utm_term=.cd0249365369.

Sanders, Bernie. "Disneyland Workers Face Ruthless Exploitation: Their Fight is Our Fight," *Guardian*, June 7, 2016. Accessed June 13, 2018. https://www.theguardian.com/commentisfree/2018/jun/07/disneyland-workers-living-wage-disney-inequality.

Sandhu, Sukhdev. "American Refugees," *Sight & Sound*, April 2014: 51.

Santos, Fernanda. "Confrontation Over *Justice for Willets Point*," *New York Times*, August 14, 2008: C13.

Saul, Stephanie. "N.Y.U. Labor Guidelines Failed to Protect 10,000 Workers in Abu Dhabi, Report Says," *New York Times*, April 17, 2016: A25, 27.

Savage, Mike, et al. "A New Model for Social Class? Findings from the BBC's Great British Class Survey Experiment," *Sociology*, 2013. Accessed May 23, 2018. http://journals.sagepub.com/doi/abs/10.1177/0038038513481128.

Scheiber, Noam. "New Labor Rules for Public Sector Workers Don't Apply to All," *New York Times*, March 20, 2015: B1–2.

Scheiber, Noam. "In Test for Unions and Politicians, a Nationwide Protest on Pay," *New York Times*, April 16, 2015: A1, B2.

Scheiber, Noam. "Raising the Floor for Wages Moves Economy into Unknown," *New York Times*, July 26, 2015: A1, B6.

Schell, Heather. "Outburst! A Chilling True Story about Emerging Virus Narratives and Pandemic Social Change," *Configurations*, 5 (1), 1997: 93–133.

Schulte, Brigid. "From the Ranks of Microsoft's Permatemps," *Washington Post*, March 29, 2015: F1, 4.

Schulman, Michael. "The Zombie Factories That Stalk China's Economy," *New York Times*, August 8, 2015: B1, B9.

Scott, A. O. "*Foreign Parts*: A Patch of Rusty Paradise that Might Be Paved," *New York Times*, March 10, 2011. Accessed December 8, 2018. https://www.nytimes.com/2011/03/10/movies/foreign-parts-about-willets-point-review.html.

Scott, A.O. "Faces on the Train Help Tell a Nation's Story," *New York Times*, August 21, 2015: C1, C5.

Schlote, Christiane, and Eckart Voights-Virchow. "Introduction: The Creative Treatment of Actuality—New Documentarism," *Zeitschrift für Anglistik und Amerikanistik*, 36 (2), 2008. Accessed June 6, 2018. https://www.degruyter.com/view/j/zaa.2008.56.issue-2/zaa.2008.56.2.107/zaa.2008.56.2.107.xml.

Seabrook, Jonathan. *In the Cities of the South: Scenes from a Developing World*. London: Verso, 1996.

Segal, David. "The People v. the Coal Baron," *New York Times*, June 21, 2015: B1, B4–5.

Sekula, Allan, and Noel Burch. "The Forgotten Space: Notes for a Film," *New Left Review*, 69, May–June 2011.

Semerene, Diego. "Downeast," *Slant Magazine*, March 9, 2013. Accessed May 23, 2018. https://www.slantmagazine.com/film/review/downeast.

Semmker, Illiana Alexandra. "Ebola Goes Pop: The Filovirus from Literature to Film," *Literature and Medicine*, 17 (1), 1998: 149–74.

Servin, Jacques, and Igor Vamos. *The Yes Men: The True Story of the End of the World Trade Association*. New York: The Disinformation Company, 2004.

Shambu, Girish. "A Double Life: One Hundred Years of Films about the Immigrant Experience Reveal the Split Personality of Modern Living," *Film Comment*, September–October 2017: 56–61.

Shaw, Deborah. "Deconstructing and Reconstructing 'Transnational Cinema'," in Stephanie Dennison, eds. *Contemporary Hispanic Cinema: Interrogating Transnationalism in Spanish and Latin American Film*. Rochester: Tamesis Books, 2013: 47–66.

Shen, Andy, and Abby McGill. *Taking Stock: Labor Exploitation, Illegal Fishing and Brand Responsibility in the Seafood Industry*. May 11, 2018. Accessed May 18, 2018. https://www.laborrights.org/publications/taking-stock-labor-exploitation-illegal-fishing-and-brand-responsibility-seafood.

Sholette, Gregory, and Oliver Ressler, eds. *It's the Political Economy, Stupid: The Global Financial Crisis in Art and Theory*. London: Pluto Press, 2013.

Silverman, Jason. "*Sleep Dealer* Injects Sci-Fi Into Immigration Debate," *Wired*, January 24, 2008. Accessed June 15, 2018. https://www.wired.com/2008/01/injects-sci-fi-into-immigration-debate.

Singer, Natasha. "Check App. Accept Job. Repeat," *New York Times*, August 17, 2014: B1, B4–5.

Slack, Paul. *Plague: A Very Short Introduction*. Oxford: Oxford University Press, 2012.

Slackman, Michael. "Belatedly, Egypt Spots Flaws in Wiping Out Pigs," *New York Times*: September 19, 2009. Accessed December 8, 2018. https://www.nytimes.com/2009/09/20/world/africa/20cairo.html?_r=1&module=ArrowsNav&contentCollection=Africa&action=keypress&region=FixedLeft&pgtype=article.

Smithson, Robert. "Entropy Made Visible," *Interview with Alison Sky*, 1973. Accessed October 6, 2018. https://www.robertsmithson.com/essays/entropy.htm.

Soomra, Marvi. "Cut from Glass: The Perilous Lives of Hyderabad's Bangle Makers," *Dawn*, November 28, 2015. Accessed March 3, 2019. https://www.dawn.com/news/1221040.

Southwood, Ivor. *Non-Stop Inertia*. London: Zero Books, 2011.

Sowunmi, Jordan. "*Marmato* Covers a Colombian Town in the Aftermath of a Canadian Mining Operation," *Vice*, October 14, 2014. Accessed July 5, 2018. https://www.vice.com/en_uk/article/gq83vx/marmato-covers-a-colombian-town-in-the-aftermath-of-a-canadian-mining-operation-903.

Spott, Greg. *Walmart: The High Cost of Low Price*. Foster City: The Disinformation Company, 2005.

Stahl, Ted. "Video Game Genres," *The History of Computing Project*, 2005. Accessed July 22, 2018. http://www.thocp.net/software/games/reference/genres.htm.

Standing, Guy. *The Precariat: The New Dangerous Class*. London: Bloomsbury, 2011.

Standing, Guy. "Who Will Be a Voice for the Emerging Precariat?" *The Guardian*, June 1, 2011. Accessed December 8, 2018. https://www.theguardian.com/commentisfree/2011/jun/01/voice-for-emerging-precariat.

Standing, Guy. *A Precariat Charter: From Denizens to Citizens*. London: Bloomsbury, 2014.

Standing, Guy. *The Corruption of Capitalism: Why Rentiers Thrive and Work Does Not Pay*. London: Biteback Publishing, 2016.

Standing, Guy. "Meet the Precariat, the New Global Class Fueling the Rise of Populism," *World Economic Forum*, November 9, 2016. Accessed July 25, 2018. https://www.weforum.org/agenda/2016/11/precariat-global-class-rise-of-populism.

Standing, Guy. "The Precariat, Populism and Robots: Is Basic Income a Political Imperative?," *World Economic Forum*, November 9, 2016. Accessed December 20, 2016. https://www.weforum.org/agenda/2016/12/the-precariat-populism-and-robots-is-basic-income-a-political-imperative.

Standing, Guy. "The 5 Biggest Lies of Global Capitalism," *World Economic Forum*, December 12, 2016 Accessed July 25, 2018. https://www.weforum.org/agenda/2016/12/lies-of-global-capitalism-guy-standing.

Standing, Guy. *Basic Income: And How We Can Make It Happen*. London: Penguin Books, 2017.

Standing, Guy. "Universal Basic Income is Becoming an Urgent Necessity," *The Guardian*, January 12, 2017. Accessed July 25, 2018. https://www.theguardian.com/commentisfree/2017/jan/12/universal-basic-income-finland-uk.

Standing, Guy. "Build a Precariat Strategy," *Albert Shanker Institute*, February 9, 2017. Accessed July 25, 2018. http://www.shankerinstitute.org/blog/build-precariat-strategy.

Starr, Amory, Luis Fernandez, and Christian Scholl. *Shutting Down the Streets: Political Violence and Social Control in the Global Era*. New York City: New York University Press, 2011.

Stone, Katherine V. W. "Unions in the Precarious Economy: How Collective Bargaining Can Help Gig and On-Demand Workers," *The American Prospect*, Winter 2017. Accessed November 18, 2018. http://prospect.org/article/unions-precarious-economy.

Sudjic, Deyan. *The 100 Mile City*. Orlando: Harcourt, Brace, 1992.

Sudjic, Deyan. "Cities on the Edge of Chaos," *The Observer*, March 9, 2008. Accessed March 9, 2008. http://www.theguardian.com/profile/deyansudjic.

Swarns, Rachel L. "Proposed Raise for Fast-Food Employees Divides Low-Wage Workers," *New York Times*, July 27, 2015: A12.

Swider, Sarah. *Building China: Informal Work and the New Precariat*. Ithaca: Cornell University Press, 2015.

Szalai, Jennifer. "The Tough Love of Austerity," *New York Times Magazine*, August 4, 2015. Accessed July 22, 2018. https://www.nytimes.com/2015/08/09/magazine/the-tough-love-of-austerity.html.

Tari, Marcello, and Ilaria Vanni. "On the Life and Deeds of San Precario, Patron Saint of Precarious Workers and Lives," *The Fiber Culture Journal*, (5), 2005: *Precarious Labor (FCJ-023)*. Accessed March 30, 2019. http://five.fibreculturejournal.org/fcj-023-on-the-life-and-deeds-of-san-precario-patron-saint-of-precarious-workers-and-lives.

Tarr, Carrie. *Reframing Difference: Beur and Banlieu Filmmaking in France*. Manchester: Manchester University Press, 2005.

Tekin, Latife. *Berji Kristin: Tales from the Garbage Hills* (1984). Trans. Ruth Christie and Saliha Paker. London: Marion Boyers, 2004.

Teixeira, Carlos, and Wei Li, eds. *The Housing and Economic Experiences of Immigrants in US and Canadian Cities*. Toronto: University of Toronto Press, 2015.

Thew, Geoff. "Review: Kentucky Route Zero Act III," *Hardcore Gamer*, May 9, 2014. Accessed July 22, 2018. http://www.hardcoregamer.com/2014/05/09/review-kentucky-route-zero-act-iii/84253.

Torres-Spelliscy, Ciara. "The History of Corporate Personhood," Brennan Center for Justice, April 7, 2014. Accessed March 22, 2019. https://www.brennancenter.org/blog/hobby-lobby-argument.

Toth, Jennifer. *The Mole People*. Chicago: Chicago Review Press, 1995.

Townsend, Anthony M. *Smart Cities: Big Data, Civic Hackers, and the Quest for a New Utopia*. New York: Norton, 2014.

The Typology of Modern Slavery: Defining Sex and Labor Trafficking in the United States. Polaris Project. National Human Trafficking Hotline. Accessed July 25, 2018. https://polarisproject.org/typology-report.

Uneven Geographies: Art and Globalisation. Nottingham Contemporary Exhibition: May 8, 2010 to July 4, 2010. Accessed May 18, 2018. http://www.nottinghamcontemporary.org/sites/default/files/UG_cat_lowres.pdf.

Unnikrishnan, Deepak. *Temporary People.* New York: Restless Books, 2013.

Urbina, Ian. "Forced Labor for Cheap Fish," *New York Times,* July 27, 2015: A1, A8–9.

Valenzuela, Abel, et al. *On the Corner: Day Labor in the United States.* Los Angeles: Center for the Study of Urban Poverty at UCLA, 2006.

Van Dam, Andrew. "Meet the Workers Tossed Aside by the Strong Economy," *Washington Post,* July 29, 2018. Accessed July 30, 2018. https://www.chron.com/business/article/Millions-of-educated-experienced-workers-have-13111220.php.

Van der Linden, Marcel. "San Precario: A New Inspiration for Labor Historians," *Labor,* 11 (1), Spring 2014: 9–19.

Van Luyn, Floris-Jan. *A Floating City of Peasants: The Great Migration in Contemporary China.* Trans. Jeannette K. Ringold. New York: The New Press, 2008.

Venugopal, Arun. "The Robert Neuwirth Interview," *Rediff India Abroad,* March 25, 2005. Accessed May 26, 2018. http://www.rediff.com/news/2005/mar/25inter.htm?print=true.

Vinik, Danny, et al. "The Real Future of Work," *Politico,* January-February 2018. Accessed July 2, 2018. https://www.politico.com/magazine/story/2018/01/04/future-work-independent-contractors-alternative-work-arrangements-216212.

Virilio, Paul. *Unknown Quantity.* London: Thames & Hudson, 2003.

Vollmann, William T. "Invisible and Insidious: Living at the Edge of Fukushima's Nuclear Disaster," *Harper's Magazine,* March 2015.

Wagner, Keith. "Historicizing Labor Cinema: Recovering Class and Lost Work on Screen," *Labor History,* 55 (3), 2014: 309–25.

Wald, Priscilla. *Contagious: Cultures, Carriers, and the Outbreak Narrative.* Durham: Duke University Press, 2008.

Walker, Rob. "Gaming the System," *New York Times,* September 3, 2006. Accessed November 13, 2018. https://www.nytimes.com/2006/09/03/magazine/03wwln_consumed.html.

Wang Bing. "Filming a Land in Flux" [Interview]. *New Left Review* 82, July–August 2013.

Weber, Max. "Entwicklungstendenz in der Lage der ostelbischen Landarbeiter" ["Developments on the Placement of the Farm Workers from East of the Elbe River"] (1894), in *Gesammelte Aufsätze zur Sozial- und Wirtschaftsgeschichte* [Collected Essays on Social and Economic History]. Tübingen: J.C.B. Mohr, 1924.

Weil, David. *The Fissured Workplace: Why Work Became So Bad for So Many and What Can Be Done about It.* Cambridge: Harvard University Press, 2014.

Weissberg, Jay. "Film Review: *Cart*," *Variety*, March 10, 2015. Accessed May 25, 2018. http://variety.com/2015/film/festivals/film-review-cart-1201448373.

Wells, Katie, Kafui Attoh, and Declan Cullen. "Uber, the *Metropocalypse*, and Economic Inequality in D.C.," *Working-Class Perspectives*, February 5, 2018. Accessed November 18, 2018. https://workingclassstudies.wordpress.com/2018/02/05/uber-the-metropocalypse-and-economic-inequality-in-d-c.

Welzer, Harald. "No Freedom Without Waste," in *Klaus Staeck—Nothing is Done*. Munich: Goethe-Institute, 2011: 59–79.

Wilkinson, Richard, and Kate Pickett. *The Spirit Level: Why Greater Equality Makes Societies Stronger*. New York: Bloomsbury Press, 2009.

Williams, Raymond. *Keywords: A Vocabulary of Culture and Society*. London: Croom Helm, 1976.

Williamson, Judith, *Deadline at Dawn: Film Writings, 1980–1990*. London: Marion Boyars Publishing, 1992.

Windham, Lane. *Knocking on Labor's Door: Union Organizing in the 1970s and the Roots of a New Economic Divide*. Chapel Hill: University of North Carolina Press, 2017.

Winkler, Adam. "'Corporations Are People' Is Built on an Incredible 19th-Century Lie," *Atlantic Monthly*, March 5, 2018. Accessed July 14, 2018. https://www.theatlantic.com/business/archive/2018/03/corporations-people-adam-winkler/554852.

Wise, Damon. "*Machines* Director Rahul Jain: 'I Was Not Interested in Giving Any Answers,'" *Variety*, November 17, 2016. Accessed July 14, 2018. https://variety.com/2016/film/festivals/rahul-jain-debut-docu-feature-machines-idfa-1201920556.

Wolfson, Andrew. "A Hoax Most Cruel: Caller Coaxed McDonald's Managers into Strip-Searching a Worker," *Louisville Courier-Journal*, October 2, 2005. Accessed December 3, 2018. https://www.courier-journal.com/story/news/local/2005/10/09/a-hoax-most-cruel-caller-coaxed-mcdonalds-managers-/28936597.

Wong, Joshua. "Scholarism on the March [Interview]," New Left Review, March–April 2015.

Wood, Jason. *Nick Broomfield: Documenting Icons*. Ed. James Wood. London: Faber & Faber, 2005.

Wright, Richard. "The Man Who Lived Underground (1942)," in *Eight Men*. Cleveland and New York: World Publishing, 1961.

Xin, Zhou. "Decline and Fall: The Broken Dreams of a Chinese Coal-Mining City Struggling to Address Industrial Overcapacity," *South China Morning Post*, April 12, 2016. Accessed May 23, 2018. http://www.scmp.com/news/china/economy/article/1935326/decline-and-fall-broken-dreams-chinese-coal-mining-city.

Yuen, Eddie, Daniel Burton-Rose, and George Katsiaficas, eds. *Confronting Capitalism*. Brooklyn: Soft Skull Press, 2004.

Zaniello, Tom. "Filming Class," In *New Working-Class Studies*, ed. Sherry Linkon and John Russo. Ithaca: Cornell University Press, 2005: 152–65.

Zaniello, Tom. *The Cinema of Globalization*. Ithaca: Cornell University Press, 2007.

Zaniello, Tom. "Cinema of the Precariat," in Michele Fazio, Christie Launius, and Tim Strangleman, eds. *Handbook of Working-Class Studies*. London: Routledge, 2019[in press].

Zaniello, Tom. "The Kopple Effect: Women Directing Documentaries," in Jeff Jaeckle and Susan Ryan, eds. *ReFocus: The Films of Barbara Kopple*. Edinburgh: Edinburgh University Press, 2019: 51–68.

Zhao, Kiki. "China's Environmental Woes, in Films that Go Viral, Then Vanish," *New York Times*, April 28, 2017. Accessed May 14, 2019. https://www.nytimes.com/2017/04/28/world/asia/chinas-environmental-woes-in-films-that-go-viral-then-vanish.html.

Zimmerman, Andrew. "Decolonizing Weber," *Postcolonial Studies*, IX (1), 2006: 53–79.

Zimmerman, Andrew. "German Sociology and Empire: From Internal Colonization to Overseas Colonization and Back Again," in George Steinmetz, ed. *Sociology and Empire: Colonial Studies and the Imperial Entanglements of a Discipline*. Durham: Duke University Press, 2011. 166–87.

Zlolniski, Christian. *Janitors, Street Vendors, and Activists: The Lives of Mexican Immigrants in Silicon Valley*. Berkeley: University of California Press, 2006.

Zuckerman, Esther. "Director Boots Riley Breaks Down the Craziest Part of *Sorry to Bother You*," *Thrillist*, July 5, 2018. Accessed August 27, 2018. https://www.thrillist.com/entertainment/nation/sorry-to-bother-you-ending-explained-boots-riley-interview.

Index

NOTE: The following topics should serve as a means to help define the scope of all the films, video games, and installations associated with the precariat. In some instances film titles may appear under more than one topic heading if appropriate.

Androids and the Cyberprecariat
    Ex Machina 103–4
    Her 104
    Humans 102–3
    I, Robot 97
    I Am Mother 104
    Moon 102
    A Robot Walks into a Bar 97
    Sleep Dealer 97
    Why Cybraceros? 96

big box stores, *see also* Walmart
    Cart 137–8
    Czech Dream 106
    Superstore 14
border crossings
    Eldorado 44
    The Girl 44–5
    The Judgment 44
    Simshar 43–4

capitalism
    The Bull Laid Bare 157
    Le Capital 125
    Capitalism 126
    Capitalism: A Love Story 122–3, 126
    Dirty Money 128
    Enron: The Smartest Guys in the Room 129, 140
    The Founder 130
    The Fountainhead 122, 130
    Last Days of Lehman Brothers 122
    The Pit 133
    The Plundering 156
    Potiche 123, 134
    Rogue Trader 134
    Saving Capitalism 122–3, 134
    The Secret of Oz 123, 134
    The Spider's Web 134–5
    Yella 122, 136
    Zeitgeist: Moving Forward 136
capitalism and politics
    The Big Sellout 124–5
    Comedy of Power 122, 127
    Corporate Coup d'Etat 128, 158
    Dark Money 122, 128
    Fly Democracy 154
    The Golden Rule: The Investment Theory of Politics 130–1
    Miss Sloan 122
    The Yes Men Fix the World 122, 136
capitalist utopia
    Falcon City of Wonders 99–100
    GM Futurama I and II 98
    King Abdullah Economic City 100–1
    New Songdo City 101–2
    The World 99
catastrophes
    The Battle of Chernobyl 69
    The Buffalo Creek Flood: An Act of Man 77–8
    Buffalo Creek Revisited 77–8
    Burn 81
    Chemical Valley 78
    Chernobyl 70–1
    The Chernobyl Diaries 71
    Cooked: Survival by Zip Code 72–5
    Deepwater Horizon 83, 128
    The Emerald Forest 83–4
    Embittered City 72
    Escape from New York 61
    Everything's Cool 73
    The First Secret City 72
    The Great Flood 75–6
    A Healthy Baby Girl 73
    The Host 131

The Last Winter 84
Middlemen 151–2
Osmosis and Excess 151–2
Pripyat 69–70
The Safe Side of the Fence 72
Snowpiercer 133
The Stalker 70, 112–13
Training Ground 151–2
Unknown Quality 151, 153
chemical industries
Blue Vinyl 73
Chemical Valley 78
Trading on Thin Air 135
child labor
Children of the Harvest 27–8
Machines 41–2
Chinese Industries
American Factory 39
Behemoth 37–8
Bitter Money 35–6
The China Hustle 126–7
The Chinese Mayor 36–7
Chingqing: Flashes of a Megalopolis 34
Coal, Money 36
Condensation: Five Video Works 32–3
Crude Oil 36
Dreamwork China 33–4
Last Train Home 34–5
Losers and Winners 38–9
The Pit 133
Tie Xi Qu: West of Tracks 36
24 City 32
commodities
Bananas Unpeeled 90
My Name Is Salt 91–2
The Price of Sugar 92
Salt: Tears of the Earth 91
Thangata 90
Up in Smoke 90
The Visible and the Invisible 122, 135
de-industrialization
Burn 81
Condensation: Five Video Works 32–3
Detropia 82
The Factory 150
Fahrenheit 11/9 82

Flint 83
From Flint: Voices from a Poisoned City 82
The Last Truck: Closing of a GM Plant 39
Poisoned Water 82
Roger & Me 82
Sollers Point 8–9, 81
Spiral Jetty 150–1
the diamond trade
Bling: A Planet Rock 89
Blood Diamond 88–9
Blood Diamonds 88
Diamonds from Sierra Leone 89–90
dystopia
Fahrenheit 451 (1953) 98
Fahrenheit 451 (1966) 98
Fahrenheit 451 (2018) 98
Minority Report 96
The Wild Blue Yonder 113

epidemic cinema
The Andromeda Strain (1971) 65–6
The Andromeda Strain (2008) 65–6
Blindness 66
Blue Vinyl 73
Cooked: Survival by Zip Code 72–5
District 9 68
Fatal Outbreak: Bird Flu in America 66
From Flint: Voices from a Poisoned City 82
The Leakers 67–8
The Omega Man 67
Outbreak 66
Pandemic 67
Panic in the Streets 65–6
Training Ground 152
28 Days Later 67
28 Weeks Later 67

fast food and restaurant workers
Burger Tycoon 108
Compliance 42–3
The Founder 130
The McDonald's Game 107
the food industry
Food, Inc. 129–30

Food Chains 29–30
The Future of Food 130
Okja 122, 133
Our Daily Bread 93
fossil fuel industries
   Addicted to Oil 84
   Deepwater Horizon 83, 128
   Gasland 80
   Kaala Patthar 80
   Petropolis: Aerial Perspectives on the Alberta Tar Sands 114
   The Promised Land 80
   Trading on Thin Air 135

Global Financial Crisis of 2008
   After the Crisis is Before the Crisis 155–6
   The Big Short 122, 124
   The Bull Laid Bare 157
   Collapse 127
   The Flaw 129
   Hank: 5 Years from the Brink 122, 131
   Inside Job 122
   The Last Days of Lehman Brothers 122
   Last Train Home 34–5
   Margin Call 131
   Master of the Universe 132
   Robbery 156
   Too Big to Fail 135, 156
   Wall Street: Money Never Sleeps 135
   We Have a Situation Here 157

homelessness
   Cathy Come Home 3–4
   Riff-Raff 3

Italian activists
   Black Block 144
   Condensation: Five Video Works 32–3
   Diaz: Don't Clean Up the Blood 144
   Disobbedienti! 154
   Now or Never 144–5
   The Summit 143–4

migratory labor
   Adios Amor: The Search for Maria Moreno 22
   Angel City 28
   Bitter Rice 35
   Bordertown 46
   Children of the Harvest 27–8
   A Desk for Billie 17–18
   Fighting for Our Lives 30
   Food Chains 29–30
   The Grapes of Wrath 19, 21–2
   Harvest of Shame 11, 17, 19–30
   Hunger in America 23–4
   Idaho's Summer Citizens 18
   In Dubious Battle 29
   The Infiltrators 95–6
   I Witness 47
   Legacy of Shame 26–7
   Migrants (1970) 24–5
   Migrants (1980) 25
   My Name Is Salt 91–2
   New Harvest, Old Shame 25–6
   A Painted House 28–9
   Poverty in the Land of Plenty 21–2
   Seniorita Extraviada 45–6
   Silenced Voices 147
   Sixth Section 95
   What Harvest for the Reaper 23
   The Wrath of Grapes 30
miners
   Blood in the Mobile 87
   Blood on the Mountain 79
   The Brave Don't Cry 28
   Gold 130
   Harlan County, USA 76–7
   Justice in the Coal Fields 78
   Kaala Patthar 80
   Marmato 85–6
   Mine War on Blackberry Creek 77
   The Pennsylvania Miners Story 78–9
   The Promised Land 80
   Strike a Rock 86

office workers
   Nine to Five 141
   Raises Not Roses: The Story of 9to5 141–2
   Two Days, One Night 4, 149
organizing
   Five Factories—Workers Control in Venezuela 154–5
   Fly Democracy 154

In Dubious Battle 29
Occupy, Resist, Produce: Scop Ti 155
Seeing Red 141
Union Maids 141

the precariat
  Beijing Flickers 39
  The Cart 137–8
  Clash 149
  Daughters of a Lesser God 41
  A Day Without a Mexican 106
  The Divide 138
  Eat Sleep Die 158–9
  Ghosts 40
  I, Daniel Blake 3
  Machines 41–2
  Manpower 10–11
  The Measure of a Man 4
  The Nightcleaners 42
  The Nothing Factory 149–50
  7 Chinese Brothers 106
  Sex My British Job 39–40
  Shoplifters 9
  Sollers Point 8–9, 81
  Songs from the Second Floor 112, 150
  Sorry We Missed You 4
  24 City 32
  The World 32, 99

protests
  Boom! 155
  Capitalism: A Love Story 122–3, 126
  Crowd Bites Wolf 145–6
  A Day without a Mexican 106
  Disobeddienti! 154
  Nine to Five 141
  The Plundering 156–7
  Prison Valley 114
  Resist to Exist 156
  Rise Like Lions: Occupy Wall Street and the Seeds of Revolution 122, 142–3
  Roger & Me 82
  Seeing Red 141
  Showdown in Seattle: Five Days that Shook the World 145
  Strike a Rock 86
  The Summit 143
  This Is What Democracy Looks Like 145, 154
  Union Maids 141

  Vacuum Room 152
  War by Other Means 135–6
  What Would Jesus Buy? 13–14
  Wisconsin Rising 147–8

real estate and gentrification
  Detropia 81
  The Little Pink House 47–8
  99 Homes 132, 139

recycling and garbage cities
  Beijing Besieged by Waste 54–5
  Chop Shop 62–3
  eDump 54
  Escape from New York 61
  Foreign Parts 61–2
  Garbage Dreams 59
  Graveyard for Giants 56–7
  The Great Gatsby 60
  Lagos/Koolhaas 49–50
  Lagos Wide & Deep 49–50
  Marina of the Zabbaleen 59
  Plastic China 55
  A Project of Peace, Painted Across 50 Buildings 60
  Recycled Life 51–2
  Shanghai Journal: At the Dump 51–2
  Shipbreakers 56
  Soylent Green 130
  We Are the Zabbaleen 58–9
  The White Train 52–3
  Willets Point Beyond the Curbline 63
  Willets Point Lawsuits: Parts One and Two 63
  Workingman's Death 56
  The Worst Job in the World: The Bhangis of India 53–4
  Zabbaleen: Trash Town 59–60

video games
  Burger Tycoon 108
  Disaffected! 107
  Dr. Langeskov, The Tiger, and the Terribly Cursed Emerald: A Whirlwind Heist 116–17
  Fort McMoney 113–15
  Kentucky Route Zero 111–13
  The McDonald's Game 107
  Minecraft 119
  No Man's Sky 119

Oligarchy 108–9
Papers Please 110–11
Papo & Yo 118
Phone Story 109–10
Red Faction 117–18
Red Faction: Armageddon 117–18
Red Faction: Guerilla 117–18
Red Faction: Guerilla Re-Mars-tered 117–18
The Stanley Parable 115–16
Virtual City 110
Virtual City Playground 110

Wall Street
 Betting on Zero 124
 Billions 122, 124
 The China Hustle 126–7
 Cleveland vs Wall Street 122, 127
 Enron: The Smartest Guys in the Room 129, 140
 Equity 122, 129
 Gold 130
 Margin Call 131
 Miss Sloan 132
 Molly's Game 124
 Money Monster 122, 132
 97% Owned 132
 Rise Like Lions: Occupy Wall Street and the Seeds of Revolution 122, 134
 Wall Street 122
 Wall Street: Money Never Sleeps 122, 135
 We Have a Situation Here 157
 The Wolf of Wall Street 122, 136
Walmart
 The Cart 137–8
 Dear Walmart 13
 Superstore 14
 Talking to the Wall 13
 What Would Jesus Buy? 13–14
 Where the Heart Is 14

www.ingramcontent.com/pod-product-compliance
Lightning Source LLC
Chambersburg PA
CBHW052044300426
44117CB00012B/1965